Micro-Negotiations

Micro-Negotiations

Tiny Talks That Save You Thousands a Year

Safiya Montrel

Mindful Pages

Published in 2026

ISBN: 9789376553938 (PB)
ISBN: 9789376554041 (eBook)

Published by

Mindful Pages
Imprint of Alpha Editions LLC
312 W. 2nd St #1834
Casper, WY 82601, USA

Content

Introduction

In December 2018, in London, the Competition and Markets Authority published a study with a strangely domestic punchline: loyalty can cost money. Not in the abstract, not as a moral fable, but as a measurable "loyalty penalty" paid by people who stayed put. The most vivid part was not the spreadsheets; it was the implied scene repeated across the country, night after night, as envelopes landed on doormats and price-rise emails arrived with their polite subject lines. A kettle clicks off. Paper smells faintly of toner. Someone reads, sighs, and pays. The hinge on a kitchen cupboard makes its small, familiar sound as a mug is put away and the moment passes. Most prices are not prices. They are proposals that survive because nobody touches them. The quiet marvel is how often a minor question alters the outcome, not because the world becomes kinder, but because the world is built from adjustable parts—scripts, thresholds, discretionary budgets, and human beings who would rather resolve than resist.

The modern consumer economy is noisy with certainty. Numbers appear as if they were laws of physics. "£49 a month." "Non-refundable." "We can't." Yet much of this certainty is theatre, and the stage directions are written for speed. Organisations do not want long conversations; they want predictable ones. They design menus of answers that fit the majority of callers, the average complaint, the most common misunderstanding. When someone accepts the first line, the system records a win: efficient resolution, minimal labour, no escalation. When someone asks again—calmly, precisely—the system sometimes reveals its second layer, and then its third. That is the territory of micro-negotiations: the tiny talks that reshape terms without requiring grand speeches, glossy confidence, or a personality transplant. People fear being difficult. The truth is more prosaic: many institutions are built to accommodate a certain amount of friction, because it is cheaper than perfect fairness and more flexible than pure rigidity.

Consider a small scene with a hard edge. In April 2010, an ash cloud from Iceland's Eyjafjallajökull volcano shut down large parts of European airspace, stranding travellers in airports from Heathrow to Frankfurt. Most people remember the headlines and the chaos; fewer remember the quiet, individual negotiations that followed—the conversations at desks and on phone lines about rerouting, accommodation, and what counts as "extraordinary circumstances". Regulation, policy, and real-world goodwill tangled together. Some passengers received hotel nights; others slept under fluorescent lights. Some were rebooked quickly; others were told to wait. The difference was not always virtue or volume. Often it was timing, clarity, and whether the person on the other end could hear a specific request rather than a general frustration. Systems under stress show their joins. They also show where discretion lives.

The point is not that everything is pliable. Some doors stay shut. Taxes, statutory penalties, and tightly regulated charges often offer little to no room for adjustment. In certain moments—safety decisions at an airport gate, clinical protocols in a hospital, safeguarding procedures in schools—trying to bargain is not merely futile but inappropriate. A micro-negotiation is not a magic spell, and pretending otherwise turns an honest skill into a superstition. Still, the mistaken conclusion drawn from the existence of immovable boundaries is that most boundaries are immovable. That leap is how quiet overpayment becomes a lifestyle. The daily economy of modern life is full of soft limits: fees imposed by default but waived on review, contracts renewed by inertia rather than intention, delivery failures handled differently depending on the channel used, workloads that expand because nobody names the scope, hotel rooms assigned by algorithm but changed by request. The real question is not whether negotiation "works". The real question is how much you are donating, invisibly, to the altar of automatic acceptance.

There is a particular type of loss that rarely appears on bank statements. It is the time-tax: the hours spent cleaning up misunderstandings, chasing a trade who assumed the wrong scope, sitting on hold because a discount expired silently, absorbing the frustration of a service that went slightly wrong and then stays wrong because nobody returns to the conversation. Trust, efficiency, and risk sound like boardroom words until they show up in the texture of a week. Trust becomes the decision to believe a fee is fair because it is printed. Efficiency becomes the choice to accept a confusing process rather than ask for a simpler one. Risk becomes the fear that speaking up will backfire, or that a request will brand you as "that customer", the one who is trouble. These are not philosophical abstractions. They are behaviours. They can be measured: the number of calls avoided by one clarifying email, the annual total of "small" monthly increases, the two hours lost to a rebooked train because nobody asked what alternatives existed, the discounted rate that never appeared because someone did not say, with calm curiosity, "Is there anything you can do on price?"

There is also a social story attached to asking. For decades, "negotiation" has been marketed as combat: a winner, a loser, a dramatic stare-down in a glass-walled boardroom. That story is gripping and mostly irrelevant. Everyday life is negotiated in quieter registers, in places where nobody wears power suits and the stakes are not acquisitions but dignity, time, and the household budget. People who dislike confrontation often assume they must choose between meek acceptance and aggressive pushing. There is a third option: small, specific conversations that respect the other person's role while refusing to treat the first answer as divine revelation. A three-minute call about a late fee is not a war. A carefully worded message that confirms what a contractor will and will not do is not an insult. A pause at a hotel desk, long enough to let the front-of-house worker check the screen again, is not entitlement. It is an act of attention.

Attention, in this context, is a kind of quiet power. Most organisations run on triage. Calls are categorised; cases are routed; scripts are followed. The person on the line is rarely authorised to reinvent policy, but they are often authorised to interpret it. Interpretation lives in the grey zone between "must" and "usually". It lives in the gap between "our policy is..." and "what I can do is...". Micro-negotiations work when they recognise this without moralising it. They ask for review rather than confession. They propose alternatives rather than issuing demands. They make it easy for the other person to say yes without feeling manipulated or ambushed. A well-framed request is like handing someone the right tool: it reduces effort, and effort is the hidden currency of modern service. When the request is precise—when it names a number, a date, a fixable term—the conversation becomes a problem to solve rather than a complaint to endure.

That precision matters most in the places people least expect to negotiate: recurring bills and subscriptions. The loyalty penalty identified by the Competition and Markets Authority in 2018 was not a scandal because companies secretly hate loyal customers. It was a scandal because of incentives. New customers are counted, tracked, and celebrated; retention is less glamorous. Introductory offers are marketing spend; continued full-price payment is "normal". The result is a structural tilt towards inertia. The household that never calls, never compares, never asks for a better rate becomes a reliable profit centre. Meanwhile, the household that makes a polite, timely enquiry becomes a cost—a small one, but enough to justify a discount if it prevents cancellation. This is not personal. It is arithmetic. Once that arithmetic is understood, a short phone call stops feeling like begging and starts feeling like routine maintenance, like checking the tyre pressure on a car. The conversation is not about winning. It is about refusing to fund other people's marketing budgets out of quiet habit.

The same logic appears, with different costumes, in repairs and trades. A quote is rarely just a price; it is a story about scope, risk, and uncertainty. When the scope is vague, the price carries a fog of unknowns, and that fog later condenses into disputes and "extras". When the scope is clear, the price becomes legible, and legibility creates fairness. This is why a few simple clarifications—what is included, what is excluded, what might change the estimate—can save far more than a dramatic attempt to haggle at the end. A contractor who is asked, early, to put assumptions in writing is not necessarily being challenged; they are being invited into a cleaner agreement. That agreement protects both sides. It lowers the risk of resentment, of surprise invoices, of that exhausted argument at the threshold of a door when the work is done and someone says, "That wasn't what I thought we agreed." The micro-negotiation, here, is not a price-fight. It is an insistence on definition.

Hotels and travel reveal a different type of discretion: situational rather than contractual. At a front desk, the allocation of rooms is part algorithm, part human judgement. A noisy room near the lift is a default assignment; a quieter room is often a choice. At an airport gate, rebooking options exist in a tree of possibilities, some visible, some hidden behind the next click. When disruptions happen, the most common response is emotional paralysis or noisy venting, both of which are understandable and neither of which reliably produces better outcomes. The micro-negotiation in travel is a disciplined shift from grievance to options. What happened? What is being offered? What else is possible within the system today? The questions are not romantic. They are practical. They respect the reality that the staff member did not cause the storm, the delay, or the overbooking, while also recognising that their job is to handle the consequences. A small, well-timed request—specific and reasonable—can change a journey from miserable to manageable.

Work, meanwhile, is where micro-negotiations become existential. Pay, promotion, workload, and job offers involve not just money but identity. People often either avoid these conversations entirely or enter them as if stepping into a courtroom, armed with resentment or rehearsed slogans. Neither approach tends to produce dignified results. The healthier stance is neither meekness nor hostility but evidence. Not vibes; facts. The market rate for a role. The documented results delivered. The expanded responsibilities quietly accepted. The moment in the year when budgets are planned rather than already spent. Even then, outcomes vary. Organisations have constraints: pay bands, hiring freezes, internal politics. A person can do everything "right" and still hear no. That is not a reason to treat the conversation as futile; it is a reason to treat it as information. A no can clarify the real structure of the workplace. It can reveal what is valued, what is possible, and what is not. The micro-negotiation, here, is the refusal to let emotion be the only language spoken about work.

There is a temptation, whenever a skill is named, to turn it into a moral identity. The world does not need more self-proclaimed "negotiators" swaggering through customer service as if every interaction were an audition for dominance. Nor does it need people so afraid of being disliked that they accept terms they do not understand, or pay fees that can be reconsidered with one simple request. The middle path is more interesting: kindness with boundaries, curiosity with backbone. It is also more realistic. Service workers are not villains; they are people operating within scripts and targets. Customers are not entitled for asking; they are participants in a system that relies on their passivity. The micro-negotiation is not a loophole. It is an acknowledgement of how modern institutions actually function: by default settings, by variance in human discretion, by categories that can be nudged from one box to another with the right phrase at the right moment.

The right phrase is not a charm; it is a design choice. Language can inflame or defuse. A sentence that starts with blame invites defence; a sentence that starts with clarification invites problem-solving. Tone is not cosmetic; it is signal. It tells the other person whether this will be a short, solvable interaction or a long, exhausting one. A calm, curious manner does not mean surrender. It means precision without heat. It means speaking in a way that preserves the other person's dignity while insisting on one's own. That combination is rarer than it should be, and it is startlingly effective. It also makes the person asking feel different. There is a particular steadiness that arrives when someone knows they can ask without collapsing into either apology or aggression. The hinge squeaks less. The moment opens.

And yet it would be dishonest to pretend that every small talk yields a saving, an upgrade, or a waived fee. Some companies have tightened policies, automated decisions, and removed discretion in the name of consistency. Some staff members are exhausted, undertrained, or simply unwilling. Some requests are poorly timed; some problems are genuinely unsolvable in the moment. The point is not to collect victories like trophies. The point is to refuse unconscious surrender. A person who never asks is not "easy-going"; they are invisible. A person who asks well is not "difficult"; they are legible. They become someone the system can respond to, because they have turned a vague dissatisfaction into a clear, answerable request.

The most intriguing part of micro-negotiations is how small they remain. They do not require a new personality, only a new posture towards the everyday. A bill is not a fate; it is a document. A policy is not scripture; it is a rule written by people, interpreted by people, and often softened by people. A job title is not an essence; it is a set of responsibilities that may have drifted over time. When the drift is named, it can sometimes be corrected. When it is not named, it becomes a quiet tax. The same is true of personal time. Scope creep in friendships, volunteer roles, and family obligations is often not the result of malice but of vagueness. "Can you help with this?" becomes "You always handle this." A boundary not stated becomes a boundary erased. The micro-negotiation is, at heart, a craft of naming: naming the term, the expectation, the mismatch, the alternative.

There is a forward tension embedded in this craft, a trade-off that never disappears. Ask too little, and the world charges you extra for your silence. Ask too much, and the world pushes back, sometimes fairly, sometimes with bureaucratic froideur. The skill is not knowing how to force a yes; it is knowing how to frame a request so that a yes becomes easy and a no becomes useful. Every micro-negotiation contains a diagnostic question, whether spoken or silent: is this fixed, or merely treated as fixed because it is convenient? A person who can answer that question—without drama, without self-betrayal—moves through modern life with a different kind of freedom. The hinge turns with less resistance, and the door, when it opens, often reveals not a battle but a better set of terms waiting behind the first, easy-to-accept line.

Chapter 1
Understanding Micro-Negotiations

A man in a polo shirt answers the phone on a Tuesday afternoon and, without thinking much about it, uses a phrase he has said a hundred times: "Let me see what I can do." Somewhere in the background there is the soft percussion of an office—keyboards, a printer clearing its throat, the faint rattle of a headset cable against a desk. The caller is not a corporate titan, not a master of persuasion, not even particularly confident. They are simply asking why their mobile bill has risen by £6 when nothing has changed. The question is plain. The tone is steady. A pause follows, long enough to make the silence feel like a decision being weighed. Then comes the quiet hinge-turn of discretion: a "goodwill credit", a matched promotional rate, a "we can extend that discount for another six months". Nothing dramatic occurs. No voices rise. And yet the terms shift. The bill is no longer the bill. It is a new arrangement made out loud.

It is strange how negotiation became synonymous with confrontation, as if the only way to change a condition is to bruise someone's ego. Most of the shifts that shape daily life happen in smaller ways, and they happen constantly. The supermarket does it with loyalty pricing. The airline does it with fare classes. The bank does it with fee schedules. Work does it with job descriptions that stretch like elastic when nobody measures them. A micro-negotiation is what happens when a person notices the elastic and, gently, pulls it back into shape. It is not theatre. It is attention applied with intention.

Most people already negotiate. They simply refuse to call it that. They ask for a later delivery slot. They request that a repair appointment be moved. They say, "Could you confirm what's included?" They ask whether a refund is possible. They do not feel like negotiators because they are not trying to dominate; they are trying to understand, adjust, or avoid waste. That is precisely the point. The everyday world is packed with terms—prices, policies, conditions, assumptions—many of which are negotiable not because anyone is being generous, but because systems are designed with flex built in. The flex exists because exceptions happen, because retention matters, because mistakes occur, because customer service has leeway, because human judgement still sits inside the machinery. The flex is real. The trick is learning to recognise it without turning into a person who treats every interaction as a contest.

To understand micro-negotiations, it helps to strip the word "negotiation" of its costume. Forget the boardroom and the high-stakes handshake. Think instead of a narrow footbridge over a stream. One side is the default outcome: the price as quoted, the fee as charged, the scope as assumed, the seat as assigned. The other side is a slightly better outcome: a lower rate, a waived charge, a clearer agreement, a more workable deadline. The footbridge is not crossed with force. It is crossed with a question, a pause, a small proposal that keeps the other person's job intact while improving your own position. A micro-negotiation is that crossing—brief, specific, and focused on changing terms rather than changing feelings.

This distinction matters because so much conversational energy is squandered on activity that resembles negotiation but is not. Complaining is not negotiating. Venting is not negotiating. Telling a story about how unfair something feels is not negotiating, even when the feelings are justified. These things may be emotionally necessary in private, and occasionally useful as signal, but they do not in themselves alter the agreement. Negotiation begins the moment a person makes a clear, answerable request for a change in terms. It can be tiny. It can fit into a single sentence. "Can you remove the late fee as a one-off?" "Is there any flexibility on the rate?" "Could you confirm whether that includes parts and labour?" "Can you move me to a quieter room?" A micro-negotiation is not defined by the subject matter. It is defined by its structure: it identifies a term and asks for it to be adjusted.

That structure is why a sixty-second query about a bill or booking is already a negotiation. In most service interactions, the default script assumes passivity. The system expects people to accept what appears on the screen, pay what appears on the invoice, click "agree" and move on. A short, calm query interrupts the script. It forces a check: is this term fixed, or merely presented as fixed? Even when the answer is no, the act of asking performs a useful function. It reveals where discretion does and does not live. It teaches the shape of the system. It turns the vague sense of being done-to into a more accurate sense of being in a transaction—because that is what most of adult life is, whether one likes the language or not.

Take the small case of a mobile bill, because it is almost insultingly ordinary. A person notices that their monthly cost has crept up. They have not changed their usage. They have not bought a new handset. The increase may be perfectly legitimate: an inflation-linked rise, an expired promotional discount, a change in tariffs. What matters is that many people treat the bill as a natural phenomenon, like weather. They may grumble. They may complain to friends. They may do nothing. The micro-negotiation begins when they pick up the phone or open a chat and say something like: "I'm looking at my last two bills and I can see it's gone up. Can you tell me what's changed, and whether there's a better rate available?" That is not a threat. It is not a plea. It is a request for explanation paired with a request for adjustment. It invites the person on the other end to move from script-reading to problem-solving. And because retention departments, promotional codes, and discretionary credits exist, that invitation sometimes opens a door.

The power of these tiny asks is not that they create miracles; it is that they reduce leakage. Most households have multiple points of leakage. Subscriptions renew silently. Insurance premiums rise annually. Energy tariffs drift. Bank fees appear because a direct debit bounced once in a busy month. Delivery charges are accepted because they are small enough to ignore. Scope expands at work because nobody clarifies what "just a quick thing" actually entails. Each leak is minor. Together, they are structural. What micro-negotiations offer is a way to treat daily life less like an unstoppable conveyor belt and more like a series of adjustable settings. A person who tweaks the settings occasionally tends to find that the whole machine runs cheaper, smoother, and with less resentment.

The compounding is not just financial. It shows up in time and in friction, the two resources modern life steals most efficiently. A clarified scope message can prevent hours of back-and-forth later. A confirmation that an appointment window is firm can save a lost afternoon. A quick check on cancellation terms can prevent an argument when plans change. A small request for an alternative route during travel disruption can shorten a delay by a day. There is a particular relief that comes from reducing friction—not by complaining louder, but by intervening earlier and more precisely. People often imagine that negotiation is something you do when you have already been wronged. In reality, the most effective micro-negotiations occur before the problem becomes personal. They are preventative maintenance for relationships and systems.

This is why the focus stays on everyday patterns rather than one-off windfalls. The internet loves the story of someone who argued for a free flight or a massive refund, as if the point were to "win" spectacularly. Those stories are entertainment, and they distort expectations. A micro-negotiation is deliberately modest. It aims for the kind of improvement that feels almost boring—because boring improvements repeat. A £6 monthly reduction is not a headline. Over a year, across several services, it becomes a meaningful figure. More importantly, it becomes a habit of attention, and habits are where real leverage hides. The person who repeatedly asks small, reasonable questions builds a different relationship with systems: less mystified, less resigned, more competent. That competence has an odd side-effect. It makes future conversations calmer, because the stakes feel manageable and the process feels familiar.

If micro-negotiations are so mild, why do so many people avoid them? The usual answer is "fear", but fear is too blunt a word. What people often fear is not the conversation itself but what it might imply about their character. They fear being rude. They fear being the sort of person who causes trouble. They fear sounding cheap. They fear being judged by a stranger who has the power to say no. Underneath those fears lies an older story: negotiation as a fight, where one person's gain is another's loss and asking is a kind of aggression. That story is reinforced by cultural stereotypes and by bad experiences—moments where someone asked clumsily, or demanded too much, or was met with hostility. The lesson drawn is: better not to ask at all.

Yet many organisations actively expect some pushback. Not because they enjoy conflict, but because their internal systems are built around it. They have queues for escalations. They have scripts for waivers. They have discretionary limits for frontline staff. They have departments whose entire job is to keep customers from leaving. None of this makes organisations benevolent, but it does make them predictable. The person who never asks is easy to process: charge, renew, move on. The person who asks once, politely, is a known category too. They are not a threat. They are a decision point. When people realise that asking is expected in certain contexts, the fear changes shape. It becomes less about morality and more about technique. Technique is learnable.

Still, there is a human truth here that deserves respect: some interactions are genuinely uncomfortable. People carry histories—of being dismissed, of being shamed for having less money, of being taught that "making a fuss" is dangerous. Some people have accents, names, disabilities, or identities that attract bias in service environments. A micro-negotiation does not erase social asymmetry. It is not a guarantee of fairness. It is a tool that can be used softly, and sometimes that softness is precisely what makes it safe. The aim is not to transform the world into perfect reciprocity. The aim is to give people a way to advocate for themselves without triggering the adrenal drama that traditional negotiation myths demand. There is dignity in a question asked well, even when the answer is no.

A helpful way to think about this is to separate asking from insisting. Asking is an invitation; insisting is a demand. Most micro-negotiations live comfortably in the realm of asking—asking for review, asking for options, asking for clarification, asking for an exception when circumstances justify it. Insisting is reserved for moments when rights and commitments are clear and the other side is failing to honour them. That boundary matters. It is the difference between being firm and being abrasive. It is also the difference between a conversation that keeps doors open and one that slams them. Many people avoid asking because they think the only alternative to silence is insistence. Once that false binary is dismantled, the space for micro-negotiations appears.

To use that space well, it helps to develop a map. Not a grand strategy, not a spreadsheet empire, but a simple mental inventory of where negotiation already lives in your week. Modern life is full of recurring decision points: contracts that renew, subscriptions that auto-charge, service providers whose prices drift, travel plans that involve policies and discretion, work tasks that expand beyond their original shape. The problem is that these decision points are often disguised as routine. A bill arrives, paid automatically. A subscription renews, unnoticed. A favour at work becomes a permanent responsibility. Micro-negotiations begin when routine is seen as a series of terms and assumptions rather than a fog of "how things are".

Mapping is a way to regain agency without becoming obsessive. It is also a way to practise safely. People who feel anxious about asking often imagine starting with the most emotionally loaded conversation—money at work, a dispute with a contractor, a tense cancellation. That is the negotiating equivalent of deciding to learn swimming by leaping into rough sea. A map changes the practice landscape. It reveals low-risk arenas where the stakes are small and the feedback is immediate: a billing query that can be made on live chat, a hotel request at check-in, a clarification message after a meeting, a question about a fee that has appeared unexpectedly. These are practice opportunities disguised as errands. They teach the rhythm of asking: the calm opening, the factual framing, the precise request, the pause that lets the other person think. Each small attempt makes the next one less charged.

The modern relevance is obvious: prices have risen, services have become more automated, and customer support has been pushed into channels designed to minimise human contact. The average person now navigates a landscape of interfaces that present decisions as final and delays as normal. The temptation is to treat the whole system as indifferent and to retreat into silent compliance or angry outbursts. Micro-negotiations offer a third response suited to the times: a way of remaining human inside automated systems, a way of turning faceless processes into conversations where discretion can still be accessed. Even when the other side is a chatbot or a rigid form, the act of framing a clear request often determines whether the case is routed into a path where a person can intervene. The world is becoming more standardised; that makes the ability to ask precisely more valuable, not less.

There is also a deeper, more timeless relevance. Negotiation, at its core, is about how people share limited resources—money, time, attention, risk—and how they decide what is fair enough. That question never goes away. It exists in markets and marriages, in workplaces and friendships, in hotel lobbies and family WhatsApp groups. Micro-negotiations simply bring that question down to human scale. They treat fairness not as a grand ideology but as a practice: noticing where a term has drifted, naming it, and proposing a small correction. They treat dignity as something expressed in language—through clarity, through calm, through the refusal to be either submissive or cruel.

A motif runs through all of this: the hinge. Most people imagine negotiation as a door being kicked in. Micro-negotiations are the opposite. They are the gentle work of finding the hinge, the point where movement is possible with minimal force. The hinge might be a timing cue—a billing cycle, a quiet moment at a front desk. It might be a policy detail—a grace period, an exception clause, a discretionary limit. It might be a simple alternative—another tariff, another appointment slot, another way to define scope. The hinge is rarely glamorous. It is often hidden in plain sight, behind the first answer that is easiest to deliver. Learning to notice hinges is a way of seeing the world more accurately. The world is not fixed; it is configured.

By the end of this chapter, the aim is not to manufacture confidence through motivational slogans. The aim is to make the whole concept feel smaller and more ordinary, which is where its strength lives. When a person can distinguish venting from negotiating, they stop mistaking emotional release for practical change. When they understand the compounding power of small asks, they stop dismissing minor savings and minor clarifications as not worth the effort. When they recognise their fears as stories—often inherited, often exaggerated—they can choose a different script. When they can map their negotiable life, they acquire a quiet menu of opportunities, a set of low-risk doors they can test without feeling they are gambling their dignity.

The page-turn momentum comes from a simple realisation: once you can see micro-negotiations, you start seeing them everywhere. A bill is no longer just a bill; it is a set of terms that can be checked. A policy is no longer a wall; it is a rule that sometimes has a gate. A work request is no longer a vague obligation; it is a scope that can be named. The choice is not whether to negotiate at all. The choice is whether to negotiate consciously, with a light hand and a clear mind, or to negotiate by default—through silence that pays whatever is demanded and time that absorbs whatever is assumed. The hinge is there. The question is whether to touch it.

Defining Micro-Negotiations

In February 2020, Ofcom introduced rules in the United Kingdom requiring mobile, broadband and pay-TV providers to send end-of-contract and annual best-tariff notifications, a nudge aimed at customers who drifted into paying more simply because they stayed put. The policy detail matters less than the small human scene it was designed to correct: a person in London, half-listening to the low hum of a fridge, glancing at a monthly bill on a cracked phone screen and thinking, without quite forming the thought, that it probably cannot be changed. The rule was a public admission of something many organisations already know in private. Defaults are powerful. So is silence.

Sixty seconds can change terms. That's the oddness. A bill feels like a fact, a policy like a wall, a price like gravity; yet a brief, well-placed question often reveals a hinge. The hinge is not generosity. It is the way systems are built: with scripts, thresholds, exceptions, retention budgets, and humans tasked with resolving problems quickly. A micro-negotiation is what happens when someone touches that hinge with care instead of pushing at the door in anger.

The boundary line is crisp, even if people blur it. Complaining is an expression of dissatisfaction. Venting is emotional discharge. Both can be understandable; neither necessarily alters the agreement. A micro-negotiation begins only when a person makes a clear request for a change in terms—price, timing, scope, fee, condition, or outcome—and does so in a way the other side can answer. The difference is visible in behaviour, not attitude. "This is ridiculous" is heat without a handle. "Can you remove the late fee as a one-off?" is a handle. One creates noise. The other creates a decision.

That distinction is more than semantics because organisations route interactions differently depending on what they hear. A complaint is often channelled into apology scripts, reassurance language, and sometimes a feedback log. A request for altered terms triggers a different internal pathway: a check of authority limits, a search of available codes, a scan of policy exceptions, a judgement about retention risk. Even when the person answering has limited power, they can often escalate a concrete request faster than they can soothe a vague grievance. Precision reduces labour. Labour is cost. Cost shapes outcomes.

The easiest way to see this is to watch a common household interaction unfold. A customer calls their mobile provider because the monthly charge has risen. They lead with a story: they have been a customer for years; they are annoyed; it feels unfair. The agent listens, apologises, and repeats policy. Nothing moves. Now watch the same interaction when the opening is engineered for decision. The customer states an observable fact—"my last bill is £6 higher than the previous one"—then asks an answerable question—"what changed?"—and follows with a specific request—"can you check whether there's a cheaper tariff for the same usage?" The story is shorter. The ask is sharper. The agent can now do their job: compare plans, search offers, apply credits where permitted, or transfer to retention. The relationship does not become friendlier or harsher; it becomes legible.

Micro-negotiations are not defined by volume or bravado. They are defined by the presence of terms. Terms are the hidden scaffolding of everyday life: "non-refundable", "admin fee", "subject to availability", "standard call-out charge", "delivery window", "reasonable wear and tear", "additional work charged at…". When those terms are left unspoken, they still operate. When they are named, they can be questioned, clarified, and sometimes adjusted. This is why a sixty-second query counts. It is not the duration of the conversation that matters; it is whether the conversation turns the implicit into the explicit.

The hinge appears again in the language people use when they believe something is fixed. They reach for moral vocabulary—"it's unfair", "it's outrageous", "you shouldn't"—as if the problem were mainly ethical. Sometimes it is. Often it is procedural. A micro-negotiation keeps ethics in the background and procedure in the foreground, not because fairness is irrelevant, but because the route to fairer outcomes usually runs through operational choices: which department can change what, which timing makes exceptions easier, which alternative options exist, which evidence makes a dispute reviewable. "Can you explain how that fee is calculated?" is a procedural question that shifts the burden from outrage to explanation. Explanation is where inconsistencies are found. Inconsistencies are where change becomes possible.

A second, checkable example makes this even clearer. In April 2010, the Eyjafjallajökull volcanic eruption in Iceland disrupted air travel across Europe, and passengers encountered a maze of policies, rerouting decisions, and responsibility boundaries. Some people spent their energy arguing about blame—who "should" fix it—while others focused on terms—what the airline was offering, what alternatives existed, what documentation was needed for reimbursement. The event was unusual, but the pattern is ordinary. When disruption hits, the system tightens. Staff revert to scripts. Micro-negotiations do not defeat disruption; they navigate it. They turn panic into a sequence of decisions: what can be changed, by whom, and under what conditions. The traveller who asks, calmly, for the earliest rerouting option via a different hub is not being dramatic; they are making the problem solvable. The traveller who only vents may be entirely justified—and still end up sleeping under airport lights.

None of this requires romantic beliefs about human nature. It rests on incentives. Most service systems are built to handle a predictable distribution of customer behaviour. Many people accept default terms. Some people ask once. A smaller number escalate. Companies calibrate effort accordingly. If everyone negotiated every line item, the system would collapse; if nobody did, margins would swell until regulators and competitors intervened. Micro-negotiations live in the stable middle: the level of friction that organisations can absorb because it keeps customers from leaving, prevents complaints from turning into reputational problems, and resolves errors before they metastasise. That is why "we can't" so often means "we can't at this level, with this framing, right now". The hinge is often organisational, not personal.

Still, a credible definition must include limits, otherwise it becomes a pep talk disguised as a concept. Some terms are genuinely fixed, not as a tactic but as a constraint. Statutory penalties, certain regulated charges, and safety-critical decisions are not the territory of micro-negotiation. A tax authority does not "discount" a legal obligation because a caller sounds earnest. A gate agent cannot override safety protocol because a passenger is persuasive. Automation can also harden boundaries. A system that applies fees automatically without discretionary override may offer no movement at all. Pretending otherwise produces the worst kind of negotiation culture: one that mistakes persistence for virtue and turns other people's constraints into personal battles.

The limitation matters because it sharpens the definition rather than weakening it. A micro-negotiation is not the belief that everything is bendable. It is the skill of testing, quickly and respectfully, whether a given term has flex. The test is diagnostic. When the answer is no, the result is still useful information: a boundary has been located. When the answer is yes, the change tends to be modest—often a credit, a matched tariff, a waived fee, an adjusted appointment, a clarified scope. The modesty is a feature. It keeps the interaction proportionate. It also keeps it repeatable, which is where the real value accumulates.

This is why micro-negotiations are distinct from bargaining in the popular imagination. Bargaining is often framed as a contest over a price tag. Micro-negotiations are broader and quieter: they occur wherever terms exist, and terms exist nearly everywhere. When someone asks a hotel desk for a quieter room, they are not contesting the room rate; they are renegotiating the conditions of stay. When someone asks a contractor to confirm whether disposal is included, they are not haggling; they are renegotiating scope. When someone asks a colleague to clarify whether a "quick review" includes rewriting sections, they are renegotiating expectations. Even silence is a negotiation, just a passive one: by saying nothing, a person accepts the other side's framing of reality.

The common objection is psychological: "That feels manipulative." It can be, if the intent is to trick. But a micro-negotiation, properly defined, is closer to a request for alignment. It says: here is what I understood; here is what I need; here is the term that matters; is there a better fit available within your system? It does not require deception. It does not require playing games. In fact, it often works best when it is transparently practical. Many staff members prefer clear, bounded requests because they reduce ambiguity, and ambiguity is what produces long calls, repeat contacts, and complaints that spiral.

A good definition also distinguishes micro-negotiations from what might be called *performative escalation*: the habit of immediately demanding a manager, threatening reviews, or implying legal action as an opening move. Those tactics can sometimes force attention, but they often poison the interaction and are unnecessary for small adjustments. Micro-negotiations are low-drama by design. They preserve future options. They allow both sides to save face. They keep the door closeable even when it opens. That restraint is not politeness for its own sake; it is strategic in the most literal sense. If the aim is a repeatable practice—something that can be used across bills, bookings, repairs, and work—then the method must be compatible with ordinary life, not dependent on adrenaline.

Return to the mobile bill, because the ordinariness is the point. Imagine the same customer at two different moments. In the first, they see the increased charge while rushing between commitments, feel a spike of irritation, and mutter to themselves about corporate greed. They do nothing. The fee becomes part of their baseline, then disappears into the blur of monthly spending. In the second moment, they notice the increase and treat it like a measurable anomaly. They open the bill, compare it to the previous month, and decide to test the hinge. They call or message, state the number, ask what changed, and request the best available rate for their usage. The entire interaction can end inside a minute. Even if the answer is no, the customer has converted passive payment into an active check. If the answer is yes, the household has reduced leakage. More subtly, the customer has trained themselves to see terms as adjustable until proven otherwise. That shift in perception is the invisible engine of micro-negotiation.

The phrase "negotiation" makes people think of dominance, but the more accurate mental model is calibration. Systems drift. Relationships drift. Terms drift. Micro-negotiations are calibration conversations: brief interventions that bring drift back into line with reality. A price increase might be legitimate, but it might also be unnecessary for a customer with low usage. A fee might be policy, but it might also be waivable once a year. A scope assumption might be reasonable, but it might also be unspoken and therefore contested later. Calibration is not confrontation. It is maintenance.

The hinge motif matters here because it keeps the definition grounded. A hinge is small, mechanical, and often ignored until it squeaks. It is also the point where movement happens with minimal force. Micro-negotiations, at their best, locate the hinge in a given situation: the discretionary rule, the alternative plan, the timing window, the department with authority, the piece of evidence that changes classification. People who do not negotiate often push at the door—anger, resignation, avoidance—because they cannot see the hinge. People who micro-negotiate do not push harder. They push smarter, and often more gently.

There is a final boundary worth naming, because it prevents the concept from becoming moralised. Micro-negotiations are not a claim that the person who asks deserves more than the person who does not. They are a claim about how systems respond to clarity. They reward the person who turns a diffuse dissatisfaction into a solvable request. That is ethically uncomfortable in a world that would prefer fairness to be automatic, but it is operationally true. The discomfort is not an argument against micro-negotiations; it is an argument for understanding them, because ignorance does not produce fairness—it produces quiet subsidy. The person who never asks subsidises the system's defaults. The person who asks sometimes receives the system's corrections.

The unresolved tension is this: if a micro-negotiation is a responsible act of attention, when does attention become exhausting? There is a line between maintaining one's terms and living as a permanent auditor of every interaction. The hinge can be touched too often until the door becomes the only thing one sees. So the forward test is not whether to ask endlessly, but whether a given moment deserves a question: is this term truly fixed, or is it merely convenient for everyone that it remain untested?

Why Small Asks Matter

In January 2022, the UK Financial Conduct Authority's "general insurance pricing practices" rules took effect, aiming to stop the quiet phenomenon known as price walking, where renewing customers could end up paying more than new customers for equivalent cover. The rule-change was a regulatory acknowledgement of a familiar domestic scene: a renewal notice arrives, a premium has risen, and the default response is a tired shrug. Somewhere in Britain, a kettle boils, a laptop fan whirs, and a person clicks "accept" because life is busy and the increase is "only" a few pounds a month. Regulators rarely intervene over trivia. They intervened here because trivia, repeated, becomes a pattern—and patterns become a cost that can be measured in household budgets and corporate profits.

Small leaks drain budgets fast. The strange part is not that money adds up; everyone knows that. The strange part is how reliably the mind downplays increments that arrive in small, predictable doses. A single monthly charge sits below the threshold of drama, and anything below drama is treated as optional attention. The same psychology shows up with time: five minutes of friction, a few times a week, becomes a background hum of wasted hours that nobody names because it never arrives as a single, obvious bill.

A modest ask matters because it changes the default. That is the core mechanism. When a person makes a small request—an enquiry about a fee, a check on a tariff, a clarification of what is included—they interrupt a system designed to run on automatic acceptance. The interruption forces a comparison: between what is happening and what could happen with minimal adjustment. That comparison is not merely financial; it is informational. It reveals how the system treats inertia, where discretion lives, and what kinds of change are considered normal inside the organisation.

Picture the ordinary household arithmetic that almost never gets written down because it looks too small to be worth the ink. A service rises by £6 a month. Another creeps up by £4. A "new customer" discount expires and a streaming bundle quietly becomes £8 more expensive than it was a year ago. None of these figures is a crisis. Taken together, they are £18 a month, which is £216 a year. That is the compounding in its least glamorous form: not windfall, but seepage. The implication is not that every rise can be reversed, only that treating seepage as unworthy of attention is a choice with a price tag attached.

Money is only one half of the story. The other is friction, the social and administrative drag that accumulates when terms stay vague. Friction is the extra email thread because scope was assumed rather than confirmed. It is the hour on hold because the wrong department received the query, and nobody asked the question that would have routed it correctly. It is the hotel room by the lift because the preference was never stated. It is the repair invoice padded with "extras" because nobody paused to define what "included" meant. These are not tragedies. They are the texture of modern life. And because they are textural, they are ignored—until someone starts treating them as measurable.

A small ask is, at heart, a measurement tool. It turns a feeling ("this seems expensive") into a checkable proposition ("what is the best available rate for this usage?"). It turns a grumble ("this process is a nightmare") into a decision point ("is there a simpler way to do this without delaying the outcome?"). This shift matters because organisations respond differently to measurement than to emotion. A complaint triggers sympathy scripts. A clear request triggers policy checks, system searches, and discretion thresholds. The implication is almost mechanical: the more precisely a request is framed, the more likely it is to be routed into a pathway where something can actually change.

The clearest evidence that small asks matter is that entire industries have built defences against them. Consider the end-of-contract notifications introduced by Ofcom in February 2020 in the UK for mobile, broadband and pay-TV providers. The rule required companies to inform customers when a contract was ending and to tell them about their best available deals. That is not a piece of etiquette; it is a structural response to a known behavioural pattern: people stay put, and staying put tends to cost them. The small ask—"is there a better rate?"—was common enough, and effective enough, that regulators sought to reduce the need for it by forcing information into the open. The implication is not that regulation replaces personal agency, but that the agency itself is recognised as economically significant.

The compounding effect becomes even sharper when the "ask" is not about price but about avoiding future work. Imagine a work task that expands because expectations are not stated. A colleague sends a message: "Could you have a quick look at this?" If "quick" is left undefined, the task can silently become a rewrite, a redesign, a mini-project with a deadline. The time cost is not paid in one lump; it is paid in scattered evenings, fragmented attention, and a lingering sense of being behind. A small ask—one clarifying question about scope—can prevent an hour of unplanned labour. Multiply that by a few times a month and the result is not simply saved time; it is reduced cognitive load, a less crowded mental calendar. The implication is that micro-negotiations protect attention, which is the resource most professionals are actually rationing.

There is a reason this kind of compounding is easy to underestimate: the human mind is drawn to events, not drips. A one-time crisis feels "real". A quiet monthly increase feels like weather. Behavioural economists have long studied how people treat small, repeated costs as less salient than a single large cost, even when the totals match. The academic language varies—salience, mental accounting, present bias—but the lived experience is the same: what does not shout, disappears. Micro-negotiations matter because they restore salience. They pull a drip into view long enough to decide whether it deserves a change.

A household scenario makes the point without romance. A person notices their mobile bill has risen by £6. They could ignore it. They could complain to friends. Or they could make a brief, measurable enquiry: why has it changed, and what are the options? If the answer is "policy, no movement", the person gains information and can decide whether the service still fits. If the answer includes a cheaper tariff, a matched offer, or a discretionary credit, the person has not merely saved money; they have reset their baseline. Next month, the lower figure becomes normal. The leak has been sealed—at least for now. The implication is not that providers are charitable, but that a quiet request can move the customer from the inertia category into the "decision point" category, where options are presented rather than withheld.

Compounding also applies to confidence, although "confidence" is too airy a word unless it is attached to behaviour. The behaviour is simple: the willingness to ask, briefly and precisely, rather than stew. Each successful small ask reduces the perceived risk of the next one. Each respectful refusal reduces fear as well, because it shows that a request can be made without catastrophe. Over time, the internal metric changes: what once felt like confrontation begins to feel like routine maintenance. The implication is that micro-negotiations create a feedback loop. The loop is behavioural, not motivational.

Still, there is a limitation that deserves daylight. Small asks are not free. They cost time, attention, and emotional energy, and those costs are not evenly distributed. A person juggling caring responsibilities, shift work, or chronic fatigue may find the mental overhead of calling a provider more expensive than the potential savings. A person who has repeatedly been dismissed or stereotyped in service settings may experience "asking" as a risk to dignity rather than a neutral transaction. Even for the well-resourced, some systems have hardened: automated fees, rigid policies, outsourced support that cannot deviate from scripts. In those contexts, asking may yield nothing but frustration.

This limitation does not undermine the value of small asks; it clarifies the criteria for making them worth it. The point is not to interrogate every drip until life becomes an endless audit. The point is to notice which drips are connected to the largest pipes. Recurring services, renewal cycles, and routine scope misunderstandings tend to be those pipes because they repeat, and repetition is where compounding lives. When a system is rigid, the information gained from one attempt can prevent repeated wasted effort. When a system is flexible, one successful adjustment can reduce leakage for months. The implication is that selectivity is part of the skill. Discernment keeps the practice humane.

The most interesting thing about "small asks" is that they alter relationships with systems as much as they alter numbers. A person who never asks becomes invisible to the mechanisms that exist precisely to handle requests—retention teams, discretionary credits, exception processes, escalation routes. A person who occasionally asks becomes legible. Legibility has practical consequences. It changes what options are surfaced. It changes how quickly a query is routed. It changes how much explanation is offered. None of this requires charm. It requires clarity.

Clarity is also what converts friction into something measurable. Consider travel, where time is often lost not to the delay itself but to the fog around it. When a flight is disrupted, the difference between waiting passively and asking a precise question—what alternative routes are available, what rebooking options exist today—can be the difference between a night in an airport and a workable itinerary. The savings here may not appear as a refund; it appears as recovered time and reduced stress. Stress can be named as a feeling, but it is also a metric: the number of hours spent uncertain, the number of contingency plans collapsed, the number of additional costs triggered by delay. A small ask can reduce those metrics even when the broader disruption remains unsolved.

The leak motif returns here because friction behaves like water. It finds the gaps in poorly defined agreements and flows through them until someone seals them. A vague booking condition becomes a dispute later. A loosely stated expectation becomes unpaid overtime. A silently renewed subscription becomes a drain. Each leak is small enough to ignore. Together, they reshape a year.

There is a deeper reason the compounding matters, and it is not money. It is agency. Not the inflated kind that gets sold as personal branding, but the quiet kind that comes from understanding that many everyday outcomes are co-produced. A bill is not simply received; it is accepted. A policy is not simply imposed; it is applied, sometimes with discretion. A scope is not simply assigned; it is negotiated through what is said and left unsaid. When small asks become part of ordinary behaviour, the world feels less like a set of fixed walls and more like a set of doors with hinges—some stiff, some loose, many unopened.

Yet the forward tension remains. If small asks can save money, time, and friction, why do most people still ignore the drips? The answer is not ignorance; it is the trade-off between attention and ease. Automatic acceptance is convenient. Asking requires a moment of presence. The diagnostic question, then, is not whether a particular fee or condition is "fair", but whether it is worth converting from background noise into a deliberate decision: is this drip small enough to ignore, or is it part of a pipe that quietly runs all year?

Common Fears About Asking

In 2004, the International Organization for Standardization—ISO, based in Geneva—published ISO 10002, a formal guideline for how organisations should handle complaints. The detail is not thrilling until its implication lands: complaint-handling is not an embarrassing exception to normal business; it is normal business, important enough to be standardised, audited, trained, and measured. Somewhere behind the document sits a thousand small scenes: a customer at a counter, a traveller on a delayed train, a client querying an invoice, an employee raising a concern—each of them hesitating at the same threshold. A system does not build a standard for something it expects never to happen. It builds one for what happens every day.

Asking feels like breaking rules. The fear is rarely about words alone; it is about the imagined social penalty attached to those words. A person can know, intellectually, that a request is reasonable and still feel a flush of shame before making it, as if politeness required silent acceptance and gratitude required compliance. The voice in the head says: don't be awkward; don't be difficult; don't make a fuss. The irony is that many of the institutions people fear offending have entire departments designed to receive exactly these moments, to process them quickly, and to offer controlled forms of relief.

The first fear is of rudeness, which often disguises a deeper fear of conflict. Rudeness, in this context, is not a matter of vocabulary; it is a matter of forcing someone else into inconvenience. The mental picture is vivid: a tired call-centre agent, a queue behind, a receptionist with a fixed smile, and the request as an act of selfishness. This fear comes from a decent instinct—nobody wants to be the person who makes someone's day worse. Yet it misreads what makes most service interactions hard. The hardest calls are not the ones where someone asks clearly. The hardest calls are the ones where someone arrives upset, tells a long story, refuses to name what would solve it, and then punishes the person on the line for not being able to read their mind. Clarity is kinder than theatre. A short, precise request can reduce labour, which is one of the few gifts a customer can give.

The hinge appears here, quietly. Many people treat "being polite" as pushing at the door as little as possible—don't disturb, don't query, don't ask for a change. But politeness can also mean touching the hinge instead of kicking the wood. A request framed as a check—what changed, what options exist, what can be done—allows the other person to do their job without being accused. The implication is simple and slightly uncomfortable: the fear of rudeness often produces behaviours that are actually less considerate, because they replace clarity with resentment.

A second fear is of seeming ungrateful. Gratitude is a social glue, and most people would rather overpay than risk being seen as entitled. That makes sense in intimate relationships where favours are personal and generosity is discretionary. It becomes stranger in commercial relationships, where the exchange is priced, contractual, and designed to be repeatable. The shop is not doing a favour by selling a product; it is doing business. The hotel is not performing charity by providing a room; it is fulfilling a paid service. The confusion arises because modern service is styled as friendliness—smiles, warm language, "happy to help"—and the brain reads friendliness as personal kindness. When the interaction feels personal, a request for improved terms can feel like ingratitude.

This is where outdated stories about negotiation do real damage. The story says: negotiation is a fight, and fights imply hostility. If the only model a person has is the aggressive haggle, then even a mild enquiry can feel morally suspect. Yet many organisational systems treat negotiation as routine triage. Retention teams exist because companies expect some customers to query price and consider leaving. Billing systems include discretionary credits because errors happen and goodwill is cheaper than churn. Complaint processes are formalised—ISO 10002 is one sign among many—because friction is inevitable and must be managed. Gratitude and negotiation are not opposites in this environment; they are often companions. A person can be appreciative of an agent's effort while still asking for a fee to be reviewed. The implication is not that gratitude is irrelevant, but that it can be expressed without surrendering terms.

The third fear is of being labelled "difficult". This fear has teeth because it imagines consequences: worse service, passive aggression, being punished later. Sometimes that fear is justified. People do get treated differently when they are seen as trouble, and not everyone has equal safety in asserting themselves. But "difficult" is a slippery label. For many organisations, "difficult" does not mean "asked a reasonable question"; it means "consumed excessive time, created uncertainty, refused boundaries, escalated emotionally". A person who is calm, specific, and respectful is often easier to handle than a person who is silent until they explode. The label attaches more readily to drama than to definition.

This is why organisations expect pushback, not because they enjoy it but because their processes assume it. Ofcom's February 2020 requirement for end-of-contract and annual best-tariff notifications in UK telecoms is one example of that expectation becoming policy. It acknowledged that customers often do not know when they can change terms, and that the information imbalance drives overpayment. The existence of such rules is a clue: the market's "normal" state includes people asking, comparing, switching, and querying. Asking is not deviance. It is a predictable behaviour that systems are built to absorb. The implication for fear is subtle: the person who asks is not necessarily stepping outside the social contract; they may be stepping into the version of the contract the organisation quietly expects.

A brief example shows how fear distorts behaviour. Two people receive the same message: a subscription price will rise next month. The first person reads it, feels annoyed, and pays anyway because the annoyance is not worth the imagined awkwardness of a call. The second person contacts support and asks, plainly, whether any retention offer exists or whether a lower tier could match their usage. The second person is not "braver" in a heroic sense. They have simply treated the interaction as transactional rather than personal, and the fear has less room to grow. When the response is positive, the outcome changes. When it is negative, the person gains information and chooses accordingly. Either way, the fear did not get to decide in advance.

Modern life intensifies these fears in a particular way: it mixes intimacy cues with automation. A chat window uses friendly language while delivering rigid policies. A sleek app encourages one-tap acceptance while burying the exit. A customer service agent speaks warmly while following a script optimised for speed. This creates a strange cognitive tension. The interaction feels personal, but the system behaves impersonally. Fear thrives in that tension because it is unclear what kind of social rules apply. Is this a relationship where asking is rude, or a transaction where asking is normal? Micro-negotiations resolve the ambiguity by focusing on behaviour rather than mood: name the term, ask for a review, propose an alternative. The implication is that clarity is not only a tool for getting better terms; it is a tool for easing the psychological discomfort of modern service design.

There is also a moral undertone to these fears, shaped by class, upbringing, and cultural scripts about "making a fuss". In some households, asking is associated with embarrassment—only "those people" haggle; decent people pay and move on. In other households, asking is normal—money is discussed openly; terms are questioned; deals are expected. Neither script is purely virtuous. The first can preserve harmony while quietly draining resources. The second can protect resources while sometimes eroding kindness. The more interesting stance is to separate the act of asking from the act of performing superiority. A micro-negotiation is not a display of cleverness. It is a request for alignment.

A credible account must also face a counter-example: there are contexts where asking carries genuine risk. A junior employee negotiating workload with a volatile manager is not in the same position as a customer querying a late fee. A tenant disputing a charge with a landlord may fear retaliation. A person with a marginalised identity may encounter bias when asserting themselves. Even in banal commercial settings, some systems punish friction indirectly: long hold times, limited channels, "computer says no". The fear is not always irrational; it can be a protective instinct.

Reconciling this does not require pretending the world is fair. It requires a more realistic definition of "safe". Safety is often about reducing exposure: keeping requests short, anchoring them in facts, choosing channels that create records, and knowing when a no is information rather than a cue to escalate. Organisations that formalise complaint processes do so partly to protect themselves, but those processes can also protect the person asking by creating a predictable pathway. The implication is that fear can be respected without letting it become a permanent veto. A person can choose when and where to ask, rather than living under a blanket rule of silence.

Notice how "trust" operates here, not as a warm feeling but as a decision under uncertainty. Trust is the decision to believe that asking will not produce punishment. Many people's trust is low because they have seen service failures and bureaucratic indifference. Micro-negotiations do not demand naive trust; they demand measured trust. Measure the stakes. Measure the likely upside. Measure the cost of asking. When the cost is low and the potential benefit is meaningful, asking becomes less a leap of faith and more a rational test. The same applies to "risk". Risk is not a mood. It is the probability and impact of a negative outcome. Fear often exaggerates both. A clear, respectful request tends to reduce actual risk because it gives the other side fewer reasons to become defensive.

"Efficiency" shows up as well, and it is often misunderstood. People avoid asking because they assume it will take too long. Sometimes it will. Yet the time cost of asking must be compared to the time cost of not asking. Not asking can mean recurring overpayment, repeated rework, ongoing annoyance, and the future labour of switching providers in frustration. Many organisations optimise for shorter calls, which perversely means that a short, well-framed request is often the most efficient way to resolve a problem. A person who vents for ten minutes and never names a request creates inefficiency. A person who asks for a specific adjustment in one sentence often creates the opposite. The implication is not that time always favours asking, but that the common assumption—asking equals hassle—is frequently based on the memory of badly structured conversations.

The fight-story about negotiation also produces a particular kind of self-sabotage: people wait until they are angry enough to justify asking, then they ask with the heat of that anger. Anger is energising, but it is also noisy. It triggers defensiveness in others and impulsiveness in oneself. When negotiation is imagined as combat, anger feels like armour. Micro-negotiations rely on a different kind of armour: structure. Structure allows a person to ask early, before resentment curdles, and to ask in a way that makes cooperation possible. The hinge is easier to turn before it rusts.

There is a final, quieter fear that rarely gets named: the fear of being seen. Asking makes the person legible. Silence is a form of camouflage. For many people, especially those trained to be "low maintenance", camouflage feels safer than visibility. But invisibility has a cost. It keeps the person out of the pathways designed to correct mistakes, offer options, and adjust terms. It also keeps them in a posture of quiet endurance, which can spill into other parts of life—accepting vague scope at work, absorbing unequal burdens at home, tolerating small indignities because naming them feels like too much. A micro-negotiation is a small act of self-recognition: a refusal to disappear from the transaction.

Organisations, for all their faults, often reward this kind of legibility because it makes cases solvable. A person who states the fee, the date, the expectation, and the requested change gives the system something to process. That does not guarantee a yes. It does, however, shift the interaction from moral drama to operational choice. This is why asking can be normalised without turning it into a personality type. Normalisation does not mean everyone asks all the time. It means asking is treated as one of the standard moves available to an adult navigating a complex system—no more shameful than querying an error on a document.

The forward test is therefore not "Am I the kind of person who negotiates?" That question invites identity politics and unnecessary guilt. The more useful question is narrower and harder: when a term feels fixed, is it truly fixed, or is it merely presented that way because silence is common—and is the fear of asking protecting dignity, or quietly selling it for convenience?

Mapping Your Negotiable Life

In September 1854, in Soho, London, the physician John Snow walked the neighbourhood with a notebook and a purpose. Cholera was tearing through streets that looked ordinary in daylight. Snow did something deceptively simple: he mapped deaths to addresses, then compared the pattern to the location of water pumps. The resulting cluster around the Broad Street pump became an argument made visible, strong enough to justify removing a pump handle and, eventually, to change how people understood disease transmission. A map did not cure cholera by itself. It changed what counted as an explanation. It turned dread into a pattern that could be tested.

Maps change what we notice.

The same principle applies to the daily, quieter epidemic of unnecessary friction: the fees that arrive because renewal is automatic, the hours lost because scope is vague, the small service failures that persist because nobody asks for a remedy that fits the system's own rules. Without a map, these costs feel like weather. They are everywhere and nowhere. With a map, they become clustered around a few pumps: recurring contracts, routine services, travel decisions, workplace tasks that expand beyond their original shape. The point is not to become paranoid about every penny. The point is to stop being surprised by predictable loss.

A negotiable-life map begins with an unromantic observation: most negotiations are not dramatic events but repeated patterns. A person who waits for a "big negotiation" will miss the dozens of tiny ones that set their baseline. Baselines are powerful because they become normal. A mobile plan that drifted up by a few pounds becomes "what it costs". A subscription bundle that doubled over three years becomes "standard". A work responsibility that crept into a role becomes "part of the job". When the baseline is accepted without inspection, the system learns that this version of reality will hold. When it is inspected—briefly, occasionally—the system is forced to reveal its alternative configurations.

The first claim is simple, and it is best shown rather than asserted. Think of a week with no obvious crises. There is a standing order for broadband. There is an insurance direct debit. There is a train booking for next month. There is a recurring meeting where tasks are assigned loosely and later "clarified" into more work than expected. Nothing about this week screams negotiation. Yet each element contains terms: renewal dates, cancellation windows, fee schedules, refund rules, scope expectations, delivery standards. Naming this is not pedantry. It is the act of locating the pump. The concept is *recurrence*: anything that repeats is where small changes compound. The implication is that attention should follow recurrence, not drama.

Mapping also changes how fear behaves. Fear thrives in the vague. "Negotiation" sounds like a confrontation with a winner and a loser; "mapping" sounds like observation. That difference matters because observation is psychologically easier to begin. A person who would never describe themselves as someone who negotiates might still happily describe themselves as someone who keeps track, who likes clarity, who prefers not to waste time. The map offers a softer entry into agency. It turns "asking" from a personality trait into a decision made at specific points, based on visible triggers.

Here is what "mapping" means in practice, without turning it into bureaucracy. Imagine setting aside a brief, bounded stretch of attention—long enough to scan, not long enough to spiral. You are not hunting for every possible negotiation. You are identifying a small number of recurring situations where a micro-negotiation would be low-risk and potentially high-yield. The visible behaviour is writing down your regular providers and obligations, then noting the next moment each can be changed: contract end dates, renewal notices, billing cycles, upcoming bookings, scheduled repairs, performance review windows. The concept is *decision points*: moments when a system expects adjustment and therefore has pathways for it. The implication is that you begin choosing your moments, rather than being dragged into them by surprise.

A useful map has a legend: it differentiates types of negotiability. Some items are "fixed unless there is an error". Others are "flexible at renewal". Others are "flexible at the moment of service". Others are "flexible when scope is unclear". This is not about creating perfect categories. It is about noticing that different systems move at different times. A gym membership may have a monthly cancellation cycle. A mobile provider may have end-of-contract offers. A hotel desk can change room allocation at check-in but not after the building is full. A work project is easiest to scope at the beginning and hardest when deadlines loom. The concept is *timing*: terms are often most pliable at particular points. The implication is that mapping prevents wasted effort, because you stop trying to move stone when the system only ever moves wood.

A second, checkable example clarifies why institutions themselves care about these decision points. In February 2020, Ofcom introduced rules in the UK requiring providers in mobile, broadband and pay-TV to send end-of-contract and annual best-tariff notifications. The intent was to reduce overpayment caused by inertia. The relevant detail for a negotiable-life map is not the politics of regulation; it is the acknowledgement of structure. These notifications mark a moment when change is anticipated. They are, in effect, signposts placed by the system itself: here is where terms can be reviewed. A person who maps their contracts and watches for these signposts is not gaming anything. They are responding to the system's own cadence.

The third claim is about scale, and it should be shown with something concrete. Many people assume that negotiating is "worth it" only if the potential gain is large. Mapping reveals a different arithmetic. A person might have five or six recurring outgoings—communications, utilities, insurance, subscriptions, transport, and perhaps a professional membership—each with modest drift over time. They might also have recurring friction points—meetings that generate unclear tasks, contractors who provide vague quotes, travel plans that contain restrictive conditions. None of these individually feels life-changing. Yet the map reveals how often the same kinds of moments occur. Frequency is a multiplier. The concept is *compounding by repetition*. The implication is that "small" becomes significant when it is no longer rare.

Mapping also guards against a common trap: mistaking busyness for inevitability. People do not ignore negotiable moments because they are foolish; they ignore them because attention is scarce. The modern economy is built around scarcity of attention. Auto-renewal, pre-ticked boxes, rolling contracts, and default upgrades are not mere conveniences; they are attention-capture mechanisms. Mapping is a counter-mechanism. It restores a small amount of deliberate choice. The visible behaviour is not obsessive monitoring but periodic review: a glance at what repeats, what has changed, and what is due for renewal. The concept is *attention budgeting*. The implication is that micro-negotiations become sustainable, because they are scheduled into life rather than triggered by irritation.

There is, however, a credible limitation that deserves honesty. Mapping can become a form of anxiety dressed as productivity. Some people, once they start seeing terms everywhere, begin treating every interaction as a potential battle over value. They measure everything and enjoy nothing. They become, effectively, their own worst compliance department. This is a real failure mode, and it is more likely in people who are already under stress, because control feels comforting when the world feels unstable. The reconciliation is not to abandon mapping, but to refine its purpose. A map is not the territory. It is a tool for choosing where *not* to spend attention as much as where to spend it. A good map helps a person ignore most things with confidence, because they have identified the few pumps that matter.

This is where the notion of "low-risk practice opportunities" becomes important, not as self-help jargon but as an operational idea. When people fear asking, they often begin with the highest-stakes scenario and then retreat after a bad experience. Mapping allows a different progression: begin where the downside is minimal. A billing query via chat is low-risk because it is brief and reversible. A hotel request at check-in is low-risk because the worst outcome is a polite no and the interaction ends. A clarification message after a meeting is low-risk because it frames expectations rather than criticises performance. Each of these can be rehearsed by life itself because the opportunities recur. The concept is *deliberate exposure*: practising a behaviour in settings where failure is not catastrophic. The implication is that the skill becomes reliable rather than sporadic.

A third checkable example underscores why mapping workplace tasks matters as much as mapping bills. In January 2022, the UK Financial Conduct Authority's rules on general insurance pricing practices came into force, aiming to curb "price walking" for renewing customers. That was about premiums, but the underlying mechanism applies in offices too: the longer someone "stays put" in a role, the more likely it is that expectations drift upward without corresponding adjustment in recognition or resources. The workplace equivalent of price walking is responsibility walking. It happens when extra tasks attach themselves to a person because they are competent, agreeable, or simply present. A negotiable-life map that includes work tasks—recurring meetings, recurring deliverables, recurring "quick favours"—is a way of noticing responsibility walking early, when it can still be discussed as scope rather than as grievance.

Mapping turns abstractions into decisions. "Trust" becomes the decision to believe that a request will be received as normal rather than as insolence; mapping increases trust by clarifying which systems expect requests and which do not. "Risk" becomes the decision to ask in a context where refusal carries little penalty; mapping lowers risk by favouring low-stakes points of contact. "Efficiency" becomes the decision to spend five minutes now to save an hour later; mapping reveals where friction repeats and therefore where time-saving is most likely. These are not inspirational claims. They are operational. They can be tested in a calendar and on a bank statement.

The most useful maps also include upcoming transitions, because transitions are where terms often reset. Moving house, changing jobs, travelling, renewing insurance, replacing a phone, organising a repair—these moments contain unusually high concentrations of adjustable terms. They are natural negotiation seasons. People often experience them as overwhelming precisely because so many decisions arrive at once. A map does not eliminate that load, but it changes the posture from reactive to prepared. The visible behaviour is noting upcoming changes early enough to reduce panic decisions. The concept is *anticipation*: meeting decision points with information rather than urgency. The implication is that micro-negotiations become calmer because they are not forced into the narrow window where everything feels urgent.

The motif of the map matters again here, because a map is only useful at the right scale. Too zoomed out, and everything looks like a blur. Too zoomed in, and the map becomes an obsession. The right scale shows roads and junctions—the decision points—without pretending you must inspect every paving stone. This is the tone a negotiable-life map aims for: broad enough to be sustainable, detailed enough to be actionable. It is a practice of seeing the joints in the week.

The forward test is therefore practical and slightly philosophical. If a week is made of terms—some fixed, some flexible—what is your chosen relationship to those terms: passive acceptance until irritation accumulates, or deliberate attention at a few key junctions? The map does not answer the question for you. It merely makes the question impossible to ignore.

Chapter 2
Timing, Tone and Leverage

In April 1970, at the height of the Apollo 13 crisis, Gene Kranz sat in Mission Control in Houston listening to clipped voices, rising numbers, and the dull, relentless hiss of radio static. The story is often told as heroism and engineering, but its most instructive detail is quieter: the discipline of communication under pressure. Words were chosen for function, not drama. Questions were timed. Decisions were framed so they could be answered. A single badly placed instruction could waste minutes the crew did not have. A single well-formed prompt could turn confusion into a plan. That, in a different costume, is the hidden mechanics of everyday negotiation too: not dominance, but the choreography of attention.

Most people who struggle to ask for better terms do not fail because their requests are unreasonable. They fail because they treat conversation like a coin toss. They call when they are annoyed rather than when the system is most receptive. They speak in the heat of moral judgement rather than the cool of shared problem-solving. They assume they have no leverage unless they can threaten, when in fact leverage often arrives disguised as mundanity: a competitor's offer, a long payment history, the ability to be flexible, the simple fact that keeping an existing customer is cheaper than acquiring a new one. Micro-negotiations begin with the hinge; this chapter is about learning where the hinge is most likely to turn, and how to touch it without splintering the door.

Timing is the first of these quiet advantages because it determines whether the person you reach is even capable of hearing you. It is fashionable to imagine organisations as machines, but most of their "decisions" are human decisions made within constraints, under clocks, with queues building behind them. A call placed at 9:03 on a Monday morning can land on someone triaging a backlog, scanning for the quickest way to clear the line. The same call placed midweek, at a quieter hour, can land in a different psychological climate: more bandwidth, more patience, more willingness to check one more screen rather than recite the first script. The request has not changed. The outcome might.

There is a philosophical discomfort here that is worth naming. We prefer to believe that fairness is independent of timing, that a rule is a rule and a fee is a fee regardless of the hour. Yet anyone who has ever tried to resolve a problem knows that systems are not pure logic; they are living arrangements between policy and people. Timing changes the friction coefficient. It changes whether discretion feels like a burden or a simple kindness. It changes whether the person on the other end has room to think. This is not cynicism. It is an observational fact about how cognition works under load. Even the most conscientious agent, clerk, or manager becomes more rigid when overwhelmed, because rigidity is faster.

Tone is the second advantage because it determines whether the other person joins you or braces against you. Tone is not the same thing as niceness. A person can be "nice" in a submissive way and still be ignored. A person can be firm in a respectful way and still be helped. Tone is the signal carried by pace, word choice, and the moral temperature of a sentence. Accusatory language invites defence. Curious language invites explanation. Explanation is where options hide. A customer who opens with "You've overcharged me" may be factually right, but they have already implied blame. A customer who opens with "I'm trying to understand this charge—can you walk me through it?" has asked for the same outcome while making it easier for the agent to assist without losing face. This is not etiquette for its own sake; it is the social engineering of cooperation.

Modern service design makes tone even more consequential because so many interactions begin in places where nobody can see you. A disembodied voice on a headset. A chat window that strips away facial cues. An email thread where the reader cannot hear your good intentions. In these conditions, tone becomes a proxy for identity. The recipient uses it to decide what kind of person they are dealing with and, therefore, what kind of effort is worth spending. People often misjudge tone because they write as if they are arguing with a system, but the system is operated by a person. The person has feelings, fatigue, limits, and sometimes genuine goodwill. Micro-negotiations work best when they acknowledge the person without flattering them and acknowledge the system without treating it as an enemy. Calm curiosity is not weakness. It is a method.

Then comes the word that makes everyone uncomfortable: leverage. It conjures threats, power plays, and that stale cultural caricature of negotiation as a contest of wills. The leverage that matters in daily life is rarely theatrical. It is the presence of realistic alternatives and the ability to choose among them. A competitor's tariff is leverage. A willingness to accept a different appointment time is leverage. A consistent payment history is leverage. The fact that a company wants to keep churn low is leverage, whether or not the customer ever uses that language. Leverage is not what you do to someone; it is what the world allows you to do for yourself. When you can leave, you do not need to shout. When you can wait, you do not need to beg. When you can compare, you can speak plainly.

Many people believe they have no leverage because they confuse leverage with status. They imagine leverage belongs to executives, celebrities, or people who enjoy confrontation. But most everyday leverage is quiet and structural. It lives in switching costs, in market competition, in how organisations measure success. Consider the internet contract that renews with a price rise: the provider's front line may recite policy, but a retention team exists because the provider has already decided that some customers are worth discounting to keep. The customer does not need to threaten; they need to be credible. Credibility comes from alternatives that are real, not invented. Even the simple act of mentioning that another provider offers a comparable package at a lower rate can be enough to shift the conversation from "policy" to "options".

There is a deeper thread here, and it is about self-possession. People often think the most powerful negotiator is the most aggressive one. In practice, the most powerful person in a conversation is usually the one with genuine exit options who does not need to perform them. A person who knows what they will do if the answer is no speaks differently. They are calmer. They ask better questions. They do not cling to the conversation as if their dignity depends on being granted an exception. That calm changes the other person's behaviour, because it removes the sense of being cornered. The paradox is that exit options often produce better outcomes even when they are never used. They are psychological scaffolding.

This chapter's focus on timing, tone, and leverage is not a self-improvement manifesto. It is a study of conditions—like studying weather before sailing. Conversations are environments. They have pressure systems. They have visibility. They have currents. A request made at the right moment, in the right tone, with the quiet confidence of alternatives behind it, travels differently through that environment. The same request made in a rush, sharpened by irritation, with no thought to what happens if it fails, often sinks. The content of the request is identical. The context is not.

The tools that shape context are often simple and therefore easy to dismiss. A pause at the right time. A question that invites explanation rather than defensiveness. A reasonable starting point that defines the frame—an anchor that is neither absurd nor timid. A bundle that links two issues into one coherent ask, so the other person can justify flexibility without feeling exploited. A clear sense of what you will accept and what you will not, not as a threat but as a boundary. These are not tricks. They are the grammar of small negotiations.

Anchoring deserves attention because it explains a common experience: a person accepts an offer that feels "better" without noticing that the frame was set by the other side. If a provider begins with the highest price and then "discounts" it, the customer can feel grateful for returning to something close to reasonable. A different anchor—one grounded in a known public offer or in the customer's existing rate—changes the psychological landscape. It gives the conversation a reference point. It makes the ask feel like alignment rather than extraction. Anchors are not lies. They are starting points. In many everyday negotiations, the side that sets the first clear starting point sets the emotional temperature of the discussion.

Bundling matters because people rarely negotiate single variables in isolation. A customer might be willing to sign a longer contract if the monthly price falls. A traveller might accept a different flight if accommodation is covered. A client might accept a revised timeline if scope is reduced. Bundling links variables so that concessions can be exchanged rather than begged for. It turns "give me" into "here is a trade". Trades feel fairer because they acknowledge constraint. They allow the other person to say yes without feeling they have surrendered. Fairness is not a mood. It is a structure.

And yet it would be dishonest to pretend these tools are always effective. Some systems have hardened. Some staff members are burnt out. Some companies prefer churn to flexibility. Some organisations train employees to resist any deviation because deviation creates precedent. There are also moments when the right thing to do is to stop talking and switch provider, decline an upsell, or accept that a policy will not bend. This chapter does not promise that timing, tone, and leverage will move every wall. It promises something less glamorous and more useful: they will help you tell the difference between a wall and a door.

The modern relevance of this difference is obvious to anyone who has tried to resolve a problem through a chatbot, a web form, or a labyrinth of automated menus. The more automated the front end, the more valuable human moments become. The person who can choose when to seek a human, and then speak in a way that makes the human's task easier, will often receive more help—not because they are special, but because they have reduced uncertainty and reduced labour. Organisations are not generous; they are efficient. If you make it easier for the system to give you a better outcome than to refuse, you have shifted the odds.

A quiet motif threads through all of this: the tide. Timing is tide. Tone is tide. Leverage is tide. A tide does not care about your arguments; it cares about conditions. Sail with it and progress feels almost effortless. Fight it and exhaustion arrives quickly. The point is not to become calculating. The point is to become observant. When you start noticing the tide—when a call centre is least loaded, when a front desk has space, when a policy window is open, when an alternative offer is credible—you stop wasting energy in dead water.

The page-turn question is therefore not whether you can "negotiate", but whether you can choose your conditions. Will you keep having these conversations at random, fuelled by irritation and urgency, or will you begin arranging them—quietly, deliberately—so that a reasonable request can land in a receptive moment, carried by a calm tone, supported by options you have already measured? The answer is not theoretical. It is a choice repeated in small moments, where the tide is either noticed or ignored.

Choosing the Right Moment

In 1917, in Copenhagen, the Danish mathematician Agner Krarup Erlang published a paper for the Copenhagen Telephone Company on a problem that sounded banal and was not: how many lines and operators are needed so callers do not wait forever. The work became the backbone of queueing theory in telephony, and its most human detail is easy to imagine even now—the click of switchboard relays, the low murmur of voices, the small irritations of being put on hold when life is already full. Erlang's mathematics did not moralise the caller or blame the operator. It treated time as a force that reshapes outcomes. When arrivals cluster and capacity stays flat, the queue grows; when arrivals spread out, the same capacity feels generous. The physics of waiting was laid bare.

Timing changes the whole outcome.

That is the first quiet truth of micro-negotiations: the same request can be granted or refused depending less on its content than on the conditions surrounding it. Most people experience this as superstition—"they were nicer last time"—but it is usually structure. A system is never equally receptive at all hours. A person is never equally patient at all moments. The question, then, is not whether timing "matters" in some sentimental sense, but *how* it matters, and how a time-conscious adult can treat it as a variable rather than an afterthought.

Begin with a scene that feels too ordinary to carry theory. A customer calls a provider at 9 a.m. on a Monday. The weekend's unresolved problems have rolled forward like a wave. Bills have landed. Services have failed. People who postponed calling now call at once, as if Monday were a reset button. The agent answers with the clipped efficiency of triage. The customer's query is reasonable, but the line is thick with urgency from other callers, and urgency narrows empathy. The agent's safest move is the fastest move: recite policy, offer minimal options, close the case. The same customer calls midweek, late morning, when queues are thinner and the agent's brain is not in sprint mode. There is more silence. Silence is bandwidth. A second screen gets checked. A discretionary credit becomes thinkable. The concept here is *cognitive load*: when someone is overloaded, they default to rigid scripts; when they have slack, they can solve. The implication is practical and slightly unsettling: much of what feels like "fairness" in service is in fact *capacity management.*

This is not unique to call centres. It appears anywhere a person is making decisions under a queue. A hotel front desk at check-in time is a queue. A gate agent during boarding is a queue. An accounts team at month-end is a queue. Even an inbox is a queue, shaped by deadlines and attention. Timing is the art of meeting decision-makers when they have room to decide. That room may be measured in minutes, not hours. It may be the difference between a refusal delivered automatically and an option surfaced deliberately.

A second, checkable example shows that this is not merely "common sense"; it is visible in research about decision fatigue. In 2011, Shai Danziger, Jonathan Levav, and Liora Avnaim-Pesso published a study in *Proceedings of the National Academy of Sciences* analysing Israeli parole decisions. They found that favourable rulings were more likely earlier in a session and after breaks, and less likely as the session wore on. The study has been debated, as any high-profile behavioural finding should be, but its value here is not as a slogan about judges. It is as a reminder that human decision-making is not constant over time. It is periodic. It is punctuated by fatigue, hunger, interruptions, and the slow accumulation of cognitive strain. The concept is *decision depletion*: as mental resources drain, risk tolerance often shrinks. The implication for everyday negotiation is modest and profound: when a request requires someone to think, to deviate, or to apply discretion, the timing of that request can change the probability of a favourable response.

Timing operates through at least three channels, each visible if one looks closely. The first is *queue pressure*, Erlang's world. When many people want service at once, the system becomes harsher—not out of spite, but out of throughput. The second is *policy windows*. Many services have cycles: billing dates, renewal dates, promotional expiries, monthly quotas, annual reviews. Requests made inside the window are processed as normal business; requests made outside it are treated as exceptions. The third is *human energy*, Danziger and colleagues' world, where the same person can be more flexible at one time and more defensive at another. None of these channels requires manipulative intent. They are structural features of work.

To see policy windows at work, consider the end of a billing cycle. An account has a rhythm: the bill is generated, sent, paid, and archived. Disputes and adjustments tend to be easiest when the transaction is still "open" in the system—when credits can be applied without reopening prior periods, when notes can be added before the next statement, when an agent can see the context without searching. The same request made months later may still be possible, but it often becomes harder simply because it requires more steps. Steps are labour. Labour is cost. The concept is *operational friction*: the more internal effort a request demands, the less attractive it becomes to grant. The implication is that timing is often less about mood and more about how many clicks the request forces inside the organisation.

The same logic applies to renewals. Renewals are moments when the system expects change—prices shift, terms are re-confirmed, services can be altered. Outside renewal, the system expects stability. A request to modify terms mid-contract might still be possible, but it is more likely to be treated as special handling. Special handling is scarce. When change is expected, it can be framed as routine. The implication is not that one must obsess over dates, but that dates are part of the negotiation environment whether or not they are acknowledged.

This helps explain why "Monday morning versus midweek" is more than a folk belief. Monday morning often combines all three channels: queue pressure (weekend backlog), policy windows (people reacting to messages received late Friday or over the weekend), and human energy (agents beginning a week with a packed slate, supervisors in meetings, teams catching up). Midweek often disperses these pressures. The system breathes. A person who plans around this is not gaming the world; they are recognising that a request is an event that lands in an environment. Environment matters.

Still, timing is not a moral right. It is a probability tool. There are moments when timing cannot be chosen, and pretending otherwise can turn a useful idea into a source of self-blame. When a flight is cancelled, the timeline is imposed. When a contractor finds an unexpected problem mid-job, the decision point arrives whether or not anyone feels ready. When a fee is charged, there may be a limited dispute window. In these moments, timing becomes a constraint rather than a choice. The credible counter-example, then, is the crisis negotiation that must happen *now*, when queues are long and nerves are short. In such circumstances, timing cannot be "optimised"; it can only be managed.

Reconciling this limitation makes the concept sharper. Timing, in everyday negotiations, is not about waiting for perfect conditions. Perfect conditions rarely arrive. It is about recognising *avoidable bad conditions* and *predictable windows*. Even in imposed timelines, small timing choices exist: whether the first contact is made immediately in the heat of panic or after ten minutes spent gathering details; whether the message is sent at midnight in a burst of frustration or in the morning when a human is more likely to read it with fresh eyes; whether escalation happens instantly or after one clear attempt at resolution. The difference between "now" and "later" may be small. Small differences compound.

One can watch timing at work in the micro-economy of hospitality. A hotel request for a different room, made at 11 p.m. when the building is full and staff are thin, is structurally hard to grant even if the staff member would like to help. The same request made earlier, when room assignments are still in motion, is easier because the system has slack. Slack is not kindness. Slack is capacity. The concept is *resource availability*: when the resource is abundant relative to demand, flexibility feels natural; when scarce, flexibility feels costly. The implication is that some "no" responses are not refusals of the person; they are reflections of the moment.

Workplaces offer a parallel example. A request for a change in scope, made after a deadline has been promised to a client, lands in an environment of reputational risk. The same request made when timelines are still internal is a different proposition. Here "risk" becomes visible: it is the likelihood of a missed deadline, a dissatisfied stakeholder, a blame spiral. Timing changes risk, and risk changes decision behaviour. The implication is that timing is not merely about catching people in a good mood; it is about catching the system before it has locked itself into commitments.

There is also a subtle, often overlooked form of timing: the sequence of information. Many conversations fail not because the request is bad, but because the request arrives before the facts. An agent, hearing an emotionally loaded opening, reaches for the fastest exit—policy, refusal, closure—before the relevant detail appears. When the detail finally arrives, the refusal has already been spoken, and reversing it requires face loss. Humans dislike reversing themselves. The concept is *commitment inertia*: once someone states a position, they tend to defend it. The implication is that timing includes timing within the conversation: leading with the clearest facts, then the request, before the emotional story expands.

This is why planning changes outcomes without requiring aggression. Planning is not a grand strategy. It is choosing the moment when the hinge is most likely to turn. The hinge motif matters because it keeps timing grounded. A hinge moves best when it is not under strain. When a door is pressed by a crowd on the other side, even a good hinge will groan. When the pressure eases, the same hinge swings easily. Timing seeks the easing.

And yet there is a tension here worth holding rather than smoothing away. If timing is real, it means the world is not purely fair in the way people wish it were. Two customers with the same issue can receive different outcomes because one called at a quiet hour and one called during a surge. That feels unjust. It is also true. The ethical response is not to pretend timing does not matter; it is to recognise that fairness in many systems is mediated by capacity, and capacity is variable. Institutions attempt to standardise, but discretion remains. Timing is a way of interacting intelligently with that reality, not endorsing it.

The deeper challenge is deciding how much life should be planned around these windows. There is a line between sensible attention and a kind of chronic vigilance. The goal is not to live with one eye always on the queue, arranging every interaction like a chess move. The goal is to stop treating timing as random, and to treat it as one of the controllable variables available in a complex world. The forward test is therefore quiet and concrete: when the next small term needs adjusting, will it be raised in the moment of maximum pressure simply because that is when irritation peaks, or will it be raised when the system has slack—when the hinge is most likely to move?

Using a Calm, Curious Tone

In May 1981, in Cambridge, Massachusetts, Roger Fisher and William Ury published *Getting to Yes*, a book that smuggled a radical idea into mainstream negotiation culture: treat the problem as the problem, not the person. The phrase is now so widely repeated that it risks becoming wallpaper, but its original impact lay in how it sounded compared to the era's negotiation mythology. It did not instruct readers to outmanoeuvre opponents. It asked them to change the temperature of conversation. That temperature shift—cooler, clearer, less accusatory—was not presented as moral purity. It was presented as an instrument. Instrumental tone is the subject here: the way voice, pace, and wording can open or close the hinge of discretion.

Tone makes decisions easier.

Most people assume tone is decoration, the social ribbon tied around a request so it looks polite. In micro-negotiations, tone is structural. It changes what the other person believes is happening. Are they being attacked or recruited? Are they being blamed or asked to think? Are they about to endure a long argument or help solve a contained problem? Those beliefs are formed quickly—often within the first sentence—and once formed they are sticky. The first impression becomes the filter through which every later fact is heard. A calm, curious tone is not timid; it is a way of making the other person's brain available for problem-solving rather than self-defence.

A concrete scene shows how this plays out. A customer sees a charge they do not recognise. They contact support and begin with an accusation: "You've taken money from my account." The agent hears threat, not information. Threat triggers procedure: the agent becomes careful, rigid, keen to protect themselves from blame. They quote policy. They insist the charge is valid. The customer's anger grows. Now replay the same scene with a different opening: "I've spotted a charge I don't understand. Can you help me identify what it's for?" The facts are unchanged. The emotional frame is not. The agent can now enter the interaction as a helper rather than as a defendant. They can search, explain, and, if appropriate, correct. The concept is *framing*: the first sentence defines whether the conversation is collaborative or adversarial. The implication is blunt: if the aim is a change in terms, starting with blame often reduces the chance of getting it.

This is not a claim about politeness as virtue. It is a claim about cognitive mechanics. Humans are exquisitely sensitive to social threat. Threat detection is fast, and it shifts the nervous system towards defence. When the other person feels threatened, they stop exploring options. They narrow. They cling to rules. They look for safe exits. A calm tone reduces threat; curiosity reduces blame; together they make cognitive space. That space is where discretion lives. Discretion is not magic. It is the ability to choose among permissible options. Tone influences whether someone is willing to do the mental work of finding an option.

The difference between accusation and curiosity can be heard in small, practical scripts. Consider a provider who has increased a bill. Accusatory phrasing sounds like: "You've put my price up again. That's outrageous." Curious phrasing sounds like: "I can see the price has gone up. What changed, and what options do I have?" The first statement declares moral judgement. The second requests explanation and invites solutions. Moral judgement may be satisfying, but it rarely helps the person on the line search their system for alternative tariffs or credits. The concept is *answerability*: curious questions are answerable, which makes them actionable. The implication is that curiosity is not softness; it is engineering.

It is also faster. An accusation tends to invite an argument about intent—did the company "take" money, did they "lie", are they "ripping people off". Those arguments are endless and usually unresolvable in a customer service interaction. Curiosity keeps the conversation on rails: what happened, what can be done, what is possible. The rails matter because modern service channels reward brevity. Agents are often measured on call duration, resolution rate, and customer satisfaction scores. A calm, structured request helps an agent resolve quickly while still helping you. This is why tone is not merely interpersonal; it is economic. A conversation that can be closed cleanly is a conversation the system is more willing to indulge.

Curious tone does not mean endless questions, nor does it mean passive acceptance. It can be firm. The firmness comes from specificity. A firm, friendly request sounds like: "I'm happy to stay if the price can be closer to what I'm seeing elsewhere. Is there a retention offer you can apply, or a tariff that fits my usage?" The firmness is in the condition—closer to what is elsewhere—and in the request for a particular pathway. The friendliness is in the absence of insult. The concept is *conditional cooperation*: willingness paired with boundaries. The implication is that firmness can be expressed without hostility, and often works better that way.

Voice and pace carry as much meaning as words. On the phone, a rapid, breathless delivery signals urgency and agitation; a slow, steady pace signals control. Control is contagious. When someone sounds controlled, the other person tends to mirror it. This is not woo. It is a well-established social phenomenon: humans unconsciously synchronise with each other's emotional cues. The same applies to written channels. Short sentences with clear punctuation read calmer than long, breathless paragraphs that spill frustration. The visible behaviour is measurable: number of sentences, number of exclamation marks, the presence of a single clear question. The concept is *emotional contagion*. The implication is that tone is a tool for shaping the other person's state, not by manipulation but by modelling.

A second named example grounds the idea in a context far from billing disputes. In September 1962, President John F. Kennedy addressed the United Nations in New York during the Cold War and spoke about arms control and the "ultimate common goal" of peace. Whatever one thinks of the politics, the rhetorical technique is instructive: the enemy was not treated as a cartoon villain in need of humiliation; the focus was on shared risk and shared survival. That is tone as strategy: the deliberate choice to reduce threat so that the other party has space to move without losing face. Micro-negotiations are not geopolitics, but they run on the same basic human machinery. People rarely shift position when they feel cornered. They shift when they can do so while preserving dignity.

Dignity matters because many everyday negotiations involve someone with limited authority. A call-centre agent may have a narrow menu of options. A hotel receptionist may be bound by occupancy. A tradesperson may be dealing with fluctuating costs and tight schedules. When a customer begins with accusation, they imply that the person they are speaking to is responsible for the system's flaws. That implication is often false and always unhelpful. Curiosity respects the difference between the person and the system. "Can you help me understand what happened?" is a way of inviting the person to step alongside you, to look at the system together. The concept is *role clarity*: recognising what power the other person likely has. The implication is that tone can compensate for power asymmetry by reducing the need for the other person to defend themselves.

There is, however, a credible counter-example that must be faced: calm curiosity can be misread as weakness. Some people respond to gentleness by giving less, not more. Some organisations are trained to interpret anything short of escalation as permission to do nothing. Some individuals are simply obstructive. In those cases, curiosity alone will not move the interaction. This is where the "firm" part matters, and where tone must be paired with structure. Curiosity opens the door; structure keeps it open. Structure looks like stating the term at issue, stating the desired adjustment, and asking a direct question about what can be done. It looks like politely repeating the request when the conversation drifts. It looks like asking, without theatrics, whether there is someone else who can authorise the change. Calm does not mean compliant. Calm means controlled.

Reconciling this limitation is not about learning to become sharper; it is about learning to be clearer. Many people equate firmness with aggression because they have seen aggression produce short-term compliance. But clarity can be more persistent than aggression. Aggression often provokes a defensive "no" followed by a grudging concession to end the call. Clarity can produce an earlier "yes" because it makes the path to yes obvious and safe. Even when clarity meets resistance, it keeps escalation clean. A person can say, in a calm voice, "I understand that's your policy. Is there any discretion available, or should I speak to someone who can review exceptions?" The tone remains friendly. The request becomes sharper. The concept is *escalation without hostility*. The implication is that calm tone does not trap you; it gives you more room to move.

The point is not to perform friendliness. People can hear performance. The point is to use a tone that matches the reality of the situation: you are in a transaction, and you are seeking an adjustment. A transaction does not require apologies for existing. It requires clarity and respect. One practical marker of that balance is the absence of moral language. Replace "you've unfairly charged me" with "I don't recognise this charge". Replace "you're trying to rip me off" with "this price is higher than the alternatives I'm seeing". Replace "this is ridiculous" with "this doesn't match what I understood". These substitutions are not cosmetic. They move the conversation from moral judgement to discrepancy. Discrepancy is solvable.

The hinge motif returns here because tone is what allows the hinge to be touched without cracking the frame. Accusation pushes at the door. Curiosity finds the hinge. When the hinge moves, it is often because the other person has found a permissible way to help: a credit code, a different tariff, an exception category, a service recovery option. Those pathways are easier to access when the conversation feels safe and bounded. Safe does not mean sentimental. It means non-threatening, precise, and brief.

There is also a social benefit to calm curiosity that is easy to overlook: it protects the person asking from themselves. Anger has a way of expanding a request into a referendum on character. The company becomes evil, the agent becomes incompetent, the whole system becomes an insult. Once the conversation turns into a referendum, any outcome short of total victory feels like humiliation. Calm curiosity keeps the stakes appropriately sized. It frames the interaction as a practical problem to be solved rather than a test of personal worth. That reduces the emotional hangover that often follows conflict. People who avoid asking frequently do so not because they fear the other person's reaction, but because they fear their own: the flush, the shaking voice, the regret afterwards. Tone is a way of regulating that internal experience as well.

The forward test at the end of all this is deceptively simple. When the next term needs adjusting, will the first sentence be an accusation that demands defence, or a question that invites thought—and will the tone carry the quiet confidence of someone seeking alignment rather than victory? The hinge will move more often for the second, but the deeper question is whether you can choose that tone even when you feel provoked.

Finding Everyday Leverage

In June 2016, the UK Competition and Markets Authority published its final report on the retail energy market and described, in unusually plain terms, how weak customer engagement could be exploited: many households did not switch, and those households tended to pay more. The report was policy, but its real subject was a familiar domestic pattern. A person stays with the same provider because changing feels annoying. The direct debit ticks over. The lights stay on. The cost rises quietly. The organisation, seeing stability, has little reason to volunteer a better deal. That is leverage in negative: the power you hand away when you signal you will tolerate drift.

Leverage is often invisible.

When people hear the word, they picture threats and bluster—someone pounding a table and insisting they will walk. That performance is not leverage; it is noise. Leverage is simply the set of credible alternatives and credible signals that shape the other side's incentives. In daily life, the strongest forms of leverage are quiet: the ability to switch provider without chaos, the ability to wait, the ability to accept a different time-slot, the history of paying reliably, the fact that you are easy to serve, the evidence that a competitor offers a comparable service. Leverage is not what you do *to* someone. It is what you can do *without* them.

The first step is to see how organisations interpret signals. Many systems are built to categorise customers. A customer who never contacts support is cheap to maintain. A customer who pays late is expensive. A customer who rings repeatedly with vague frustration is expensive. A customer who asks a clear question once, with evidence, is a different category: potentially at risk of leaving, but also easy to resolve. These categories are not moral; they are operational. The concept here is *incentive alignment*: the other side's willingness to adjust depends on whether adjustment is cheaper than refusal. The implication is that leverage is often less about your charisma than about the shape of the choice you present.

This is why "loyalty" can be leverage, but only if it is framed correctly. Loyalty alone is not leverage; loyalty plus credible leaving is. Organisations do not reward loyalty out of gratitude. They reward it when the cost of losing you exceeds the cost of keeping you. The difference matters because many people mention loyalty as if it were a moral claim—"I've been with you for years"—and then stop, hoping the other side will feel shame. Shame rarely helps. What helps is the operational translation: "I've been with you for years, and I'd prefer to stay, but the price is now out of line with what I'm seeing elsewhere." That sentence converts loyalty into a decision point. It is a signal with teeth, but not a threat. The concept is *credible preference*: an expressed desire to stay paired with a clear condition. The implication is that loyalty becomes useful when it is linked to a boundary.

"Flexibility" is leverage in the same way, and it is often stronger than people realise because it reduces cost for the other side. A person who can take a call at a quiet hour, accept installation on a weekday afternoon, or tolerate a slower but cheaper service tier offers something valuable: reduced strain on capacity. Capacity has a price inside organisations. Call-centre staffing, engineer time, appointment slots, and expedited shipping all have internal costs. When you offer flexibility, you lower those costs, which can make concessions easier. The visible behaviour is concrete: a customer agreeing to an off-peak installation window, a traveller accepting a different flight time, a client agreeing to a longer turnaround in exchange for a lower fee. The concept is *cost reduction*: making it cheaper for the other side to say yes. The implication is that leverage sometimes comes from giving up the most scarce resource—peak-time demand—in exchange for better terms.

Competing offers are the most obvious form of leverage, but they are often mishandled. People either avoid mentioning them because they fear seeming aggressive, or they brandish them like weapons. Both approaches miss the point. A competing offer is not a threat; it is a reference point that makes your request legible. If you say, calmly, that another provider offers a similar package at a lower rate, you are not insulting anyone. You are describing the market. Markets exist whether or not we talk about them. The concept is *comparability*: the ability to compare like with like. The implication is that leverage improves when you can name the comparison in concrete terms—speed, data allowance, contract length, service level—rather than waving at a vague "better deal".

An internet contract provides a clean example because it contains all the usual ingredients: recurring payments, renewal cycles, and widely advertised alternative offers. Imagine a household in Manchester with broadband that has crept up in price over time. They receive a message that their contract is ending. They can do nothing and be rolled onto a higher standard rate, or they can contact the provider. The household's leverage is not a dramatic speech. It is the fact that multiple providers compete for their address, that switching is administratively possible, and that retention teams exist to reduce churn. The household's quiet strengths include being a low-maintenance customer—few support calls, on-time payments—and being flexible about installation timing if they did switch. These strengths become leverage only when they are signalled.

A clumsy approach signals only irritation: "Your prices are ridiculous. I'm leaving." The agent hears anger and bluff. Bluff is common. The safe response is to recite policy or offer a small token discount. A more effective approach signals alternatives without performance: "My contract's ending and the price is rising. I'd like to stay if you can bring it closer to the offers I'm seeing from other providers for similar speed. What's the best rate you can apply for an existing customer?" That sentence does three things. It shows the situation (contract ending, price rising). It names the concept (a preference to stay). It introduces leverage (competing offers) without threat. The implication is that the agent now has a reason to search for retention offers and a conversational frame that makes a concession feel routine rather than coerced.

Leverage also includes the simplest alternative of all: the ability to do nothing, briefly, without panic. People often negotiate poorly because they negotiate with urgency they cannot afford. If your service must be restored immediately, the other side knows time is your constraint. If you can wait, you are less exploitable. Waiting is not always possible, but when it is, it is a form of leverage because it changes the balance of impatience. The visible behaviour is measurable: a person who can schedule a call rather than taking the first offered slot, a person who can accept delivery next week rather than paying for tomorrow, a person who can postpone a purchase rather than buying under pressure. The concept is *time as bargaining power*. The implication is that calm often comes from having a timeline, not from having courage.

A second checkable example broadens the frame beyond utilities. In January 2022, the Financial Conduct Authority's rules on general insurance pricing practices took effect in the UK, aiming to curb the practice of charging renewing customers more than new customers for equivalent cover. Again, the policy detail is less important here than the mechanism. Insurers were responding to customer inertia. The counterweight to inertia is the credible possibility of switching, which becomes leverage the moment it is real enough to be acted upon. Many people never switch; some threaten to switch; fewer are ready to switch. The insurer's internal calculus responds most to the third group. The implication is plain: leverage is strongest when alternatives are not merely imagined but prepared.

Preparedness, however, has a cost. This leads to a necessary limitation. Some people cannot easily switch services because of complicated needs, location constraints, bundled products, or sheer overload. A rural household might have few broadband options. A person with accessibility requirements might depend on a specific provider's features. A small business might be locked into a contract where switching would disrupt operations. In these cases, the "walk away" alternative is weaker, and pretending otherwise can backfire. An empty threat, once detected, reduces credibility. The reconciliation is not despair. It is to look for other forms of leverage that do not depend on leaving: flexibility on timing, willingness to adjust scope, long payment history, or the ability to accept a different configuration of the same service. Leverage is plural. If one form is weak, another may still exist.

There is also a moral hazard worth naming. When people discover leverage, they can become intoxicated by it, using it to extract small gains at the expense of basic decency. That is not only ethically unappealing; it is strategically short-sighted. Many frontline workers have limited discretion, and they will use it more readily for someone who treats them as a person rather than as a gatekeeper to be bullied. The goal is not to intimidate. It is to make the "yes" feel safe and reasonable. Leverage, used well, is a way of aligning incentives, not weaponising them.

The cleanest way to keep leverage human is to treat it as information, not menace. Mention alternatives as facts. Mention loyalty as history. Mention flexibility as an offer. Keep the tone calm. Keep the ask specific. These are not "tips"; they are the social mechanics that allow the other person to concede without humiliation. Humiliation makes people rigid. Safety makes them resourceful.

The hinge motif returns because leverage is, ultimately, about where the hinge is bolted. If the hinge is bolted to a competitive market, alternatives matter. If it is bolted to a capacity constraint, flexibility matters. If it is bolted to a retention metric, loyalty and churn risk matter. If it is bolted to a policy exception, evidence matters. The point of "finding everyday leverage" is to stop imagining leverage as a personality trait and start seeing it as a feature of situations—features that can be observed, named, and quietly signalled.

The forward test is uncomfortable precisely because it is practical. Before making a request, what would you do if the answer were no—and is that alternative real enough to keep you calm, or is it a fantasy that will collapse under pressure? The quality of your leverage is the quality of your alternatives. The rest is just performance.

Anchors, Bundles and Exit Options

In 1974, in Eugene, Oregon, psychologists Amos Tversky and Daniel Kahneman published a paper in *Science* describing a cognitive quirk that has since escaped the laboratory and taken up residence in daily life: people's judgements are pulled towards a starting point, even when that starting point is arbitrary. They called it anchoring. The original experiments used numbers and estimates, but the practical echo is everywhere. A menu lists a "premium" option first and the "standard" one looks reasonable by comparison. A landlord mentions the highest rent they think they can get and the negotiation begins in that gravitational field. A service provider quotes a renewal price and, suddenly, everything else is discussed in relation to it. The first number spoken does not merely describe reality. It shapes it.

Anchors change the air.

If micro-negotiations are the craft of touching hinges, anchors, bundles, and exit options are the tools that make the hinge move with less strain. They are not tricks. They are ways of structuring choices so that the other side can say yes without feeling ambushed and you can hear no without feeling cornered. The three belong together because each addresses a different vulnerability in everyday bargaining. Anchors handle the starting point. Bundles handle the trade. Exit options handle the emotions.

Anchors are the easiest to misunderstand. Many people assume an anchor is an aggressive gambit: start outrageously low or outrageously demanding and "meet in the middle". That may work in some bazaars. In most modern service environments it backfires, because the other side has scripts designed to resist obvious manipulation. A ridiculous anchor makes you look unserious. It signals that the conversation will be long. Long conversations are costly. The art is to set a *reasonable* anchor—one that feels grounded, legible, and within the range of what the system might plausibly do. Reasonable does not mean timid. It means defensible.

A reasonable anchor has three features. It refers to something checkable: a published offer, a known tariff, a previous price, a competitor's comparable package, a documented market rate. It is expressed as a clear term: a monthly figure, a fee waived, a time window, a specific add-on removed. And it is tied to a decision: what happens if it cannot be met. The visible behaviour is specific language—"I'm currently paying £X", "your website offers £Y for new customers", "Provider Z is offering £W for similar speed"—rather than vague dissatisfaction. The concept is *reference framing*: deciding what the conversation is "about" before the other side does. The implication is that the anchor you choose determines whether you will spend the interaction defending your request or exploring options.

A scene makes this concrete. An internet contract is up for renewal. The provider offers a new price, higher than before. If the customer says, "That's too expensive," they have offered no anchor. The agent must now invent one, and the agent's invented anchor will favour the company's revenue targets. If the customer says, "I can see you're offering a similar package at £X to new customers; I'd like to renew at that level," the customer has anchored the conversation to an internal, checkable reference point. The request is now not "give me something"; it is "align my terms with a known benchmark". The agent may still refuse, but the path to yes has been made simpler because the anchor is already part of the company's own pricing universe.

Anchors also shape behaviour through a subtler route: they reduce ambiguity. Ambiguity is the enemy of discretionary help because it forces the other person to guess what will satisfy you. When people guess, they choose the safest guess, which often means minimal change. A clear anchor tells the other person what "success" looks like. It becomes a target for their search through tariffs, credits, and offers. That search, if it happens, is a sequence of internal decisions: can I apply this code, can I move them to this plan, can I extend this promotion? When the goal is clear, the search is easier. The implication is that an anchor is not just a psychological trick; it is operational guidance.

Bundling is the next tool because everyday negotiations rarely involve a single variable. People often ask for one thing and are told it is impossible, not because the organisation is cruel, but because the request is costly with no compensating benefit. Bundling introduces compensation. It links items so the other side can justify flexibility. This is not about "getting more". It is about making trade-offs explicit.

Consider the difference between "lower my monthly price" and "lower my monthly price and I'll commit to a longer term" or "lower my monthly price if I drop the sports add-on" or "lower my monthly price and I'll move my mobile line to you as well". Bundling transforms a one-sided demand into an exchange. Exchange is easier to approve because it can be explained internally. A supervisor can sign off a discount that is paired with a commitment, because the discount now has a narrative: retention, increased lifetime value, reduced churn, simplified account management. The language of "value" sounds abstract until it is attached to a concrete decision: a contract extension, an additional service, a reduced support burden. The concept is *trade architecture*: designing a request so that concessions can be traded rather than gifted. The implication is that bundling increases the number of ways to reach agreement, which matters when the first option is blocked.

Bundling also protects you from a common trap: the false bargain. Companies often offer "discounts" that are merely rearrangements—lower monthly cost paired with higher installation fees, cheaper broadband paired with an unnecessary bundle, an attractive first six months paired with an inflated standard rate. Bundling allows you to control the trade rather than accept the company's. If you propose the bundle, you can choose which variables move and which stay fixed. That is not paranoia; it is clarity. The visible behaviour is asking in linked terms: "If we can keep the monthly cost at £X, I'm happy to renew for twelve months," or "If that price is fixed, I'd like the router fee removed." The concept is *conditional agreement.* The implication is that bundling gives structure to "yes" and makes "no" more informative.

Exit options are the third tool and, for most people, the most emotionally important. An exit option is not a dramatic threat to storm out. It is the quiet knowledge of what you will do if the answer is no. This knowledge changes your physiology. People who have no exit option tend to negotiate with desperation, and desperation leaks into tone—faster speech, repeated pleading, excessive justification. People who have a real alternative tend to speak slowly, ask better questions, and stop when it is time to stop. The concept is *emotional regulation through alternatives.* The implication is that exit options improve outcomes even when they are never used, because they stop you performing need.

Exit options can be obvious, like switching providers, but they can also be internal. You might decide to downgrade a service tier. You might choose to delay a purchase. You might accept a different date. You might keep the current terms and set a reminder to revisit later. The key is that the option must be credible to you. A bluff is worse than silence because it destroys trust. The visible behaviour is being able to say, calmly, "If that's the best available, I'll need to think about switching," and meaning it, or being able to end the conversation without spiralling. The concept is *credibility.* The implication is that the ability to walk away is not only practical; it is psychological scaffolding.

This brings us to a limitation that needs daylight. Not everyone has strong exit options. A rural household may have only one viable broadband provider. A person may depend on a specific service for accessibility reasons. A business may be locked into a contract where switching would disrupt operations. In such cases, "exit" is weaker, and pretending otherwise can produce humiliation when the bluff collapses. The reconciliation is to widen the notion of exit. If switching providers is not possible, perhaps switching *terms* is: a different plan, a different payment schedule, a temporary credit, a reduced add-on package, a different service channel. If even that is fixed, the exit option may be internal: deciding not to spend energy on this battle now and focusing on other negotiable areas where the hinge is looser. Exit options do not have to be dramatic to be real. They have to be honest.

Anchors, bundles, and exit options also interact in a way that explains why some conversations feel effortless and others feel like wrestling fog. Without an anchor, the other side sets the reference point. Without a bundle, the other side sees your request as a pure cost. Without an exit option, you negotiate with tightness in your voice and a willingness to accept poor terms to avoid discomfort. The three tools together create a different posture: you begin with a clear reference, you offer a trade, and you know what you will do if the trade is refused. That posture often produces a calmer, shorter, more productive conversation because it reduces uncertainty for everyone.

A short script can show the integration without turning into theatre. Imagine the internet renewal call again. The anchor might be a known offer. The bundle might be a commitment. The exit option might be a credible switch. The script, spoken in a steady pace, could be: "My contract's ending and the new price is higher than I expected. I can see comparable packages at around £X. If you can renew me at £X, I'm happy to sign for twelve months. If that isn't possible, I'll need to look at moving to another provider. What's the best you can do?" There is nothing clever here. It is almost plain to the point of boredom. That is why it works. It defines the reference point, proposes an exchange, and names the alternative without hostility.

Notice what this script does not do. It does not insult the agent. It does not exaggerate. It does not demand impossible discounts. It does not pretend to have already left. It makes the agent's task clear:

search for a way to meet £X, perhaps by applying a retention offer, changing the plan, or adding a credit, and if that fails, allow the customer to leave. The agent can proceed without guessing. The conversation becomes procedural, not emotional. Procedure is where outcomes change.

The hinge motif matters once more. Anchors decide where your hand lands on the door. Bundles decide whether the door is being pushed or eased. Exit options decide whether your grip is desperate or relaxed. Each tool reduces strain at a different point in the mechanism. Used together, they turn a vague hope—"maybe they'll give me something"—into a structured request that can be evaluated and, sometimes, approved.

The forward test is not whether you can recite a script. It is whether you can choose an anchor you can defend, design a bundle that feels fair, and name an exit you can actually live with. When the next renewal, booking, or bill presents a term you dislike, will you let the other side set the starting point, or will you set it yourself—quietly, reasonably, and with a door you can truly walk through if it stays closed?

Chapter 3
Lowering Bills and Subscriptions

In October 2022, Ofgem announced that the UK's energy Price Cap would rise again, and the news landed not in Parliament but in kitchens: on phones at the edge of the worktop, on laptops balanced beside a mug, in the quiet after dinner when someone finally opened the email and saw the direct debit changing. The language was bureaucratic—caps, bands, typical usage—but the experience was intimate. A household budget is not an abstract. It is a set of promises made to the future: rent, food, transport, warmth. When a bill rises, it is not merely an expense. It is a renegotiation imposed by default.

A subscription is a small contract with amnesia. That is its genius and its cruelty. You sign once, often in a moment of convenience or optimism, and then the charge dissolves into the background hum of modern life. A streaming service, a mobile plan, cloud storage, insurance, broadband, a gym membership—each is individually manageable, which is why they accumulate. The same is true of the subtle price rises and expiring promotions that arrive dressed as routine. A few pounds here. Another few there. Nothing worth a fight. And yet, over months, the arithmetic becomes a quiet siphon: money leaving your account not because you chose it, but because you did not notice the hinge.

This chapter lives in that hinge. It is about reducing leakage without becoming obsessive, and about treating bills as editable documents rather than as weather. The premise is not that every price is negotiable or that every provider is waiting to be charmed into generosity. The premise is narrower and therefore more useful: a large portion of recurring household spend is shaped by inertia, by information gaps, and by systems designed to reward those who ask at the right moment with the right facts in front of them. A short, disciplined interaction—often a single call or chat—can change a year's baseline. The difference between "I suppose that's what it costs now" and "What are my options?" is not personality. It is posture.

Preparation is the first form of power in these conversations because it replaces vague resentment with measurable discrepancy. Most people approach a provider from memory—"it feels like it's gone up"—and memory is a weak witness. Organisations respond to the record. The record is the bill, the dates, the line items, the renewal notice, the tariff name, the usage pattern. When those are in front of you, a call becomes a technical discussion rather than a moral one. Technical discussions are easier to resolve. They allow staff to search, compare, and apply the options they actually control. They also protect you from the most common self-sabotage: agreeing to a new deal without realising you are simply swapping one hidden cost for another. Clarity shrinks the space for accidental consent.

There is a particular form of preparation suited to intelligent, busy people: the kind that is light but decisive. Not a weekend of spreadsheets, not a forensic audit of every penny, but a short gathering of essentials—the last two or three bills, a note of any recent increases, the name of your current plan, and a glance at publicly available offers that establish a reasonable anchor. The aim is not to become an amateur analyst. The aim is to arrive at the conversation with enough facts to make the other person's job easy and your own choices clean. In practice, the difference between an unprepared call and a prepared one is often the difference between being "managed" and being offered options.

The next layer is understanding who you are actually speaking to. Billing teams and retention teams are not moral categories; they are functions. Billing resolves errors and explains charges. Retention reduces churn. Different functions have different tools. A billing agent might be able to correct a mistake or apply a one-off credit. A retention agent might be able to match an offer, extend a discount, shift you to a different plan, or restructure a contract. Many people never reach retention because they never signal, calmly, that they may leave. They complain, they vent, they accept. The system hears "not leaving" and behaves accordingly. A small change in phrasing can route you to the part of the organisation built to negotiate.

This is where tone matters again, not as performance but as engineering. A cooperative opening line does two things at once: it keeps the interaction human and it makes the request legible as a decision point. It sounds like this: respectful greeting, clear issue, specific ask. The structure is almost boring, which is precisely why it works. Staff in these roles are trained to deal with emotion; they are also trained to respond to contained problems. The conversation that begins with a clear request is the conversation that gets processed. The conversation that begins as an accusation becomes a debate about fairness, and fairness debates are time-consuming. Time is what the system is designed to minimise. In a strange twist, the most effective way to receive help from an efficiency-obsessed machine is to speak in a way that reduces its effort.

Price rises and expiring promotions are the most common triggers for these conversations, and they carry their own psychological traps. A price rise notice arrives and people respond as if it were a verdict: either swallow it or rage. But these notices are often starting guns for a negotiation window because they formalise change. They provide a reason to contact the provider and a clear reference point for your request. Promotions expiring are similar. A discount ending is not an insult; it is a predictable event. The question is whether you treat it as fate or as a prompt to ask what else is available. This chapter pays attention to the language of these moments because language determines whether you are perceived as a customer to be soothed or a customer making a rational choice.

The modern relevance is sharp. Many households are managing tighter budgets alongside an expanding menu of subscriptions, and many services are designed to stay unnoticed once set up. Auto-renewal is frictionless, which is another way of saying it bypasses deliberation. Deliberation is how values are expressed. If the charges in your life renew by default, your values are quietly outsourced to whatever pricing algorithm happens to be in force. That is not a moral failure; it is the predictable result of living with too many small commitments to track by feeling alone. The remedy is not paranoia. It is periodic review, targeted conversations, and a willingness to change providers when the cost-benefit no longer makes sense.

Leaving deserves its own seriousness because it is both a negotiating tool and a real decision. Switching can save money, but it can also create hidden costs: installation delays, service disruption, administrative hassle, the loss of features you actually use. Some people stay out of inertia; others leave out of spite. Both are forms of being pushed around by emotion. The more dignified approach is measured: consider the switching costs, consider the service quality, consider your appetite for change, and then decide. A calm, final notice is not a tantrum. It is closure. It signals that you have compared terms and made a choice.

The chapter's through-line is simple: the goal is not perfection; it is movement. In the real world, some calls end with an improved rate. Some end with a partial win—a smaller rise, a temporary discount, a fee removed. Some end with a clean no, which is still useful because it reveals the provider's true flexibility and forces a decision about staying. The emotional payoff is not merely money saved, though money saved matters. It is the sense of being less at the mercy of automatic drift. Bills become something you can touch. Subscriptions become something you can choose. The hinge stops squeaking because you stop letting the door hang open by default.

The question that carries you into the chapter is not whether you can lower every bill. It is whether you will treat your recurring charges as living agreements that deserve occasional re-reading—or as background noise that quietly renegotiates itself against you, month after month, while you are busy living your life.

Preparing Numbers and Options

In February 2020, Ofcom introduced rules in the UK requiring mobile, broadband and pay-TV providers to send end-of-contract and annual best-tariff notifications. The policy was regulatory, but its practical meaning was almost domestic: customers were being nudged to stop treating recurring charges as background noise. In a flat in Leeds, a person could open an email, hear the faint whirr of a laptop fan, and see the words that most households rarely see in plain daylight—*your contract is ending; here are your options*. The important detail is what the rule quietly assumed. Prices do not only rise because markets change. They rise because people do not compare.

Paper changes the conversation. Five words.

Preparation is not about turning a phone call into an ordeal. It is about replacing a foggy feeling—"this seems higher"—with a small set of facts that a provider can actually respond to. When people contact a company from memory, they offer the company a gift: vagueness. Vagueness forces the agent to lead, and the agent will usually lead towards the easiest, fastest close. When people contact a company with a few numbers in front of them, the interaction shifts. It becomes a technical discussion rather than a moral quarrel. Technical discussions have handles: plan names, dates, usage patterns, contract end points, line items. Handles make it easier for a system to move.

The first claim is best shown through the smallest possible scene. Someone calls their mobile provider and says, "My bill's gone up." The agent replies, truthfully, "Bills can change," and asks what they mean. The customer rummages in their mind for the last statement they half-glanced at. The conversation lengthens. The agent offers a generic explanation. The customer grows irritated because the irritation was the only fuel they brought. Now replay the same call with the customer looking at the last two bills. They can say, calmly, "Last month I paid £34. This month it's £40. The increase looks like it's on the plan charge, not usage. Can you tell me why, and whether there's a tariff closer to what I was paying?" The claim is that numbers do the heavy lifting. The name for this is *specificity*. The implication is simple: specificity reduces the effort required to help you, and systems tend to reward lower effort with more options.

"Research" can sound like homework, which is why many intelligent, busy people avoid it. They imagine hours lost in comparison websites, small print, and the peculiar despair of modern tariffs. But preparation for micro-negotiation is not a doctoral thesis. It is closer to packing a bag before a journey: a few essentials gathered so you are not stranded. The essentials are not mysterious. A recent bill or two. The plan name. The date of the last change or the start of the contract. A rough sense of usage or consumption. The question that matters: what exactly are you asking to change? The concept here is *readiness*: arriving at a conversation able to answer basic questions without rummaging. The implication is that readiness keeps you in control of pace, which keeps you calmer and the other person more willing to engage.

Preparation also protects you from a particular kind of organisational magic trick: reframing. Many providers will respond to "this is too expensive" by offering a deal that sounds attractive because it is framed against a high anchor. "We can reduce it by £5" sounds generous when the current price is treated as inevitable. If you know what you paid three months ago, or what the provider publicly offers for comparable service, the frame changes. The reduction is no longer a gift; it is a return to market. The concept is *reference points*. The implication is that preparation stops you accepting a discount that is still bad value.

A second, checkable example makes this broader than a single bill. On 1 January 2022, the UK Financial Conduct Authority's general insurance pricing practices rules took effect, designed to prevent renewing customers from being charged more than new customers for equivalent cover. Whether one applauds the policy or debates its side-effects, it signals something crucial about preparation: renewal pricing had become complicated enough, and opaque enough, that relying on "loyalty" without checking was predictably costly. The point is not to turn every renewal into conflict. The point is to treat renewal as an information moment. A person who has their current premium, their renewal premium, and a couple of comparable quotes can talk in terms a firm is structurally prepared to answer. A person who only feels betrayed can talk for ten minutes without changing a line on the policy.

The quality of preparation should match the size of the decision. That sounds obvious until you watch how people actually behave. Many under-prepare for recurring expenses that compound over years, then over-prepare for one-off purchases that do not. Preparation for bills and subscriptions should be light but consistent, because the goal is to change baselines, not to win one dramatic skirmish. The visible behaviour is brief comparison repeated occasionally: noting a price rise when it happens, saving a screenshot of a public offer, keeping the last bill accessible. The concept is *maintenance.* The implication is that small preparation done regularly is more powerful than intense preparation done rarely.

A useful way to think about this is the "one-page" rule, not as a literal sheet of paper but as a constraint on attention. If the key information will not fit on a single view—on one screen or one notepad—you are probably slipping into overwork. Overwork breeds resentment. Resentment leaks into tone. Tone changes outcomes. The goal is to have a compact cheat-sheet beside the phone: the numbers you can quote, the dates you can reference, and the option you can credibly mention. That cheat-sheet is not about appearing clever. It is about avoiding cognitive strain mid-conversation. Cognitive strain makes people sloppy, and sloppiness is expensive.

There is, inevitably, a limitation: too much preparation can become paralysis. Some people keep comparing until they can no longer decide. Some people chase the "perfect" deal and end up spending hours to save pennies. Some people read so much small print that they become suspicious of everything and trust nothing. This is a genuine risk, especially for the conscientious. The reconciliation is to treat preparation as a filter rather than a quest. A filter asks, "Is this worth a call?" not "Have I exhausted the universe of offers?" A good filter produces a short list of plausible alternatives. Plausible is enough. The implication is that preparation should serve action, not replace it.

The question then becomes: what counts as "enough" preparation in the everyday? Enough means you can state the current term, identify the change you want, and justify it with a reference that is not imaginary. In telecoms, that might be your current monthly charge and a comparable public offer. In energy, it might be your recent direct debit and whether you are on a fixed or variable tariff, alongside a public tariff from a major competitor or the supplier's own advertised rate. In subscriptions, it might be the list of what you actually use and the next renewal date. The visible behaviour is having those items ready before you contact anyone. The concept is *pre-commitment*: deciding what you will ask for before the conversation begins. The implication is that you avoid being steered into an upsell when you came to reduce leakage.

A home energy example makes the process tangible without turning it into an instruction manual. Picture a household that notices its direct debit has increased. The person preparing does not need to become an energy analyst. They simply open the last two statements, note the tariff name and whether it is fixed-term, and note the date of the last change. They check the supplier's own website for current tariffs and glance at one competing supplier's public offer for the same payment method. They do not attempt to model usage with scientific precision. They only need enough to frame a clear question: "My direct debit has risen from X to Y; I'd like to understand what's driving that, and whether there's a tariff that better fits my usage." The claim is that minimal preparation produces maximal clarity. The name for this is *bounded information gathering*. The implication is that bounded gathering allows a conversation to stay short and specific.

This preparation also changes how you listen. When you have numbers ready, you are less likely to be hypnotised by what sounds good and more likely to notice what matters. A provider might offer a lower monthly price paired with a longer contract. That may be fine. It may also be a trap if the contract includes mid-term rises or add-ons you do not want. Preparation lets you ask the next question quickly: "Is that price fixed for the term, and what happens after the promotional period?" Those questions are not aggressive. They are clarifying. Clarifying questions are a form of self-respect. They also signal to the provider that you are alert, which can reduce the temptation to offer cosmetically attractive but structurally costly deals.

Trust is often invoked around these conversations, as if trust were a personality trait. In practice, trust is a decision made under uncertainty. Preparation allows you to trust without being naive, because it gives you something to test against. If the agent claims there are no better deals available, you can compare that claim to a public offer you have already seen. You do not have to accuse. You can simply ask, with calm curiosity, how the public offer differs from your situation. The visible behaviour is referencing a specific deal rather than a vague sense of being overcharged. The concept is *verification*. The implication is that preparation reduces the need for suspicion, because you can check instead.

Risk, similarly, becomes concrete. The risk in these conversations is not just "they'll say no". The more common risk is you will agree to something you do not actually want because the conversation moves quickly and you feel pressured to decide. Preparation reduces that risk by giving you a pre-chosen anchor and a pre-chosen boundary. If your aim is to keep the monthly cost around a certain figure, you know what you are trying to achieve. If your aim is to avoid a longer contract, you know what you will not accept. This is not rigidity. It is psychological safety. The implication is that preparation guards you against the subtle risk of momentum.

The cheat-sheet motif matters because it keeps preparation humane. A cheat-sheet is not a dossier. It is a small set of truths you can hold in working memory. If a conversation is pushing you beyond that—into clauses you have not seen, fees you did not know existed, conditions you cannot check—it is a sign that a pause may be wiser than a rushed agreement. Time, here, becomes part of preparation. If you can afford to call at a time when you can focus, you reduce error. If you call while distracted, you increase the chance of agreeing to the wrong thing. Focus is not virtue. It is accuracy.

There is also a deeper benefit to preparation that rarely gets named: it changes self-perception. People who avoid negotiating often do so because they feel unqualified, as if the provider knows everything and they know nothing. Preparation narrows that asymmetry. When you can quote your own bill back to the company, you are no longer a passive recipient of information. You become a participant. That shift is small, but it has consequences. It makes your voice steadier. It makes your questions sharper. It makes you less likely to accept the first framing offered.

None of this guarantees a concession. Some providers have hardened policies. Some markets are less competitive. Some services genuinely cost more. Preparation cannot create money out of thin air. What it can do is ensure that any refusal is real rather than convenient. It can also ensure that any offer is understood rather than merely accepted. The difference between "no movement" and "no movement after a proper check" is the difference between resignation and decision.

The forward test is therefore not "Have I researched enough?" That question invites endless browsing and the illusion of control. The better test is tighter: do you have a cheat-sheet that makes your request answerable—your current term, the change you want, and one credible reference point—and if you do, will you use it to steer the conversation, or will you still allow the provider's framing to become your reality by default?

Talking to Billing and Retention

In June 1990, in *Harvard Business Review* in Boston, Frederick Reichheld and W. Earl Sasser Jr. published "Zero Defections", arguing—against the prevailing obsession with constant acquisition—that keeping existing customers could be the more rational commercial focus. The essay helped popularise a managerial shift that now shapes almost every subscription economy: organisations build machinery not only to sell, but to stop people leaving. That machinery has names, scripts, and targets. It also has doors. One door says "Billing". Another says "Retention". The customer who does not understand the difference knocks randomly and wonders why nothing changes.

Routing decides what happens next.

This is the quiet advantage: many "no" answers are not moral judgements but misroutes. A billing team is often designed to explain charges, correct errors, and apply narrowly defined credits. A retention team—sometimes called "customer options", "cancellations", or "disconnections"—is designed to prevent churn by adjusting price, plan, or terms within pre-approved limits. The same person, with the same issue, can receive a different outcome depending on which desk they reach. The system is not being coy. It is being organised.

Begin with what billing actually is, when it is working properly. Billing is the part of the organisation that protects the integrity of the account ledger: what was charged, why it was charged, whether it matches the contract, whether a payment was received, whether a fee was triggered, whether an adjustment is permitted. When people ring billing with a complaint—"you're too expensive"—they are asking the wrong function to do the wrong job. Billing cannot redesign prices to make someone feel better; it can usually only fix what is incorrect or apply limited relief where policy permits. The concept is *authorisation*: what a person is allowed to change inside a system. The implication is that frustration often comes from demanding a change from someone who has no permission to make it.

Retention is different. Retention exists because churn is measurable and costly. Customers who leave reduce future revenue, increase acquisition costs, and create knock-on effects in forecasts and staffing. Retention teams are built to reduce that loss by making selective concessions: a discount, a matched offer, an extended promotion, a plan change, a one-off credit paired with a commitment. These concessions are not charity; they are a controlled investment in keeping an account. The concept is *selective flexibility*. The implication is that price discussions belong, structurally, closer to retention than to billing.

This division explains a common confusion. A person contacts a provider, asks for a better price, and is told there is "nothing available". They assume the provider is lying. Sometimes it is. Often it is simpler: the person they spoke to either cannot see the relevant offers or is trained not to mention them unless certain words are said—cancellation, renewal, switching, ending the contract. Organisations do this because they cannot discount everyone by default; they reserve concessions for customers who signal departure. The signal does not need to be theatrical. It needs to be legible. The concept is *trigger language*. The implication is that the way you frame your call determines which internal menu is opened.

A second, checkable example shows that this expectation of customer movement is not a conspiracy theory but a regulatory fact. In February 2020, Ofcom brought in rules in the UK requiring end-of-contract and annual best-tariff notifications for mobile, broadband and pay-TV providers, an attempt to reduce overpayment caused by inertia. Whether one loves regulation or loathes it, the policy signals something crucial: the system is designed around the assumption that informed customers *will* review their options. Companies anticipate it. They plan for it. Retention exists because leaving is normal behaviour in a competitive market. The implication is that mentioning alternatives is not impolite. It is participating in the market logic providers already use internally.

Where does this leave the person who wants a better outcome without becoming aggressive? It leaves them with a simple discipline: treat the conversation as a routing exercise. You begin by reaching the right function, then you speak in a way that makes your request answerable, then you invite options. A good call is not a performance. It is a sequence.

The opening matters because it tells the other person whether this is going to be messy. Messy calls are avoided. Clean calls are processed. The most reliable "clean" opening has three moves: greet, state the issue, ask what is possible. It is boring in the way good engineering is boring. The greeting is not flattery; it is a signal of basic respect. The statement of the issue is factual—numbers, dates, plan names—because facts can be checked. The question invites options rather than demanding concessions, because options are what the person on the line can actually provide. The concept is *containment*: keeping the interaction bounded so it can be resolved. The implication is that containment reduces defensive behaviour and increases the chance that discretion is used.

Contrast two openings. One sounds like a moral attack: "You've put my bill up again and I'm sick of it." The other sounds like a solvable problem: "Hi—could I check something on my account? My bill has risen from £X to £Y this month and I'd like to understand why, and whether there's a better tariff available." The second does not surrender any firmness; it simply removes blame. Blame pushes people towards policy recitation. Questions pull people towards explanation. Explanation is where flexibility hides.

The same logic applies when the aim is to reach retention. Many people fear that mentioning leaving is rude, as if they are threatening the person who answered. It is more accurate to treat it as classification. Retention is built for the "might leave" category. If you do not place yourself in that category, the system has less reason to spend money keeping you. The wording can be calm and factual: "I'm reviewing my options because the price has risen," or "I'd prefer to stay, but I'm seeing lower offers elsewhere." The concept is *credible review*. The implication is that you can signal departure without drama, which keeps the tone friendly while still opening the right door.

A practical example makes this precise. Imagine a broadband contract ending. You contact the provider and you reach billing or general customer service. If you say, "Can you lower my bill?" you are presenting a pure cost: give me less revenue for the same service. If you say, "My contract is ending, the new price is higher than I expected, and I'm comparing alternatives," you are presenting a retention scenario. The agent may now transfer you or access different offers. The difference is not your personality. It is your classification.

This classification also affects what the agent believes is worth attempting. If they believe you will stay regardless, searching for a discount is wasted labour. If they believe you may leave, searching becomes an investment. Organisations measure labour. They measure churn. They design workflows to minimise one and reduce the other. That is why "efficiency" is not a vague corporate virtue here; it is a visible pressure on every call. Short calls are praised. Repeat calls are punished. A well-formed request is aligned with the agent's incentives because it increases the chance of a single-call resolution. The implication is that you are not begging for help; you are offering the system a clean path to closure.

There is, however, a limitation that needs honesty. Not all retention is generous, and not all industries have meaningful retention flexibility. Some markets are weakly competitive, and a provider may know you have few alternatives. Some organisations outsource customer service to agents with minimal authority. Some accounts have complications—arrears, contract breaches, recent discounts already applied—that reduce what can be offered. In these cases, the "retention magic" people talk about may not appear. The reconciliation is to treat the call as information gathering rather than as a test of self-worth. If there is no flexibility, you have still learned something real about the provider's posture. That knowledge makes later decisions cleaner: stay without illusions, or leave without anger.

Tone still matters even when flexibility is limited, because it preserves the ability to escalate without burning bridges. A calm call can end with a transfer, a supervisor review, or a note placed on an account for follow-up. An angry call often ends with a hardening of position, because staff are trained to reduce risk when a customer appears hostile. "Risk" here is not philosophical; it is operational risk: complaints, chargebacks, social media escalation, formal disputes. When risk rises, organisations become procedural. Procedure is often rigid. The implication is that calm tone is not merely manners—it is a way of keeping the system in its flexible mode.

To make this even more concrete, it helps to understand what "billing" can usually do, as a matter of role. Billing can typically explain a charge, correct an error, reverse a duplicate payment, clarify a pro-rata adjustment, or apply a one-off credit if policy permits. Retention can typically adjust the ongoing plan, extend a discount, apply a new offer, change contract length, or bundle services in a way that affects price. There will be overlap, and there will be exceptions. But the categories are stable enough to use as a navigation tool. The concept is *functional literacy*: knowing which desk handles which type of change. The implication is that you stop wasting energy trying to negotiate price with a team designed to keep the ledger clean.

The best opening lines are therefore not "clever". They are legible to the system. They do not attempt to compress your entire life story into the first minute. They do not begin with insult. They begin with a checkable discrepancy and a request for options. In spoken form, they sound like ordinary competence. That ordinariness is precisely what makes them powerful: it signals that you can follow through, that you will understand the offer, and that you will make a decision.

A short, adaptable script can carry all of this without theatrics. Imagine the call begins and you have your numbers ready. You might say: "Hello—thanks for taking my call. I'm calling because my monthly charge has gone from £X to £Y, and I'm reviewing whether this plan still makes sense for me. I'd like to stay if there's a better rate available for the same service. Can you tell me what options you can offer, or connect me to the team that handles renewals and cancellations?" It greets. It states the issue. It signals credible review. It asks what is possible. It also gives the agent a graceful route: either solve it where they are or transfer you without embarrassment.

Notice how this script uses firmness without aggression. The firm part is the decision posture: reviewing options, willing to leave, asking for the team with authority. The friendly part is the lack of blame and the acknowledgement of the other person's role. It does not demand a discount; it invites the agent to present the best available configuration. That invitation matters because agents often have discretion over *how* they search: which offers they check, how long they spend, whether they escalate. People do not spend effort for someone who treats them as an enemy. They sometimes spend effort for someone who makes effort feel worthwhile.

The unresolved tension is this: if billing and retention are doors, which door are you actually knocking on when you feel a charge is "wrong"? Sometimes you need correction, not negotiation. Sometimes you need negotiation, not correction. Sometimes you need both. The forward test is whether you can name, before you speak, what kind of change you are seeking—fixing the record, or changing the terms—and route your words accordingly, so the system hears you not as noise, but as a decision it is equipped to make.

Handling Price Rises and Promotions

In October 2022, Ofgem confirmed that the UK energy Price Cap would rise sharply again, and the numbers rippled out through the country in a predictable pattern: suppliers emailed, direct debits adjusted, households recalculated. The cap itself is a regulatory artefact, but the most instructive part is the choreography. A notice arrives. A figure changes. Most people absorb it silently, as if a higher bill were a kind of weather system. Yet those notices are not merely information. They are a moment when terms are being altered. A moment when the hinge is exposed.

Price rises are not personal. Five words.

That sentence is not meant to soothe. It is meant to clarify. Most households experience a price rise notice as a small moral insult—*they're taking advantage*—and that emotional framing pushes people towards two unhelpful responses: resignation or rage. Resignation accepts the new term without inspection. Rage turns the interaction into a referendum on ethics, which the frontline agent cannot adjudicate and the organisation has no incentive to resolve. A more effective posture is procedural: treat the notice as a trigger for review. Review does not guarantee reversal. It does, however, create the possibility of movement.

Promotions have their own psychology. They are sold as gifts—"introductory offer", "limited-time discount"—and when they expire, the higher price is treated as the natural state. This is clever design. It makes the end of a deal feel like the end of generosity rather than the start of overpayment. The micro-negotiator reads promotions differently: as time-bounded pricing experiments whose expiry creates a decision point. The concept here is *baseline drift*: the gradual normalisation of higher terms through time and habituation. The implication is that the most important moment in a promotion is not the day you sign up; it is the day the promotion ends.

Language matters here because it determines whether the other person hears you as a complaint or as a customer making a rational choice. A price rise notice can be met with indignation—"How can you justify this?"—or with a structured query—"I've received the notice; can you explain the increase and tell me what options exist to keep my monthly cost closer to what it has been?" The second approach does not erase the frustration; it channels it into an answerable request. The concept is *answerability*. The implication is that your outcomes improve when you speak in terms the system is built to process.

There is also a subtle social fear at work: mentioning competing offers feels like threatening. People imagine it makes them sound disloyal or petty. In fact, mentioning competing offers is often the most neutral thing you can do because it is about external reality, not internal blame. Markets have prices. You are comparing. A provider that wants to keep you should expect that. The difference between a threat and a comparison is tone and specificity. A threat sounds like, "Match this or I'm gone." A comparison sounds like, "I'm seeing comparable packages at around £X; I'd like to understand what you can do." The concept is *credible reference*. The implication is that a comparison can be both firm and courteous.

History—your own history with the provider—is another form of credibility, but it must be handled with care. When people invoke loyalty as entitlement—"I've been with you for ten years, so you owe me"—they invite resistance. When they invoke history as evidence—"I've been with you for ten years and I've paid on time; I'd prefer to stay, but the price change means I need to review options"—they invite problem-solving. The difference is moral temperature. Entitlement demands compensation. Evidence invites a trade. The concept is *reputation as signal*. The implication is that your history becomes persuasive when it is connected to a decision point: staying if terms remain reasonable.

A second checkable example shows how institutional structures acknowledge this dynamic. In February 2020, Ofcom's rules on end-of-contract and annual best-tariff notifications came into effect in the UK telecoms sector. The rule exists because providers had little incentive to volunteer better deals to customers who did nothing. The regulation tried to reduce that asymmetry by forcing disclosure. The key lesson for handling promotions and price rises is that disclosure moments are built into systems, sometimes by regulators, sometimes by internal design. Your task is to use those moments. When the provider itself signals change—contract ending, discount expiring, price increasing—it is also signalling that the account is entering a state where adjustments are administratively easier to justify. The implication is that the notice is not only a warning; it is a window.

This is where "getting some movement rather than perfection" becomes the realistic goal. Many people approach these conversations as if only two outcomes exist: full victory or total defeat. That binary is a recipe for unnecessary disappointment and, worse, for escalation that damages relationships. The real world offers a spectrum: a smaller increase, a temporary credit, a different plan, a longer-term fix, the removal of an add-on, an extension of a discount, or simply a clear confirmation that nothing can be done. Movement can be partial and still valuable, because it changes the baseline or clarifies the decision. The concept is *incremental gain.* The implication is that a partial yes is not failure; it is information and often money.

Brief examples help because this subject is essentially about phrasing. Imagine a streaming service that has announced a price increase. A person might say, "This is ridiculous, I'm cancelling." That can work if cancellation is desired, but it often ends the conversation before options appear. A calmer, more fruitful line might be: "I've received the notice about the increase. I'm weighing whether to keep the service. Are there any current offers or cheaper tiers that would keep my monthly cost closer to what it has been?"

The phrase "I'm weighing whether to keep the service" signals churn risk without melodrama. The question "are there any offers or cheaper tiers" invites the agent to search options rather than defend a policy. Success might look like a discounted rate for a period. Partial success might look like being pointed to a cheaper tier that removes features you do not use. Both outcomes shift your position from passive acceptance to active choice.

Now consider a mobile plan whose promotional discount is expiring. The customer calls and says, "My discount is ending; I'd like to stay on a similar monthly cost if possible. I'm seeing comparable plans at around £X elsewhere. What can you do to keep me close to my current rate?" This includes three critical elements: it references a specific trigger (discount ending), it expresses a preference (stay), and it introduces a benchmark (comparable plans at £X). It also invites the provider to propose options rather than forcing you to invent the solution. The concept is *option solicitation.* The implication is that asking for options is often more effective than asking for a specific discount code, because it lets the other side choose the easiest concession they can justify.

Of course, not all outcomes are favourable. A credible counter-example is the industry-wide cost shock, where a provider's flexibility is genuinely constrained. During periods of sharp cost increases—energy markets being the obvious recent case—providers may have limited room to cut prices beyond regulated structures. In those moments, asking may yield little movement on the headline figure. The reconciliation is to expand what counts as movement. If the price itself cannot change, perhaps the payment schedule can be adjusted, a billing error corrected, a tariff clarified, an unnecessary add-on removed, or a more suitable plan identified. This is not pretending that a payment plan is the same as a price cut. It is recognising that the household's lived experience of cost includes predictability and timing, not just totals. The concept is *dimensional negotiation*: when one variable is fixed, other variables may still move. The implication is that even in rigid contexts, language that invites alternatives can reduce friction and improve fit.

Tone remains central because these conversations often sit close to resentment. People feel tricked by promotions because the marketing is loud and the expiry is quiet. They feel punished for loyalty because new customers get better deals. Those feelings are understandable. But a conversation that begins with moral accusation often ends with policy recitation. A conversation that begins with curiosity—"help me understand" and "what are my options"—often reveals the organisation's actual menu. That menu may still be disappointing, but disappointment is easier to manage when it is specific. Specific disappointment becomes a decision. Vague resentment becomes a loop.

This chapter's earlier tools—anchors, bundles, exit options—show up again here in miniature. A price rise notice gives you an anchor: the previous price, the new price, the delta. A promotion expiry gives you an anchor: the discounted rate and the standard rate. Competing offers supply another anchor. Bundling allows you to trade: "I'm happy to renew for twelve months if the monthly cost stays near £X." Exit options provide calm: "If there isn't flexibility, I'll need to consider switching." None of these need to be spoken dramatically. Drama makes staff defensive. Calm makes them search.

There is also a hidden timing element. Price rises and promotions often have effective dates. Contacting a provider before the change takes effect can be easier because the account is still in a pre-change state. The request can be framed as avoiding a future problem rather than correcting a past one. That is not just psychological; it can be operational. Many systems allow plan changes prospectively with fewer internal adjustments than retroactive credits. The concept is *administrative simplicity*. The implication is that early contact can increase the number of available options.

Yet the most important part of "handling" these notices is philosophical rather than tactical: refusing to treat them as verdicts.

A notice is an invitation to either accept, query, adjust, or leave. Many people default to acceptance because the alternative feels like hassle. But hassle is often smaller than imagined when the conversation is framed cleanly. It becomes a short exchange between a customer and a system: here is the change; here is my benchmark; here is my preference; what can you offer? The conversation does not need to prove anyone wrong. It needs to locate the hinge.

The forward test is therefore a question about posture under mild provocation. When the next price rise or expiring promotion arrives, will you treat it as weather—sigh and absorb—or as a timed invitation to review terms, anchored in your own history and the market's reality, and voiced in language that makes movement possible even when perfection is not?

Deciding When to Switch

In June 2017, the UK's Competition and Markets Authority announced a package of measures for the retail banking market following its investigation, and one theme sat beneath the policy language: customers were not moving. Even when better terms existed elsewhere, many people stayed put. The reasons were rarely ideological. They were mundane. Switching felt like hassle; the benefits felt uncertain; the risk of something going wrong felt larger than the certainty of overpaying. In a branch in Birmingham, or on a sofa with a laptop open, inertia looked like prudence. It often wasn't. It was simply the default winning.

Leaving is also a negotiation.

That sentence is not romance. It is a description of what organisations already understand. A customer's departure is the clearest signal a market allows. It changes incentives. It triggers retention scripts. It shapes future pricing strategies. It is also, for the individual, a decision with consequences: time spent, disruption endured, attention diverted. Switching is not a virtue. Staying is not a sin. The skill is choosing deliberately, so that you neither remain trapped by convenience nor flee in a burst of irritation that leaves you worse off.

The first claim is easiest to show through a common end-of-contract scene. A customer receives a renewal notice: the price will rise, the discount will end, the terms will roll forward. They contact the provider and ask for movement. The provider offers a small concession—perhaps a token discount, perhaps a short-term credit. The customer feels a pinch of pride at "getting something" and a pinch of exhaustion at the thought of switching. They accept. Six months later, the price rises again. This cycle can repeat for years. The customer is not foolish; they are busy. The concept is *drift management*: the provider controls the rhythm of gradual increases while the customer responds sporadically. The implication is that negotiating without a switching threshold can become an endless series of minor concessions that preserve the provider's advantage.

To decide when to switch, you need a different lens: total cost, not just monthly price. Total cost includes time, risk, and the friction of change. This is where many people miscalculate. They compare the new monthly rate to a cheaper advertised rate elsewhere and assume switching is obviously rational. Then they remember the last time something went wrong—missed installation, a service outage, a payment error—and they retreat. The right question is not "Is it cheaper?" but "Is it cheaper *after* switching costs?" Switching costs are not always monetary. They are often cognitive: the hours spent on admin, the inconvenience of downtime, the mental clutter of another set of terms to read. The concept is *transaction cost*, in the economist's sense: the cost of making an exchange happen. The implication is that switching should be evaluated as a project with an overhead, not as a magical teleport to a better price.

Service quality is the second factor because a cheap service that fails at the wrong time is expensive in disguise. People often treat "quality" as vague, but it can be measured through behaviour and consequence. How often does the broadband drop? How quickly are problems resolved? How clear are bills? How frequently do unexpected charges appear? How reliable is the service during the hours you most need it? Quality is not an abstract feeling; it is the number of failures per month, the number of minutes lost, the number of unresolved tickets, the number of times you have had to chase. The concept is *reliability as value.* The implication is that switching decisions should include an honest account of how much friction the current provider creates, not just how much they charge.

Your appetite for change is the third factor, and it deserves respect because it is not a weakness; it is a resource constraint. Some periods of life can accommodate switching projects. Others cannot. A household in the middle of moving, caring responsibilities, or intense work deadlines may have no spare attention for new contracts and installation windows. In such periods, paying a little more to avoid disruption may be a rational choice. The danger is when "I can't face it right now" becomes "I'll never face it", and the extra cost becomes permanent. The concept is *capacity*: the bandwidth you have for admin and uncertainty. The implication is that the best switching decisions often happen when you plan them into calmer periods, rather than waiting until irritation peaks.

These three factors—switching costs, service quality, appetite for change—form a practical triad. They also produce a dilemma that is not solvable by slogans: the cheapest choice is not always the best choice, and the easiest choice is often the most expensive over time. This is why a calm decision beats an angry one. Anger makes the future invisible. Anger narrows attention to punishment: "I'm cancelling to teach them a lesson." The provider does not learn a lesson. The customer bears the switching cost. The wise question is always: what outcome do you want for your own life, not for the provider's moral education?

A second named example helps to show why switching can be structurally difficult even when it is rational. In energy, the UK introduced the domestic supplier switching programme to move towards faster switching, and in 2022 Ofgem confirmed a move towards quicker switching arrangements via new systems. The specifics of implementation can be debated, but the policy direction reflects a long-standing reality: switching has historically been slowed by process, and slow processes discourage movement. When switching is slow, the perceived risk rises, because a customer imagines being stuck between providers. The implication is not that one must master regulatory detail; it is that systems often create friction that makes staying feel safer than it truly is. Recognising that structural friction helps you interpret your own reluctance more accurately. Sometimes reluctance is rational caution. Sometimes it is a reaction to a system designed to make leaving painful.

This brings us to the counter-example that keeps the discussion honest: there are situations where switching is a bad move even if the monthly price is lower. A new provider may offer an attractive introductory rate but impose sharp increases later. A bundled offer may include features you do not need, locking you into complexity. A cheaper service may have weaker support, meaning a single failure can cost you hours. In some cases, the current provider's stability, familiarity, or quality makes the "overpayment" a kind of insurance premium against hassle. The reconciliation is to treat switching as a hypothesis to be tested, not as a default virtue. You compare. You weigh. You decide. You do not romanticise movement for its own sake.

One practical way to avoid inertia and anger alike is to set a switching threshold in advance, expressed in terms you can measure. Not a dramatic "I'll leave if you don't match this exactly," but a private line that turns dithering into decision. The line might be financial—an annual difference that feels worth the hassle. It might be qualitative—an unacceptable number of outages, repeated billing errors, a pattern of poor service. The point is not to create rigid rules; it is to prevent the endless half-life of indecision where you keep paying more because you keep meaning to review later. The concept is *decision criteria.* The implication is that criteria protect you from mood-based choices.

The act of switching also reveals something about negotiation itself. Many people use "leaving" as a threat while having no intention of leaving, which is not leverage; it is theatre. Theatre is brittle because the other side can sense it, and once they sense it your credibility shrinks. A genuine willingness to switch, by contrast, has a calming effect even if you never execute it. It gives you an exit option that stabilises your tone. It makes you less likely to accept a poor deal out of discomfort. It also changes how you hear offers. A retention discount that once felt like a victory may now look like a short postponement of drift. The implication is that the possibility of switching makes your negotiation more honest.

When you do choose to switch, the final notice matters more than people think, not because it is a moral performance but because it shapes your last interaction and can affect practical details: final bills, cancellation dates, equipment returns, and the avoidance of accidental renewal. A calm final notice is a tool for clean closure. It contains the essentials without insult. It confirms the choice. It asks for the process. It avoids the temptation to litigate the past. The language can be plain: "I've reviewed my options and I'm going to cancel at the end of the current term. Please confirm the effective cancellation date and any steps required on my side." The tone is not submissive. It is decisive. It treats the relationship as contractual rather than emotional.

This is also where "partial success" becomes a useful lens. Sometimes switching is not the outcome; the decision to switch prompts a retention offer that genuinely meets your threshold. If the offer meets it, staying becomes a deliberate choice rather than inertia. If it does not, leaving remains clean. Either way, you have escaped the worst posture: being dragged along by default. The concept is *controlled optionality*: keeping choices open until a decision point. The implication is that switching is not a failure of negotiation; it is often the completion of it.

The motif here is the door. Some doors open with a small hinge-touch. Some are swollen and stuck. Sometimes the wise move is to stop pushing and use another exit. The door you choose determines your next year's baseline: the bills you will pay, the friction you will tolerate, the time you will spend dealing with errors. The forward test is therefore uncomfortably concrete: when a provider refuses meaningful movement, will you stay because change feels like a nuisance, or will you leave because you have measured the nuisance against the ongoing cost—and can you do it without anger, as a clean decision rather than a flare of emotion?

Chapter 4
Retention Deals and Service Bundles

In May 2018, after the Financial Conduct Authority's market study into general insurance and the subsequent scrutiny of "loyalty penalties", a quiet truth became harder to deny in Britain: staying put could cost more than leaving. The language of regulators was cautious, but the lived experience was blunt. A renewal notice arrived, the premium rose, and the customer who had paid faithfully for years discovered that fidelity was not a currency automatically redeemed. The most revealing part of the story was not the outrage it provoked but the system it exposed: an economy of discounts designed to appear only when a customer's departure became plausible.

Most "best deals" are conditional. That is the deal.

This chapter is about learning to read that conditionality without cynicism and without naïveté. Retention offers and service bundles are not minor quirks of modern commerce; they are architectural features. They exist because organisations calculate lifetime value, churn probability, acquisition cost, and support burden with a cold eye. They design incentives accordingly. The result is a strange theatre in which the customer who asks, politely and credibly, often receives a different menu from the customer who stays silent. It is not fair in any grand philosophical sense. It is, however, predictable, and what is predictable can be navigated.

Retention deals are often misunderstood because people imagine them as spontaneous generosity. In reality, they tend to be pre-designed options, approved within limits, and offered through specific channels at specific times. A first-line agent may be trained to protect margin, offer minimal concessions, and only escalate when the customer signals cancellation. A retention specialist may be measured on saving accounts and may have access to more flexible tools: credits, matched rates, contract adjustments, add-ons.

The same company can therefore sound rigid at first contact and surprisingly pliable later. Many people interpret this as dishonesty. Sometimes it is. More often it is organisational design: different desks are paid to care about different outcomes.

The hinge here is polite persistence, a phrase that can sound like moral advice until it is seen as an operational method. Persistence is not repeating the same demand louder. It is re-stating the request clearly, checking whether another option exists, and, when appropriate, moving to the channel where discretion lives. Politeness is not submissiveness. It is the choice to keep the interaction in the realm of problem-solving rather than humiliation. Humiliation makes people rigid. Rigidity is expensive. The odd thing about retention is that it rewards calm. The customer who can hold their ground without theatre often hears, a few minutes later, a different set of possibilities.

Loyalty, too, needs reframing. In popular imagination, loyalty is a moral claim: "I have been good, therefore you should reward me." Organisations rarely respond to moral claims. They respond to signals. Loyalty becomes a strong signal when it is treated as evidence of low risk and low cost: you pay reliably, you do not generate endless support tickets, you can be retained with a sensible adjustment. Framed this way, loyalty is not a plea for gratitude. It is a case for efficiency. "I'd like to stay and I've been with you for years; can you review what you can offer to keep my rate reasonable?" is an invitation to the company to do what it already wants to do—retain profitable customers—without forcing anyone to pretend it is charity. The emotional payoff of this reframing is subtle but real: it removes the sting of feeling like you are begging for recognition. You are negotiating terms.

Then come bundles, those seductive packages that promise simplicity while quietly altering the balance of power. Bundling can save money. It can also obscure costs, lengthen commitments, and make switching harder later. A bundle is not just a price; it is a set of interdependencies. When broadband is tied to streaming, and streaming is tied to mobile, and mobile is tied to a handset contract, the household has traded flexibility for a temporary discount. This can be sensible. It can also be a trap. The only way to know is to understand what is actually being bundled: which components you genuinely use, which ones are padding, what happens when the promotional period ends, and how easily each component can be removed without breaking the entire structure.

The modern relevance is sharper than ever because the subscription economy has matured into a kind of domestic infrastructure. Entertainment, connectivity, insurance, cloud storage, software, home security, fitness, even meals—many of the services that used to be one-off purchases now renew by default. Bundles are the natural response of firms seeking to deepen relationships and reduce churn: the more services you take, the less likely you are to leave. The customer's interest is often different: keep what is valuable, discard what is not, and preserve exit routes. This chapter sits at that intersection. It is about designing your relationship to bundles so they serve you, rather than quietly turning you into a captive account.

There is also a psychological trap that makes bundles and retention offers especially potent: they are presented as time-limited gifts. "Special offer" language creates urgency, and urgency is the enemy of careful choice. Under urgency, people accept add-ons they do not need because rejecting feels like losing. They accept free trials that later auto-renew because "it's free now". They agree to longer terms because the monthly cost drops, without measuring the total commitment. What looks like a bargain becomes a slow leak. The solution is not suspicion of every offer. It is the ability to pause—"Let me think about that"—without embarrassment, and then return with a clearer counter-proposal. That pause is a micro-negotiation in itself: a refusal to let someone else's timetable become your decision-making engine.

This chapter is therefore less about hunting discounts and more about learning a new literacy: reading the menus organisations do not advertise, understanding what retention teams can and cannot do, framing loyalty as an asset rather than a grievance, and treating bundles as structures with trade-offs rather than as shiny savings. It asks you to notice how companies signal what they value—long contracts, reduced churn, higher lifetime spend—and to decide what you value in return—predictable cost, flexibility, clean service, and the ability to leave without drama when the relationship no longer fits.

The emotional stakes are not trivial. Many people feel vaguely ashamed when they ask for a loyalty reward, as if it reveals pettiness. Others feel righteous and become abrasive, as if the company has committed a personal betrayal. Both postures distort the conversation. The most effective posture is neither servile nor furious. It is clear-eyed. You are not asking for kindness. You are asking for terms that make continued business rational for both sides. That stance allows you to be courteous without being pliable, and firm without being theatrical.

The page-turn momentum in this chapter comes from a sober promise: once you understand how retention and bundling actually work, you will stop being surprised by "no" that later becomes "yes", by discounts that appear only at the edge of cancellation, and by bundles that look cheaper until you price their components. You will start seeing the hidden architecture beneath the offers—the approval limits, the churn calculations, the scripts designed to delay concessions—and you will learn to move through that architecture with minimal friction.

The question that carries you forward is not whether you deserve the best deal. That question leads to moral frustration. The better question is procedural and liberating: when an organisation offers you a set of terms, are you seeing the full menu—or only the menu shown to customers who never threaten to leave, never pause to compare, and never ask what else is possible?

How Retention Deals Work

In February 2020, Ofcom's new rules on end-of-contract and annual best-tariff notifications came into force for UK mobile, broadband and pay-TV providers. The policy language was tidy; the lived reality was messier. In a living room in Glasgow, a person could open an email, hear the faint tick of a radiator, and see a company admitting—without saying it outright—that different customers were paying different prices for broadly similar service. The message was framed as helpful disclosure. Its subtext was sharper: the best deals often appear only when leaving becomes plausible.

Discounts are rationed. They always were.

Retention deals work because churn hurts and discounting costs. Every company that sells recurring services is caught between those two forces, and most resolve the tension by building a gate: discounts are kept behind it, accessible through specific triggers, channels, and scripts. The gate is not personal. It is managerial. It exists to prevent "margin leakage"—discounts given away to customers who would have stayed anyway—while still allowing concessions for customers who are likely to leave. Retention, then, is not the spontaneous kindness of a well-meaning agent. It is a controlled system for deciding when a concession is cheaper than a cancellation.

Start with the simplest show-and-name. A household has pay-TV. The bill has risen over time. They call customer service and ask for a reduction. The agent explains that prices have increased and offers a minor adjustment or none at all. The household accepts, irritated but busy. This is the default track. Now imagine a second household with the same provider. They call near the end of a contract, mention they are comparing alternatives, and ask to cancel unless the price can be brought closer to current market offers. They are transferred to a cancellations or retention team. The tone changes. Options appear. The concept is *churn triage*: the organisation prioritises concessions where the risk of losing revenue is highest. The implication is uncomfortable but liberating: a "no" at the wrong desk is often a routing outcome, not a final truth.

The internal logic of retention is surprisingly mathematical, even if the language presented to customers is warm. Companies estimate customer lifetime value—how much revenue an account is likely to generate over time—and compare it to the cost of acquiring a new customer. They also estimate the probability that a customer will leave, based on signals: contract end dates, price rises, competitor offers, service complaints, payment history, even the channel used to contact them. These estimates do not need to be perfect to be useful. They only need to be better than guessing. The concept is *probabilistic pricing*: decisions made under uncertainty using estimated risk. The implication is that your words and timing affect not only the mood of the person on the line but the category the system places you in.

This is why "polite persistence" works. Politeness keeps the interaction in the zone where staff can help without fear. Persistence ensures the request is actually processed by the part of the organisation designed to make concessions. Without persistence, many customers accept the first "no" because they assume it is absolute. Often it is not. It may be a boundary of authority—what that agent can do—or a boundary of script—what that agent is trained to offer without escalation. Polite persistence is the method of testing those boundaries without setting the room on fire.

Consider how approval often works. Many frontline agents have limited discretion: a small credit cap, a narrow set of tariff changes, a fixed script for renewal conversations. They are measured on speed and compliance. Retention agents, by contrast, may have broader levers: larger discretionary credits, promotional extensions, "save offers" that apply only in cancellation pathways, and the authority to restructure bundles. They are measured on "saves"—accounts prevented from leaving—and sometimes on revenue retained. The concept is *authority gradients*: different roles have different powers because organisations control risk. The implication is that the customer who wants better terms must often reach the role that can legally and procedurally grant them.

A concrete pay-TV pattern illustrates this without melodrama. The customer calls and asks, "Can you reduce my bill?" The first agent offers a modest discount tied to a longer contract or suggests removing channels. The customer says they would like to cancel. The agent either transfers them or attempts a "save" on the spot. The retention agent then offers a more substantial discount, often for a limited period, sometimes paired with a contract extension. If the customer declines, the agent may make a final offer—still within constraints, but better than the first. This staircase of offers is not improvisation. It is often designed: initial offers to test willingness, later offers reserved for higher churn risk. The concept is *offer sequencing*. The implication is that the first price you hear is often not the best price available, and the system expects some customers to climb the staircase.

The staircase is also why people sometimes feel manipulated, and that feeling deserves respect. It is disorienting to be told "there's nothing we can do" and then to hear, minutes later, that something can be done after you mention cancellation. The disorientation comes from the clash between social norms and commercial design. Socially, we expect straightforwardness. Commercially, companies optimise. Retention is optimisation. That does not make it evil. It does mean the customer should stop treating the first answer as a moral statement. It is an opening bid shaped by internal rules. The implication is that understanding the design reduces emotional whiplash. You can treat the conversation as a process rather than as a personal affront.

A second named example anchors the insurance side of the story. In January 2022, the Financial Conduct Authority's general insurance pricing practices rules took effect in the UK, restricting the ability of firms to charge renewing customers more than new customers for equivalent cover. This regulatory intervention matters here because it shows that retention and renewal pricing had become structurally skewed. Firms had been able to apply different pricing logic to new and existing customers, often relying on inertia. The rule attempted to limit that, but it did not eliminate all variation in pricing, nor did it remove the need for customer engagement. The implication is that institutions themselves acknowledge the economic power of customer passivity—and they legislate around it when the imbalance becomes too visible.

Retention offers are also constrained by budgets, and budgets are not just financial; they are reputational and procedural. Companies set limits on how much discount can be offered without triggering supervisory approval. They set limits on which customers are eligible for which offers. They set limits on how often an account can receive "goodwill" credits. These limits exist because, from the company's perspective, excessive discounting trains customers to ask more and erodes price integrity. From the customer's perspective, limits create unpredictability. The concept is *controlled generosity*: concessions are permitted, but only within guardrails. The implication is that retention deals are not endless; they are bounded, which is why knowing your alternatives matters.

Alternatives matter because retention is fundamentally a cost comparison. The company asks, implicitly: is it cheaper to discount this customer than to lose them? You ask, implicitly: is it worth staying if the discount is temporary, partial, or tied to conditions? This is where exit options calm the voice. If you can leave, you can listen to offers with a cooler head. If you cannot, you are vulnerable to accepting whatever is placed in front of you because the emotional cost of confrontation feels too high. The visible behaviour is not threatening to leave. It is being able to leave. The concept is *credible exit.* The implication is that retention works best for the customer when it is backed by real choice, not performance.

Yet there is a limitation that keeps the story honest. Some markets are not meaningfully competitive, and some customers have weak exit options: rural connectivity constraints, specialist needs, contractual lock-in, or the simple fact that switching costs are high. In such cases, retention offers may be minimal because the provider knows, statistically, that leaving is unlikely. There are also providers whose systems are rigid or whose customer service is outsourced with limited authority. For them, retention may be more theatre than substance. The reconciliation is not to abandon the idea of retention but to treat it as one possible mechanism among others: plan downgrades, add-on removals, payment schedule adjustments, or, in the long run, deliberate switching when capacity allows. The implication is that retention is a tool, not a guarantee.

This is why polite persistence must include an ear for diminishing returns. If you keep pressing after the best offer has been stated, the conversation can sour. Not because you are rude, but because the agent can do no more and must protect the boundary. A skilled negotiator recognises when a boundary is real. Real boundaries are usually consistent: the agent repeats the same constraint, offers to cancel, and cannot provide new options after checking. Imagined boundaries wobble: "nothing available" becomes "maybe a small credit" becomes "actually there is a retention offer" after a specific trigger. The concept is *boundary testing.* The implication is that persistence is not endless; it is targeted at locating where discretion ends.

A small, realistic script shows how to climb the staircase without becoming theatrical. A customer might say, calmly: "I've been happy with the service, but the price has risen and I'm comparing alternatives. I'd prefer to stay if you can bring the monthly cost closer to £X. If that isn't possible, I'll need to cancel at the end of the term. What options do you have?" The script does not accuse. It signals churn risk. It sets an anchor. It names an exit. It invites options. It gives the agent a safe route: either present a retention offer or proceed with cancellation. This is not bluffing. It is structuring the decision.

The motif worth carrying through is the gate. Retention offers sit behind a gate because companies must ration discounts. The customer's task is not to batter the gate. It is to find the latch: timing, routing, calm tone, credible alternatives. When the latch is found, the gate opens with surprising ease, not because the company has suddenly become benevolent, but because you have reached the part of the system designed to make a trade.

The forward test is therefore stark. When you hear "there's nothing we can do," will you treat it as a verdict and surrender to drift—or will you treat it as the first answer from the first desk, and decide whether the gate is worth trying again, politely, with a clearer signal of choice behind your words?

Asking for Loyalty Rewards

In January 2022, the Financial Conduct Authority's general insurance pricing practices rules took effect in the UK, restricting firms from charging renewing customers more than new customers for equivalent cover. The change was technical, but its cultural echo was loud: the long-standing assumption that loyalty would be rewarded had been unreliable enough to require regulation. In a kitchen in Bristol, someone could hold a renewal letter, feel the paper's thin sheen between finger and thumb, and realise that "staying" had not been interpreted as devotion. It had been interpreted as probability—probability of inertia, probability of not switching, probability of accepting drift.

Loyalty is a signal. Not a virtue.

That distinction matters because it changes the emotional posture of the person asking. When loyalty is treated as virtue, the request becomes moral: "I've been good, so you should be good back." When loyalty is treated as signal, the request becomes operational: "I'm a reliable customer; can we align the terms so it remains rational for me to stay?" The first posture invites disappointment, because organisations are not built to reward virtue. The second posture invites negotiation, because organisations are built to respond to incentives.

Most people carry loyalty as a quiet identity: "I'm not the sort of person who shops around." It can feel elegant, even dignified, to keep relationships stable. There is something human in familiarity—knowing how the service works, having a direct debit that behaves, not having to reset passwords and learn new interfaces. The problem is that many subscription businesses do not experience your stability as dignity. They experience it as predictability. Predictability reduces their costs. It also reduces their motivation to offer concessions. This is not personal. It is accounting.

To ask for a loyalty reward without sounding entitled, you have to translate your history into the language of cost and risk. A reliable customer is lower risk. A reliable customer is cheaper to serve. A reliable customer is a safer revenue stream. These facts are not sentimental; they are measurable in the same way that churn is measurable. When you frame your history as an asset, you are giving the organisation a story it can use to justify making an exception. The concept here is *internal justification*: the reason a concession can be approved without making the agent feel reckless. The implication is that your phrasing should make it easy for the other side to explain, to themselves and their systems, why helping you is sensible.

A scene shows the difference. A customer calls their broadband provider. They are angry because the bill has risen. They say, "I've been with you for eight years and you treat me like this. You should be ashamed." The agent hears accusation. Accusation triggers defence. Defence triggers policy. The customer's history, which could have been valuable information, has been turned into a weapon. Now replay the call. The customer says, "I've been with you for eight years and the service has been solid. I'd like to stay, but the new price has pushed it beyond what I'm willing to pay. Can you check whether there's a loyalty offer or a tariff adjustment available for long-term customers?" The facts are identical. The emotional frame is not. The concept is *credible preference*: an expressed desire to stay paired with a boundary. The implication is that this frame invites a search rather than a standoff.

The phrase "loyalty offer" can feel faintly embarrassing to say, as if you are asking to be patted on the head. It helps to remember that many firms already have such categories, whether or not they call them that in public. They have retention budgets. They have "save" offers. They have "existing customer" tariffs. They have discretionary credits that can be applied under certain conditions. You are not inventing a new idea when you ask. You are asking the firm to check a menu that may not be displayed unless prompted. The concept is *menu visibility*. The implication is that the act of asking changes what you are shown.

A second checkable example anchors this beyond insurance. In February 2020, Ofcom's end-of-contract and annual best-tariff notification rules came into effect for UK mobile, broadband and pay-TV providers. The measure was partly about consumer awareness, but it also reveals something about loyalty rewards: regulators recognised that the market had been structured in a way that disadvantaged those who stayed without checking. The entire logic of these notifications is that "staying" and "paying" are not, by themselves, enough to ensure a fair outcome; information and action matter. The implication is not that loyalty is foolish. It is that loyalty must be accompanied by periodic review if it is to be economically sane.

The most effective loyalty requests are specific about what "reward" would mean. "Can you do something for me?" is too vague. "Can you reduce my bill?" is clearer but still frames the concession as a gift. Better is to ask for a particular kind of adjustment that the organisation might already be authorised to provide: a discount, an add-on, a more flexible term, a fee waived, a plan change without penalty, an extension of a promotion. The visible behaviour is naming one or two plausible outcomes rather than begging for mercy. The concept is *concession design*. The implication is that specificity narrows the search space, which makes help easier.

It also avoids a common trap: the false loyalty reward that costs you more later. Some "loyalty" deals are just repackaged bundles with longer commitments. A lower monthly price paired with an extended contract may be fine, but only if you understand the trade. A "free" add-on that auto-renews at a higher price is not a reward; it is a delayed charge. A premium channel for six months may be useless if you never watch it. The loyalty request should therefore include a quiet insistence on fit: the reward should be something you value, not something that pads the provider's metrics. The concept is *value alignment*. The implication is that loyalty rewards should be evaluated by your usage, not by their marketing language.

There is a social danger here, too: entitlement. Entitlement often comes from a reasonable place—people do feel hurt when years of custom are met with indifference—but once expressed, entitlement tends to poison the interaction. It implies the other person is morally obligated. Moral obligation is hard to satisfy in a transactional setting because the agent has limited authority and limited incentive to absorb blame. Entitlement also makes you less flexible, because it frames the interaction as justice rather than choice. Justice has only one acceptable outcome. Choice allows trade-offs. The concept is *moral narrowing*. The implication is that dropping entitlement is not about being nicer; it is about keeping more options available.

Appreciative asking is not flattery. It is a recognition of the other person's position. "I appreciate you checking" is not grovelling; it is a way of keeping the agent in a cooperative posture while they do the work of searching options. Appreciation also makes it easier for the agent to go a little further, to check one more screen, to ask a supervisor, to explore a retention pathway. People are more willing to expend discretionary effort when they are not being treated as an obstacle. The concept is *discretionary effort*. The implication is that appreciation can increase the amount of work someone is willing to do on your behalf, which is often the difference between "nothing available" and "there is an offer, but it's not advertised".

A credible counter-example keeps the picture honest. There are contexts where loyalty rewards are structurally weak. In markets with little competition, a firm may not need to offer much because leaving is hard. In periods of rising costs across an industry, firms may have limited margin to share. In heavily regulated products, price flexibility may be constrained. In those cases, the loyalty request may yield little. The reconciliation is to treat the request as an information probe rather than as a test of your worth. If no loyalty benefit exists, that fact itself is valuable; it clarifies the firm's posture and informs the decision to stay, downgrade, or eventually switch. The implication is that asking for loyalty rewards can be productive even when the answer is no, because it converts uncertainty into knowledge.

The simplest way to keep the request clean is to make it a three-part statement: history, preference, boundary. History: how long you have been a customer and, if relevant, that you pay reliably. Preference: that you would like to stay if terms remain reasonable. Boundary: the point at which you will not continue—either a price threshold, a comparable market benchmark, or the fact that the increase is too steep. Then a question: what can be done. That structure sounds almost too plain to be powerful. Plain is powerful. It keeps the conversation from becoming a therapy session about disappointment and makes it into a solvable problem.

A short script can show the contrast between entitlement and appreciative asking without turning into theatre. Entitlement sounds like: "I've been with you for years, so I deserve your best deal. If you don't give it, I'll tell everyone how awful you are." Appreciative asking sounds like: "Hello—thanks for your time. I've been with you for several years and I've paid on time. I'd like to stay, but the renewal price is now higher than comparable offers I'm seeing. Can you check whether there's a loyalty discount or a way to adjust my plan so the monthly cost is closer to £X? I'd appreciate you looking." The second script contains firmness—there is a benchmark and a boundary—without hostility. It invites options. It leaves the agent room to help. It also leaves you room to decide if the option offered is good enough.

The deeper work here is psychological. Asking for loyalty rewards forces you to confront a mildly painful truth: organisations do not love you back. They cannot. They are systems. Yet you can still have a dignified relationship with a system if you treat it honestly—as an exchange with terms that must make sense for both sides. Loyalty, then, becomes something you choose because the service is worth it, not because you are owed gratitude for staying. That choice is cleaner. It also makes leaving less dramatic when leaving is warranted.

The forward test is therefore not whether you can deliver a polite script. It is whether you can hold the paradox without flinching: to value stability and still insist on fair terms, to appreciate good service and still compare, to mention your history without turning it into a grievance. When your next renewal arrives, will you speak as someone seeking a reward for virtue—or as someone offering a reliable relationship on the condition that the numbers remain sane?

Designing Smart Service Bundles

In November 2014, in London, the Competition and Markets Authority published its report on the private motor insurance market and, among other findings, warned about "add-ons" sold alongside the main product—extras that could deliver value but were often poorly understood at the point of sale. The word "add-on" belongs to insurance, yet the structure now shapes much of the subscription economy. A bundle is, in effect, a main product plus a necklace of extras: streaming with broadband, cloud storage with a phone contract, device insurance with a handset, "premium" support with software, a rewards programme with a bank account. The sales copy promises simplicity. The accounting often produces complexity.

Bundles feel neat. They rarely are.

A bundle is a deal made of two deals: the price reduction you can see and the dependency you cannot. The visible part is a lower monthly figure or a "free" add-on. The invisible part is the way services become tied together, so that changing one becomes harder. This is why bundles can be brilliant and dangerous at once. They can cut cost and cognitive load, reducing the number of invoices, logins, and renewal dates. They can also trap you in a relationship that becomes expensive later, because the bundle turns a set of independent choices into a single knot.

The first claim is easiest to show with a household scene that almost everyone recognises. A person is offered broadband plus streaming for "only a little more". They already pay for broadband. They already pay for streaming, perhaps through a separate provider. The bundle promises a discount, an upgraded router, a better package, perhaps a few months "included". The person imagines future evenings made smooth by convenience: one bill, one call, one provider. They accept. Months later, they notice they are watching the same few programmes as before, and they are paying more overall because the bundle included channels they do not use and locked them into a higher broadband tier than they needed. The concept is *overbuying through bundling*: purchasing capacity or features because they are packaged attractively rather than because they are used. The implication is that the bundle's savings must be measured against actual behaviour, not against imagined consumption.

This is why "designing" a bundle matters. The word is deliberate. Most bundles are designed by companies for companies. They are built to increase average revenue per user, reduce churn, and deepen dependence. A customer who wants a smart bundle must design from the opposite direction: from usage, from flexibility, from future options. The customer's bundle is not "whatever the provider offers". It is a configuration that fits the household's real habits and preserves the ability to change later. That is what "on your own terms" means in practice.

A smart bundle starts with a simple measurement: what is used, and how often. Not in the moralistic sense of "should I watch less television", but in the descriptive sense of "what am I paying for, and what do I actually consume?" Usage is not an abstraction. It is the number of streaming platforms you open in a month, the number of devices connected to broadband, the amount of mobile data you use outside Wi-Fi, the number of times you have called support. The visible behaviour is checking recent bills and looking at app usage histories. The concept is *behavioural accounting*. The implication is that bundles become less seductive when you view them as a mirror of your habits rather than as a promise of a better identity.

The second claim is that bundles should be evaluated over time, not at the promotional moment. Bundles are often sold with introductory pricing: "six months included", "£X off for a year", "free trial". Promotional periods create a distorted picture of cost, because they front-load value and back-load expense. The household sees the discount and forgets the reversion. The reversion is the real relationship. The concept here is *price reversion*: the tendency of bundled deals to become more expensive after an initial period. The implication is that the only meaningful comparison is the cost across the full term, including what happens when the promotion ends.

A third claim follows: a bundle that is cheaper can still be worse if it increases switching costs. Switching costs are not only fees; they are the practical difficulties of leaving. If broadband and streaming are tied, switching broadband may also disrupt streaming access, email addresses, hardware, or support relationships. The more entangled the bundle, the higher the switching cost, and the more power the provider has at renewal. This is where "risk" becomes visible: the risk of being stuck, the risk of accepting a future price rise because leaving would be painful. The concept is *lock-in through interdependence*. The implication is that a smart bundle preserves seams—points where services can be separated later with minimal disruption.

A broadband-plus-streaming example can show how to preserve those seams. Imagine a household considering a provider's offer: broadband plus a streaming subscription for a slightly higher monthly rate. A naive evaluation compares only headline numbers: current broadband cost plus current streaming cost versus the bundled cost. A smart evaluation asks a different set of questions: is the streaming subscription in the bundle identical to the one you would buy independently, or is it a restricted version? Does it include adverts? Does it include multiple screens? Does it limit resolution? Is the streaming service billed separately or fused into the broadband bill? Can it be cancelled independently? Does taking the bundle extend the broadband contract length? Does the broadband price change if the streaming add-on is later removed? Each question is a lever disguised as curiosity. The concept is *seam testing*: checking where the bundle can be split. The implication is that the best bundles are those you can unbundle without punishment.

This is where language matters. Providers often describe bundles as "simple", "all-in-one", "everything you need". Those phrases are designed to stop you asking seam questions. The person designing a smart bundle is not hostile; they are precise. They ask, calmly, for the cost of each component within the bundle, and for the terms attached to removing each component. Not because they enjoy small print, but because they want to know whether the bundle is truly cheaper or merely rearranged. A true discount lowers total cost without raising future exit costs too sharply. A false discount lowers the first bill while raising the cost of leaving. The concept is *true versus cosmetic savings*. The implication is that the smartest question in bundling is often, "What happens if I remove this later?"

A second named, checkable example helps explain why firms structure bundles this way. In February 2020, Ofcom's end-of-contract and annual best-tariff notification rules took effect in the UK telecoms sector. The rules were designed to counter inertia and reduce consumer overpayment. One effect of bundling, however, is to complicate those comparisons. When a customer holds multiple products with one provider, it becomes harder to compare like with like. The provider's price becomes less transparent because it is an amalgam. This does not mean bundles are inherently bad. It means the customer must insist on comparability: what does each part cost, and what is it replacing? The implication is that bundles often work by reducing your ability to compare, and that a smart bundle restores comparability.

There is also a psychological trap that deserves a name: *the "free" illusion*. "Free months of streaming" feels like a gift, and gifts make people reluctant to scrutinise. Yet "free" is often simply a temporary transfer of cost from you to the provider in exchange for a longer commitment or higher future payments. This is not necessarily exploitative; it can be a fair trade. The problem is the way "free" bypasses calculation. Calculation is what keeps you in control. A person who designs a smart bundle treats "free" as a time-shifted price. They ask when the charging starts, what the price will be then, and whether the service can be cancelled before the charge begins without affecting the rest of the contract. The concept is *time-shifted pricing*. The implication is that "free" becomes meaningful only when you know the terms that follow it.

A credible counter-example keeps the discussion grounded: some bundles are genuinely valuable because they reduce administrative friction more than they reduce price. A household might gladly accept a small premium to have one bill, one support channel, and one integrated service experience—especially if the provider's service quality is strong and the household's life is already stretched. In such cases, the bundle's value is time and simplicity, not just money. The reconciliation is to treat simplicity as a real benefit, but to price it honestly. If you are paying for convenience, know that you are paying for convenience. Do not mistake convenience for savings. The implication is that the best bundle is sometimes the one that costs a little more but saves you hours of management—and sometimes the best bundle is no bundle at all.

To avoid overbuying, it helps to separate "capacity" from "need". Providers love to sell headroom: faster broadband than you require, unlimited data when you rarely exceed modest use, premium channels you never watch. Headroom feels safe. Safety sells. But headroom that is never used is simply cost. The visible behaviour is the mismatch between plan capacity and actual consumption: a high-tier broadband plan for a household that streams casually, or a premium television package for someone who watches two programmes and the news. The concept is *capacity inflation.* The implication is that smart bundling begins with an honest inventory of what you actually do, not what you might do in an imagined, more aspirational life.

The tone for these questions matters because bundling discussions can feel like sales encounters. Sales encounters can make people defensive or submissive. Neither posture is useful. The aim is steady curiosity: "Can you break down the monthly cost of each component?" "Is the streaming add-on cancellable independently?" "What happens to the broadband price if I remove it after the promotional period?" These questions are not aggressive. They are structural. They also signal that you are a customer who will notice later if the deal does not match what was implied. That signal, in itself, can improve the quality of the offer you receive, because it reduces the temptation to sell you something fragile.

A smart bundle is therefore less a bargain hunt than a design problem. You are designing a relationship between services: which ones should be tied, which should remain independent, and how easily you can change your mind. A bundle that respects your future self—your future needs, your future time constraints, your future desire to switch—is a bundle worth considering. A bundle that assumes you will never review terms again is the one that quietly extracts value later.

The motif to carry through is the knot. Bundles tie knots. Some knots secure things that belong together; they reduce loose ends. Some knots tighten over time, making it harder to move. The forward test is a simple question with sharp edges: if you accept this bundle, how easily can you untie it when the promotion ends, your habits change, or the provider's service declines—and are you choosing the knot because it genuinely fits, or because "free" and "simple" have temporarily made calculation feel impolite?

Avoiding Traps and Upsells

In March 2019, the UK Competition and Markets Authority published its final report on online platforms and digital advertising, and one of its recurring concerns was not merely market power but the ways digital design can shape consumer choices. The report sits at the level of systems, yet its effects land in small domestic moments: a checkout page that nudges, a pop-up that offers "free" extras, a trial that begins with one click and ends with an unexpected charge. In a hallway in Sheffield, a phone in hand, someone can accept an add-on while the kettle boils, hardly noticing the tiny shift from *choice* to *commitment.*

The trap is the default.

Upsells and traps thrive because they exploit a predictable human weakness: we are bad at noticing small, future costs when the present moment offers convenience or status. "Special offer" language is designed to shorten thought. It compresses time. It makes deliberation feel like needless fuss. Many traps are not illegal; they are merely engineered to take advantage of the fact that most people are busy. This section is about preserving agency in those moments without becoming suspicious of everything. Suspicion is exhausting. Clarity is lighter.

Begin with the most common trap: the free trial that auto-renews. The show is familiar. A provider offers a "free" month, sometimes with a card required "for verification". The customer accepts because free feels harmless. The month passes. The charge appears. The customer, startled, either pays because it is now "only" a small amount or spends time cancelling and feels vaguely foolish. The concept is *time-shifted cost*: the price is deferred to a moment when you are less attentive. The implication is that the real question is not "Is it free?" but "What happens next, and how is the next step triggered?"

Another common trap is the bundle padded with rarely used extras. A customer contacts a provider to reduce cost. The provider responds by offering a "better deal" that includes additional features: extra channels, device insurance, priority support, a premium router, a rewards programme. The monthly price may drop slightly or remain similar, and the customer feels they are "getting more". The trick is that the extras create stickiness and future cost. They also make it harder to compare prices later because you are no longer comparing a simple service to a simple service. You are comparing a tangle. The concept is *complexity as camouflage*. The implication is that the more complex the offer, the more you must ask what you are actually buying.

The modern subscription economy is built on this camouflage. It is not built primarily through villainy; it is built through metrics. Companies track conversion, retention, and average revenue per user. Extras and bundles increase those numbers. Trials increase conversion because they lower the psychological barrier to entry. Auto-renewal increases retention because it turns an active choice into a passive continuation. The customer's problem is not that companies behave this way; the problem is that the customer often behaves as if every choice is isolated, when the company has designed it as a sequence. The concept here is *choice architecture*, a term popularised in behavioural economics and public policy. The implication is that you are not simply choosing a product; you are often entering a designed pathway.

The single most protective phrase in this environment is surprisingly simple: "Let me think about that." It works because it punctures urgency. It returns the decision to a calmer time. It also changes the other person's behaviour. A sales script relies on momentum; a pause breaks the script. The phrase does not accuse. It does not reject. It merely creates space. Space is where you can measure, compare, and decide. Five words again: "Let me think about that."

This phrase can feel awkward because many people fear being seen as difficult. They accept upsells to avoid social friction, especially when speaking to a human being who seems friendly. Yet the social awkwardness is often a mirage. Sales staff expect hesitation. They are trained for it. The goal is not to embarrass the other person; it is to avoid embarrassing yourself later with an unwanted recurring charge. The concept is *social pressure*. The implication is that pausing is not rude; it is sane.

Pausing is only part of control. The other part is returning with a clearer counter-proposal. This is where micro-negotiation becomes a design exercise. Instead of absorbing a bundle as offered, you propose a bundle that fits your actual preferences: the service you want, without the extras you do not. This is not about being stingy. It is about being precise. Precision protects you from what the French economist Frédéric Bastiat called "the unseen"—the costs that are not immediately visible. Bastiat wrote in 1850 in his essay "That Which Is Seen, and That Which Is Not Seen" about how people focus on immediate effects and ignore hidden consequences. Upsells are modern lessons in Bastiat's principle: the visible benefit is immediate; the unseen cost arrives later, quietly, in a bank statement or renewal email.

A before-and-after example shows how counter-proposals can remain courteous. The provider offers: "We can give you a special deal that includes premium support and device insurance." The customer's unhelpful response is either instant acceptance or sharp rejection. A controlled response keeps the tone warm while tightening terms: "Thanks—could we look at the price for the core service on its own? I don't need insurance, and I'd rather keep the monthly cost lower." This does not insult the offer. It reframes the aim. The concept is *scope control*. The implication is that you can say no to an extra without turning the conversation hostile.

The red flags are not mysterious once you know where to look, but "where to look" matters. A free trial is a red flag when it requires a payment method upfront and when cancellation is buried behind friction. A bundle is a red flag when it cannot be broken later without penalty, or when the discount applies only if you keep every component. An "exclusive" offer is a red flag when it expires in minutes and depends on your immediate verbal consent. These red flags are not proof of bad faith; they are proof of designed momentum. The visible behaviour is urgency and bundling. The concept is *commitment capture*: turning a moment of attention into a long-term revenue stream. The implication is that your defence is not suspicion but questions that slow the capture.

A second checkable example helps anchor this in policy, not just anecdote. In February 2020, Ofcom's end-of-contract and annual best-tariff notification rules came into effect in UK telecoms. One practical reason such rules matter is that bundles and promotions can otherwise keep customers on suboptimal terms indefinitely. Notifications attempt to restore periodic moments of clarity. Yet the existence of these rules also reveals the persistence of the problem: many customers do not actively review, and companies can profit from that passivity. The implication is that you should treat "special offers" as part of a continuous renewal system, not as isolated generosity.

There is an ethical dimension here, and it is important not to overstate it. Not every upsell is a trap. Some extras are genuinely useful. Device insurance can be worthwhile for certain people. Premium support can matter for a small business that cannot afford downtime. A bigger data plan can reduce hassle. The question is not whether an extra is inherently bad. The question is whether it is wanted, used, and priced fairly relative to alternatives. The credible counter-example is the customer who benefits from a bundle because it matches their actual life and reduces friction they genuinely experience. The reconciliation is to treat add-ons as hypotheses: "Would this change my life in a way worth the cost?" Not as trophies, not as insults.

This returns us to measurement, the quiet theme of the book. You measure what you use. You measure what you pay. You measure how often the extra would have helped you in the past month. You compare that to its cost. This is not financial advice; it is common sense sharpened. The visible behaviour is a simple mental audit: how many times did I need this feature? The concept is *utility*. The implication is that many upsells collapse under the weight of one honest question: "When would I use it?"

Control also comes from recognising your own vulnerable moments. People accept upsells when they are tired, rushed, embarrassed, or eager to end a call. These moments are predictable. They are also avoidable more often than we admit. Choosing the moment to negotiate—when you are not hungry, not distracted, not trying to cook dinner—reduces the chance you will accept an unwanted extra simply to make the conversation stop. This is not moral discipline; it is managing cognitive load. The concept is *decision fatigue*. The implication is that timing protects you not only from other people's tactics but from your own tiredness.

A practical, courteous posture emerges from combining all of this. You listen to the offer. You pause. You ask the seam questions: what happens after the trial, what is the full-term price, can the add-on be removed without penalty, what is the cost of each component. You decide whether the offer matches your usage. If it does, you accept knowingly. If it does not, you return with a counter-proposal that narrows scope and protects the future: core service, clean price, minimal lock-in. You do all of this without accusing anyone of trickery. Accusation wastes time. Precision saves it.

The motif to thread through is the latch. Traps work because the latch is hidden: the default renews, the trial converts, the extra sticks. "Let me think about that" is a way of finding the latch and refusing to let it click shut behind you. The counter-proposal is a way of choosing which doors you will actually walk through.

The forward test is therefore uncomfortably ordinary. When the next "special offer" appears—on a call, on a checkout page, in a renewal email—will you accept momentum as if it were inevitability, or will you create a pause, ask the seam questions, and return with a cleaner proposal that fits your real life rather than the provider's revenue design?

Chapter 5
Late Fees, Refunds and Rights

In April 2014, the UK's Consumer Rights Act received Royal Assent in London, consolidating and clarifying key protections around faulty goods, services, and digital content. That fact feels distant until it collides with the smallest modern indignity: a parcel that arrives damaged, a subscription that renews unexpectedly, a ticketing company that insists "no refunds" as if it were a law of physics. The moment tends to happen in a kitchen or on a train: someone scrolls through an email thread, hears the dull buzz of notifications, and realises that the argument is not really about money. It is about permission—who is allowed to say no, and on what grounds.

Policy is not fate. It is a draft.

This chapter is about that draft: the fine-print terms, the "grace periods", the "goodwill gestures", the exceptions that exist precisely because life is messy. Most people treat policies as walls. Many policies are, in practice, gates. They look absolute until you approach them with the right words and the right evidence. Not because organisations are secretly generous, but because policies are written for scale, and scale cannot anticipate every human detail. Discretion is the patch that keeps the machine humane. Learning to find discretion—without theatrics—is one of the most financially consequential skills in everyday life.

Late fees are the clearest example of how the machine expresses its values. A fee is not only a charge; it is a message: pay on time, follow the process, do not create admin. When you miss a payment, the system does not merely note it. It responds. Yet late fees also exist in a world where people have erratic cashflow, family emergencies, confusing billing cycles, and, sometimes, genuine mistakes. The tension is obvious. Organisations need rules. Humans live in exceptions. The art is knowing when an exception is plausible and how to ask for it without sounding like you are asking to be excused from responsibility.

Refunds are where emotion and policy most often collide. People want refunds when something feels unfair. Companies grant refunds when their procedures allow it. The gap between "unfair" and "allowed" is where arguments happen, and arguments waste energy. A more effective approach is to translate the complaint into the category the system can process. A faulty product is not the same as a change of mind. A service that was not delivered is not the same as a service that was delivered but disappointing. A cancellation before a deadline is not the same as one after. These categories are not pedantry. They are the scaffolding of decisions. When you can name the category correctly, you stop fighting the system and start steering within it.

That steering begins with reading, not skimming. Most people skim policy terms because they are boring and because boredom feels like a signal that the content is unimportant. In reality, boredom is often a camouflage for leverage. Policies contain seams: a time window, a definition of "faulty", a clause about "cooling-off", a mention of "goodwill", a reference to "discretion". These seams are rarely highlighted. They sit in plain sight, waiting for the person who will actually notice. Reading a policy is not about being legalistic. It is about finding the hinge.

Modern life increases the stakes because so much commerce is now frictionless at the point of purchase and complicated at the point of reversal. One click buys. Five screens cancel. Trials auto-renew. Event tickets carry terms that feel punitive. Deliveries pass through multiple subcontractors, so responsibility becomes blurred. The customer's anger is understandable. But anger is a poor tool for navigating blurred responsibility, because anger makes people speak in moral absolutes while systems respond to defined categories. This chapter offers a different posture: factual description, specific requests, and calm escalation when needed. The point is not to "win". The point is to get to a reasonable outcome with minimal damage to relationships and minimal waste of time.

There is also a deeper philosophical question beneath late fees and refunds: what is a fair transaction when both sides face constraints? A small business cannot refund everything without going under. A large company cannot investigate every case in depth without drowning in admin. A customer cannot accept every error without becoming resigned. Fairness, then, is negotiated through process: policies that are strict enough to be scalable and flexible enough to remain defensible. When you understand that, you stop treating a refusal as a personal rejection and start treating it as a first pass through a decision tree. Sometimes the tree has another branch. Sometimes it does not. Either way, you can move through it with more agency.

The chapter also addresses the uncomfortable reality that the first answer is often not the last. Many organisations train frontline staff to protect policy boundaries. It reduces risk. It reduces cost. It also means that a polite, clear request can sometimes be refused simply because the first person cannot approve it or is not encouraged to. Escalation becomes necessary. Yet escalation, mishandled, can scorch the earth: insults, threats, public shaming. Those tactics may produce occasional results, but they tend to degrade future interactions and can trigger defensive procedures. Escalation done well is almost boring: a request for review, a request for a supervisor, a written summary, a calm pause and return. It is firmness without contempt. It keeps the door open.

This chapter is, in a sense, about language as a tool for dignity. It teaches how to acknowledge a fee without grovelling, how to request a refund without implying someone is a thief, how to say "I need this reviewed" without making the staff member your enemy. It also teaches the difference between rights and requests. A right is a claim grounded in a recognised standard—what the policy says, what the law says, what the contract says. A request is an appeal to discretion—goodwill, exception, flexibility. Confusing the two creates conflict: demanding discretion as if it were a right, or pleading for a right as if it were a favour. The emotionally intelligent move is to know which you are making, and to speak accordingly.

The motifs from earlier chapters return in a new form. The hinge is still there, but now it appears in the fine print. The gate is still there, but now it is called "policy". The pause is still there, but now it is the moment you choose to stop arguing and start escalating with precision. The aim is not to turn every dispute into a campaign. The aim is to shorten the distance between problem and resolution.

The momentum at the end of this chapter is a promise of practical confidence. Once you see how policies are written, where discretion hides, and how to ask without hostility, you begin to experience fees and refusals differently. A late fee becomes a negotiable event rather than a shameful verdict. A refund request becomes a structured conversation rather than a fight. A "no" becomes information rather than humiliation.

The question that carries you forward is deceptively small: when a policy is used against you—late fee, cancellation charge, "non-refundable" stamp—will you accept it as a wall, or will you read closely enough to find the seam, then speak calmly enough to test whether the seam opens into discretion, review, or a right you can claim without apology?

Understanding Typical Policies

On 26 March 2015, the UK's Consumer Rights Act 2015 received Royal Assent in London, gathering a thicket of consumer protections into a clearer shape. The legislation is public, grand, and searchable. The moment most people meet its spirit, however, is private and small: a cracked screen on arrival, a cancelled train, a delivery that never turns up, a "late fee applied" line on a statement. A person sits at a table, the paper thin under their fingertips, and stares at a sentence that feels final—*non-refundable*, *subject to charges*, *no exceptions*. The sentence is meant to end the conversation. It rarely deserves that power.

Policies are written to scale. Life is not.

That is the essential tension. A policy is a mechanism for processing thousands of cases without reading each story in full. It must be simple enough to train staff, consistent enough to defend, and broad enough to cover the common failures of human behaviour—forgetfulness, delay, misunderstanding, impulse. The customer, by contrast, experiences the policy at the level of one case: their order, their refund, their cancellation, their missed payment. When these two levels collide, people assume one must be lying. In practice, both are doing what they were built to do. The question is not whether a policy exists. The question is how it is framed, where it allows discretion, and how to read it like a person who understands that "rules" often contain seams.

Reading a policy is not an exercise in reverence. It is a form of preparation. Most policies have two layers: the hard boundary and the soft boundary. The hard boundary is the part that is meant to be applied uniformly—time limits, proof requirements, definitions of fault, cancellation procedures. The soft boundary is the part that acknowledges the world's untidiness—grace periods, goodwill gestures, managerial discretion, "we may" clauses that create room for judgement. Many people skim and see only the hard boundary, because it is written in bold. They miss the soft boundary, because it is written in the language of contingency. The concept here is *policy elasticity*: the degree to which a rule can stretch without breaking. The implication is that you negotiate more effectively when you know where the elastic is.

The first thing to notice is what policies are trying to protect. Companies do not write late-fee policies because they enjoy punishing people. They write them to protect cashflow and reduce admin. Companies do not write refund exclusions because they despise customers. They write them to limit fraud, prevent resale abuse, and keep costs predictable. Event organisers insist on strict cancellation terms because a seat unsold is revenue lost forever. These are not moral defences. They are practical constraints. When you see what is being protected, you can speak in a way that reassures the other side while still requesting movement. The concept is *constraint literacy*. The implication is that you can frame your request as compatible with the organisation's needs rather than as an attack on them.

Take late fees. The typical policy has several moving parts: when a payment is considered late, what fees are applied, whether there is a grace period, and whether a waiver is possible. A grace period is a policy's admission that the world does not run on perfect timing—bank transfers fail, weekends intervene, people misread dates. Grace periods are often short and sometimes informal, but their existence matters because it gives you a foothold. Similarly, many organisations retain a "one-off courtesy waiver" not because they expect to use it frequently, but because they know that strict application without any human relief creates churn and complaints. The visible behaviour you look for is the wording: "may waive", "can remove", "at our discretion", "as a goodwill gesture". The concept is *discretion clauses*. The implication is that your best argument is often not emotional but categorical: you are asking to be treated as an exception case the policy already anticipates.

Refund policies are even more categorical. They typically distinguish between faults, dissatisfaction, and change of mind. A faulty product has different obligations attached to it than a product you simply no longer want. A service that was not delivered has different remedies than a service that was delivered poorly. A cancellation made within a defined window is treated differently from a cancellation made after the window. These distinctions can feel pedantic when you are annoyed. Yet pedantry is how systems decide. The policy is a decision tree. The customer who wants a refund must place their case on the right branch. The concept is *categorisation*. The implication is that describing your issue in the wrong category can turn a valid claim into a rejected one.

A delivery example makes this concrete. A parcel arrives damaged. The customer's instinct might be to write, "This is unacceptable, I want my money back." That statement expresses feeling, not category. A more effective approach begins by naming the category: "The item arrived damaged; the packaging was torn and the product is unusable." Those details are not melodrama; they are evidence of fault. Evidence matters because it reduces the organisation's risk of refunding opportunistically. You are not asking them to trust your indignation. You are offering verifiable conditions that fit the policy's definition of a problem. Trust becomes visible here as behaviour: photographs, timestamps, delivery notes, the order number, the specific defect. The implication is that policies are easier to negotiate when you speak their language of proof.

Events and tickets reveal another standard policy shape: the non-refundable clause. People see "no refunds" and assume the conversation is over. Yet many event policies include exceptions—rescheduled dates, cancellations, significant changes to the line-up, venue alterations, or legal requirements around cancellation. Even when refunds are not offered, credits or transfers may be permitted. The trick is that these allowances are often in separate sections: "force majeure", "rescheduling", "changes", "customer support". A person who skims only the headline sees a wall. A person who reads two more paragraphs may find a gate: a credit note, a transfer option, a partial refund under specific conditions. The concept is *policy topology*: where in the document the permission is located. The implication is that negotiating often begins by finding the right paragraph, not by finding the right emotion.

This is also where organisational design meets human habit. Policies are often written long not because companies enjoy verbosity but because they want coverage: every exception described, every risk hedged. Customers skim because they are tired, busy, and not paid to read contracts. The result is a predictable asymmetry: the organisation knows its own terms; the customer does not. The asymmetry can be softened in two minutes by reading with a particular focus. Not everything matters. What matters are the thresholds and triggers. When does a fee apply? When can a cancellation occur? What counts as "faulty"? What counts as "used"? What evidence is required? What is the deadline? Where is discretion mentioned? These elements are not a list of chores; they are the handles you need to move the conversation away from "I feel wronged" and towards "I meet the criteria for X, and I'm requesting Y."

A second named, checkable reference helps anchor why policies in the UK have become more legible over time. The Consumer Contracts (Information, Cancellation and Additional Charges) Regulations 2013, which came into force on 13 June 2014, strengthened obligations around pre-contract information and introduced cancellation rights for many distance and off-premises contracts. Again, one need not be a lawyer to grasp the practical point: many policies include mandatory elements because regulation requires them. That means certain terms—cooling-off periods, information requirements, cancellation processes—are not merely company preferences. They are compliance artefacts. The implication is that when a policy seems oddly specific about deadlines and procedures, it is often because those details are meant to be enforceable and auditable. You can use that specificity to your advantage by aligning your request with it.

A credible counter-example is necessary, because reading policies does not guarantee flexibility. Some policies are genuinely rigid for good reason: perishable goods, bespoke items, last-minute cancellations that destroy resale value. Some companies enforce strict terms to prevent abuse, and they may prefer occasional customer anger to systemic exploitation. In such cases, you may read and find very little elasticity. The reconciliation is that reading still helps. It can tell you early that your request is unlikely to succeed, saving time and emotional energy. It can also reveal what *is* possible—credit instead of refund, transfer instead of cancellation, partial remedy instead of full reversal. Knowledge prevents futile escalation.

"Goodwill" is the most misunderstood word in this territory. Customers hear "goodwill gesture" and assume it is either a bribe or a condescension. Organisations use the phrase as a bookkeeping category: a discretionary concession that does not admit legal liability. The distinction matters. A company may be willing to offer goodwill precisely because it allows them to be generous without setting a precedent or admitting fault. If you demand a refund as a matter of right, you may force the organisation into a defensive stance. If you request a review and leave space for goodwill, you may receive relief more quickly. This is not about abandoning your rights. It is about choosing the pathway that produces a workable outcome. The concept is *face-saving mechanisms.* The implication is that sometimes the fastest route to relief is allowing the other side to help you without confessing wrongdoing.

The practical effect of understanding policies is a change in how you speak. You stop saying, "You can't do this," and start saying, "I believe this falls under your policy on X," or "I'm within the window specified," or "The service wasn't delivered as described; could you review the options available?" These phrases are not magic; they are categorisation cues. They signal that you have read, that you are not improvising, and that you are asking for a decision rather than a debate. They also keep the conversation human, because they remove the need to accuse. Accusation is usually a symptom of ignorance—when you do not know what the policy says, you try to force a result through outrage. When you know what it says, you can ask with calm precision.

The motif to carry is the seam. Policies present themselves as solid fabric—firm, unyielding, written in small print to discourage touch. Yet most contain seams where fabric is joined: deadlines, definitions, discretion clauses, exceptions. The seam is where negotiation happens, because seams are where systems acknowledge complexity. Your task is not to tear the fabric. It is to find the seam and pull gently, with evidence in hand.

The forward test is therefore deceptively simple. When the next fee or refusal appears, will you skim the headline and accept the wall—or will you take three minutes to read until you find the seam, then decide whether your case fits the policy's own category for flexibility, discretion, or remedy?

Getting Late Fees Waived

On 13 June 2014, the UK's Consumer Contracts (Information, Cancellation and Additional Charges) Regulations 2013 came fully into force, tightening expectations around what businesses must disclose and how contracts should treat consumers in distance sales. It is not a "late fee" statute, yet it marks a broader shift in modern consumer life: a growing insistence that charges should be transparent and processes defensible. Late fees, by contrast, often arrive like stealth weather. A statement lands in an inbox in Newcastle, the small line item sits beneath the larger numbers, and the word *fee* feels like a judgement rather than an administrative consequence. The amount may be modest. The sensation is not.

Fees sting. Even small ones.

A late fee is a particular kind of irritation because it implies failure. It hints—sometimes accurately, sometimes not—that you were careless, disorganised, or unreliable. Many people, even highly competent ones, feel an immediate urge to defend themselves: to explain at length, to justify, to plead. Others feel the opposite urge: to accuse the company of pettiness or predation. Both responses are understandable. Both are usually unproductive. Waivers are not typically granted to the person who performs the strongest emotion. They are granted to the person who makes a clear, low-risk case that an exception is reasonable.

To understand how to ask for a waiver without sounding defensive, it helps to understand what a late fee does inside an organisation. A fee serves three functions. It disciplines behaviour by creating a cost for delay. It compensates for administrative effort and, in some contexts, for financing costs. It also signals to staff and systems that a rule has been applied consistently. Consistency matters because inconsistency creates disputes. The company's fear is not your individual story; it is precedent. If they waive fees too freely, people learn to pay late and ask for forgiveness. The concept here is *precedent anxiety*. The implication is that a waiver request must reassure the organisation that this is an exception, not a new habit.

The most effective waiver requests therefore begin with acknowledgement. Not apology-as-theatre, not self-abasement, but simple recognition that a fee has been applied and you understand why it exists. Acknowledgement is a strange power move because it removes the company's need to defend itself. Once you acknowledge the logic of the fee, you become someone who is speaking within the rules rather than attacking the rules. The concept is *alignment*. The implication is that when you remove defensiveness on both sides, discretion becomes easier to use.

After acknowledgement comes brief explanation. Brief is crucial. People over-explain because they think volume of detail proves sincerity. In systems, volume often reads as complication. Complication raises the risk of granting a waiver, because it suggests there may be more to the story. A brief explanation gives context without inviting a debate. It might be a genuine mistake—misread date, bank transfer delay, travel disruption, a card replaced, a direct debit not set up properly. It might be a cash-flow crunch—payday timing, unexpected expense, temporary squeeze. The point is not to dramatise. The point is to provide a plausible reason that fits the category of "one-off". The concept is *plausibility*. The implication is that you are helping the staff member place your request into a familiar, approvable pattern.

Then comes the invitation to review. This is where language does the real work. You are not demanding the fee be removed as if it were an injustice. You are requesting a discretionary waiver, often framed explicitly as a one-off or occasional concession. "Could you review whether this can be waived as a one-time courtesy?" is a very different statement from "You need to remove this fee." The first invites a check; the second invites a fight. The concept is *request framing*. The implication is that the same outcome—fee removal—can become more reachable when framed as an exception rather than as a correction of wrongdoing.

A sample phone opening can show the structure cleanly. "Hello—thanks for taking my call. I can see a late fee on my account for this month. I understand it was applied because payment came in after the due date. This is unusual for me; I've paid on time historically. Could you check whether it can be waived as a one-off goodwill gesture?" There is no grovelling. There is no accusation. There is acknowledgement, brief context, and a clear request. It also includes a visible metric—payment history—because "I usually pay on time" can often be verified on their screen. The concept is *verifiability*. The implication is that when the staff member can see the evidence of reliability, they can justify the waiver without trusting your character.

The same structure adapts to a tight cash-flow month without turning into a confessional. Money strain often carries shame, and shame pushes people into defensive over-explanation. Yet many organisations have policies for hardship or temporary difficulty precisely because they want to reduce default and maintain customer relationships. You do not need to narrate your life. You need to name the situation as temporary and show intent to resolve. "I can see the late fee on my statement. This month was unusually tight for me, and the payment landed after the due date. I've now paid, and I'm aiming to keep things regular going forward. Could you review whether the fee can be waived this once?" Again: acknowledgement, brief explanation, invitation to review. The tone is steady. The company hears: payment is complete, the delay is exceptional, the customer is not trying to game the system. The concept is *risk reduction*. The implication is that when the company's risk feels low, discretion is easier to grant.

A second checkable example anchors the broader context of late fees as behavioural design. In March 2019, the UK Financial Conduct Authority published its final report on the credit card market (following its earlier work in this area), focusing in part on persistent debt and how firms communicate with customers. While not a "late fee manual", the FCA's attention to customer communications reflects a recurring regulatory interest: financial charges and customer outcomes are shaped not only by numbers but by processes and prompts. Late fees sit in that world. They are part of how systems steer behaviour. The implication is that a waiver request is not a plea to suspend reality; it is a request to apply an exception mechanism that exists precisely because communication and timing are imperfect.

It is also important to understand why some waiver requests fail even when the customer is polite. Some accounts have repeated late payments, making the request less credible as "one-off". Some fees are contractually defined and hard-coded, with limited discretion. Some staff roles have no authority to waive fees. Some companies require specific triggers—first late fee within a certain period, a particular payment method, a certain account status. These are not moral rejections; they are system constraints. The reconciliation is to treat a refusal as information. If the first person cannot waive, you can ask, calmly, whether anyone can, or whether there is any other remedy available—credit, adjustment, payment plan, change of due date. "Is there any flexibility on this, or is it fixed by policy?" is not aggressive. It is a clarifying question that helps you locate the edge of discretion.

This is where escalation, used lightly, can matter. A waiver may require a supervisor's approval, or it may require the account to be handled by a different team. A skilled approach does not leap to escalation as punishment. It treats it as routing. "If you don't have the authority to waive it, could you connect me with someone who can review exceptions?" That sentence preserves the relationship with the frontline agent and keeps the request procedural. The concept is *role sensitivity*. The implication is that you can pursue the same goal while leaving the agent's dignity intact, which often improves cooperation.

There is another, quieter factor: timing. Late fees are easier to waive when the payment has already been made, because the request is about removing a penalty, not about excusing continued delay. If the payment is still outstanding, the company may treat a waiver request as riskier, because it could be seen as rewarding non-payment. This is not a moral judgement; it is how incentives are managed. The visible behaviour here is paying first when possible, then requesting a review. The concept is *sequence*. The implication is that the order in which you act can change the likelihood of a waiver.

The language of "goodwill" deserves a brief, unromantic note. Many companies use "goodwill gesture" as a category that allows them to help without admitting they were wrong. That is useful. It means you can accept a waiver without forcing the company into a defensive legal posture. If you frame your request as "you are wrong and must correct this", you may trigger the company's need to prove it is right. If you frame it as "can you waive this as a one-off", you allow the company to help while remaining consistent with its own policy story. The concept is *face-saving*. The implication is that face-saving language often unlocks relief faster than righteous language.

A credible counter-example keeps the ethics clear. Some customers try to treat waivers as a routine discount: pay late, request waiver, repeat. Systems learn. Companies tighten discretion. The result is worse for everyone, including those who genuinely make a rare mistake. This is why the most effective waiver request is restrained. It does not try to normalise exceptions. It acknowledges that the rule exists and asks for mercy precisely because mercy is meant to be rare.

The implication is that your tone should signal respect for the system's need for consistency, even as you ask for an exception.

The motif from earlier chapters—the seam—reappears in a new form. Late fees look like hard edges, but most systems contain seams: grace periods, one-time waivers, discretionary credits, date adjustments. The seam is where you place your request. You do not tug wildly. You tug gently, with evidence.

The forward test is small and exacting. When a late fee appears, will you respond with defence or accusation—trying to argue your virtue—or will you acknowledge the rule, state the exception cleanly, and invite a review that allows the other side to remove the fee without feeling they have rewritten the policy for everyone else?

Requesting Refunds with Grace

On 13 June 2014, the UK's Consumer Contracts (Information, Cancellation and Additional Charges) Regulations 2013 came into force, creating clearer cancellation rights for many distance and off-premises purchases and tightening what traders must disclose before a contract is made. The legislation sits in Westminster's realm of clauses and committees. Its practical theatre is far smaller: a customer in Manchester, thumb scrolling through an order confirmation at midnight, the faint hiss of rain on the window, realising that the item arriving tomorrow is wrong for the job, or that the "free trial" has quietly converted, or that the promised delivery date has slipped beyond usefulness. The urge is immediate and human: *I want my money back.*

Refunds are about categories.

That sentence sounds cold. It is also kind. Most refund conversations go wrong because the customer speaks from feeling while the system listens for classification. Feeling produces accusation—"this is outrageous"—or shame—"I'm sorry to bother you"—and neither maps cleanly onto policy. Classification does.

Faulty product. Poor service. Change of mind. Non-delivery. Misdescription. Each category comes with different expectations, different evidence, different degrees of discretion. The customer who names the right category early often receives a faster, calmer resolution. The customer who stays vague often ends up arguing with a wall.

Grace, here, does not mean softness. It means accuracy without hostility. It means describing what happened in a way that preserves everyone's dignity while still insisting that the outcome should change. Most people fear that politeness weakens a refund request. In practice, politeness often strengthens it, because it keeps staff in problem-solving mode and makes it easier for them to use discretion without feeling coerced. When a conversation turns accusatory, the organisation tends to become procedural. Procedure is where the word "no" lives.

Begin with the simplest differentiation: fault versus regret. If a product is faulty—broken, defective, unusable in normal conditions—that is one branch of the policy tree. If you simply changed your mind—wrong size, wrong colour, no longer needed—that is a different branch. Conflating them is tempting because both end with the same desire: not to pay. Yet conflating them creates friction because it forces the other side to test your honesty. "Faulty" implies the seller has failed; "changed my mind" implies you have altered your preference. The concept here is *moral temperature*: how blame-laden your category is. The implication is that if you mislabel regret as fault, you may provoke resistance and scrutiny that you could have avoided by describing the situation accurately.

The same is true of service. Poor service can mean late delivery, incorrect delivery, damaged packaging, misleading information, or inadequate performance of a contracted task. Poor service is not the same as "I didn't enjoy it". Systems are built to remedy concrete failures: a missed delivery date, a cancelled booking, a service not provided as described. They are less built to remedy dissatisfaction that cannot be measured. This is where a factual description becomes the hinge. "The delivery date was stated as Tuesday; it arrived Friday" is measurable. "This was a disappointment" is not. The concept is *evidence readiness*. The implication is that your request becomes stronger when you attach it to checkable facts rather than to mood.

An online purchase example grounds this. Imagine a customer orders noise-cancelling headphones. The product arrives. The box is intact. The headphones power on. Yet the left ear cup emits a crackling sound at certain volumes. The customer could write an angry email: "You sold me junk." Or they could write a polite, factual message: "Order number X arrived on [date]. The headphones power on, but the left ear cup produces a crackling noise at moderate volume. I've tested with two devices and the issue persists. Please advise how you'd like to handle a refund or replacement." The second message contains no insult, yet it is firmer because it is precise. It presents a verifiable problem and invites a remedy. The concept is *remedy invitation*: asking what can be done rather than insisting on a specific outcome before the facts are processed. The implication is that you make it easier for the seller to resolve the issue quickly because you have already done some of the diagnostic work.

Notice what is absent: theatrical outrage. Outrage can feel energising, but it often makes the recipient defensive, especially if they are a frontline employee who did not "sell" you anything and cannot undo all harms. Outrage also makes it tempting to exaggerate. Exaggeration is poison in refund conversations because it shifts the dispute from "what happened?" to "is this person trustworthy?" Trust is not an abstraction here. It is a decision made by someone who will be judged internally for approving refunds too easily. Your job is to reduce their perceived risk.

Risk appears in visible behaviours: you provide the order number, the date, the condition, and, when appropriate, photographs or screenshots. You describe the failure in plain terms. You avoid imputing motive. You signal willingness to return the item if required. These behaviours make you legible as a reasonable customer rather than as a potential fraudster or a habitual complainer. The concept is *credible claimant behaviour*. The implication is that credibility is performed through detail and tone, not through assertions of virtue.

When the issue is poor service rather than a faulty product, the language must shift accordingly. Suppose you paid for next-day delivery and the item arrives a week later, missing the occasion you needed it for. The grievance is not that the product is broken; it is that the service promise was not met. If you call it a "fault", you muddle categories. Better is to name the promise and the breach: "I paid for next-day delivery on [date]. The item arrived on [date]. That delivery delay meant the product was no longer useful for my purpose. What options are available for a refund of the delivery charge, and for returning the item if needed?" This ties the request to a specific metric: a date and a purchased service level. The concept is *promise tracking*. The implication is that policies often have clearer remedies for missed promises than for general dissatisfaction, but only if you name the promise correctly.

Change of mind is the most socially awkward category, because it feels like you are admitting you made a mistake. Many people therefore try to disguise it as something else. This is a false economy. When a company allows returns for change of mind—often within a time window and with conditions—the process is frequently smooth if you simply state the facts. "The item arrived, but it's not the right size. It's unused and in original packaging. I'd like to return it; please confirm the return process." There is no shame in this. It is a normal commercial event. Where it becomes complicated is when the window has passed or the item has been used. Then discretion may be needed, and discretion responds better to honesty than to creative storytelling. The concept is *honest framing*. The implication is that honesty can invite flexibility, whereas an implausible fault claim can shut it down entirely.

A second named, checkable anchor helps place this in the UK's broader consumer landscape. The Consumer Rights Act 2015, which received Royal Assent on 26 March 2015, strengthened and clarified rights around goods that are not as described, not of satisfactory quality, or not fit for purpose, and also covered services to be performed with reasonable care and skill. Again, this is not legal advice; it is context. The key point is that modern consumer rules formalise the categories that everyday refund conversations already rely on. "As described", "fit for purpose", "reasonable care" are essentially classification tools. They help transform "I'm upset" into "this falls under a recognised standard." The implication is that you are not being pedantic when you choose your words carefully; you are aligning your request with the way decisions are structured.

There is also a credible limitation that must be acknowledged. Some sectors are designed to be non-refundable because the product is time-bound or easily abused: event tickets, travel bookings, digital downloads, bespoke goods. Even within these sectors, however, there is often more nuance than "no refunds" suggests. Rescheduling, credit notes, partial refunds, transfers, or exceptions for significant changes can exist. The reconciliation is to treat a refusal as a prompt to refine the category. If the ticket is non-refundable by default, but the event is rescheduled, the category changes. If a flight is cancelled, the category changes. If a service was not provided, the category changes. Even when the money cannot be recovered, other forms of remedy may be possible. The implication is that a "no" is often a boundary within a category, not the end of categorisation itself.

Grace also matters because many refund conversations involve a person who did not design the policy. The frontline agent is the messenger. Treating them as the villain creates needless conflict. Conflict is a poor tool for changing policy outcomes. A respectful tone keeps the agent willing to search, to check exceptions, to escalate. The phrase "What can you do?" is powerful precisely because it assumes the other person has agency without demanding a specific concession. It invites them to become an ally within their constraints. The concept is *collaborative posture.* The implication is that collaboration often surfaces options that a hostile approach would never reveal.

The most useful script structure, therefore, is almost austere. You state the order or booking reference. You describe the facts in one or two sentences. You name the category—fault, service failure, change of mind—without melodrama. You ask what options are available, and you signal readiness to follow the process. The "process" is not a humiliation; it is the system's way of protecting itself. When you cooperate with process, you reduce the chance the system will punish you with delay.

A brief contrast makes this vivid. Accusatory version: "You people are scammers; I want a refund now." Graceful version: "I'm contacting you about order X. The item arrived on [date] and it's damaged; the screen is cracked on arrival. I can provide photographs. Please confirm whether you'd like to arrange a return for a refund or replacement." The graceful version is not softer; it is sharper. It gives the company what it needs to approve a remedy. It also gives you something to stand on if escalation becomes necessary: a clear written record that you described the problem promptly and factually.

The motif to carry through is the ledger. Refunds are, in the end, edits to the ledger. A company must justify those edits internally. You help them justify the edit by making your case legible: facts, category, evidence, calm tone. You do not need to convince them you are a good person. You need to make it easy for them to say yes without fear.

The forward test is therefore a choice about your own posture under mild provocation. When something goes wrong—an item fails, a service disappoints, a purchase proves mistaken—will you reach for accusation or for classification? Will you write from wounded pride, or from factual clarity that invites remedy? The money matters, but so does the manner: the question is whether you can ask for reversal with enough grace that the other side can agree without feeling attacked, and enough precision that the answer can be "yes" on the first pass.

Escalating Without Burning Bridges

In July 2015, the UK Government opened Alternative Dispute Resolution (ADR) requirements more broadly across consumer disputes, reinforcing a simple public idea: disagreements should have ladders, not cliffs. The policy sits in the realm of regulators and ombuds schemes, but its everyday echo is a smaller choreography: a call in Leeds that ends with "there's nothing we can do", a chat window that closes, an email reply that cites "policy" like a sacred text. The customer feels heat rise in the chest. The agent sounds bored or exhausted. A decision must be made in a few seconds: escalate, or surrender.

Escalation is a craft.

Most people treat escalation as either aggression or defeat. Aggression looks like threats, accusations, public shaming. Defeat looks like compliance: paying the fee, accepting the loss, moving on resentfully. Both miss a third option: escalation as disciplined routing. Routing is the unglamorous heart of micro-negotiation. When the first answer is no, you are often not meeting malice; you are meeting limits—limits of authority, limits of policy, limits of the person's time, limits of what can be approved without scrutiny. Escalation is the method of moving the problem to the place where those limits are different, without turning the interaction into a moral trial.

The show-and-name begins with a familiar scene. A customer asks for a late fee waiver or a refund. The frontline agent says no, citing policy. The customer feels a choice: argue or comply. Arguing often fails because the agent's job is to repeat policy boundaries, and because the agent may not have permission to deviate. Compliance feels safe but expensive, and it trains the customer to accept "policy" as a wall. The alternative is a calm escalation phrase that acknowledges the agent while signalling you need a higher review: "Thanks for explaining. Could you tell me who can review exceptions, or transfer me to a supervisor?" The concept is *authority escalation*. The implication is that you can seek a different decision-maker without insulting the first one.

A key distinction is between challenging a person and challenging a decision. People burn bridges when they make escalation personal: "You're useless" or "You're refusing to help me". Those lines provoke defensiveness and procedural hardening. Challenging a decision keeps the focus on process: "I understand that's the current policy position. I'd like this reviewed." The difference sounds subtle. It is enormous. The concept is *depersonalisation*. The implication is that you preserve cooperation by treating the agent as an intermediary rather than as an adversary.

This is where gratitude becomes a strategic virtue, not a performance. Many customers fear that thanking an agent will weaken their stance. In reality, it often strengthens it, because it prevents the agent from feeling attacked while you insist on review. "Thank you for checking. I appreciate what you can do. I still need this escalated." That sentence holds two truths at once: the agent may be constrained, and your request remains. It signals maturity. It also signals that you are likely to be reasonable with a supervisor, which makes an agent more willing to transfer you rather than stonewall. The concept is *relationship preservation*. The implication is that politeness can increase the probability of being routed upward.

A second named, checkable example anchors the institutional logic. In October 2015, the Financial Ombudsman Service became the recognised resolver for certain disputes under defined conditions, reflecting a wider UK tradition: structured escalation exists because markets and contracts produce predictable conflict. One does not need to invoke ombuds schemes in everyday interactions. The point is simpler: formal systems expect escalation steps. Companies have complaint procedures, supervisor tiers, written channels, and sometimes external routes. Escalation is not a tantrum; it is a normal part of the machine, and treating it as normal changes your tone. The implication is that when you escalate calmly, you align yourself with the organisation's own process rather than fighting it.

The most effective escalation begins with a diagnostic question: is the "no" a policy boundary or an authority boundary? Policy boundary means the rule itself is strict. Authority boundary means the rule may have exceptions, but the person you are speaking to cannot approve them. The difference often reveals itself in language. Authority-bound "no" sounds like, "I'm not able to do that" or "I don't have access to those options." Policy-bound "no" sounds like, "We don't do refunds after X days" or "Fees apply in all cases." Even then, the categories blur. Still, the diagnostic helps. If it is authority-bound, a supervisor review may unlock movement. If it is policy-bound, escalation may require a different argument: proof you fit an exception, or a request for goodwill, or acceptance that the remedy will be something other than a full reversal.

Written channels are often underrated as escalation tools because they feel slower. They can be slower. They are also clearer. A written summary creates a record, and records change how organisations behave. Call centre conversations can be messy; written complaints are often routed to teams trained to handle complexity and to document outcomes. Written channels also allow you to present facts cleanly: dates, order numbers, screenshots, policy excerpts. This is not about threatening. It is about reducing ambiguity. Ambiguity is where "no" thrives. The concept is *record creation*. The implication is that writing can convert a dismissive "no" into a reviewed decision because it forces the organisation to respond to specifics.

The simplest written escalation is not long. Long messages often read as venting and trigger defensive templates. A short, structured note tends to perform better: reference, timeline, issue, request. The rhythm matters because it signals that you are organised. Organisation reduces perceived risk. Risk, here, is the fear that granting you a concession will lead to more work: follow-up emails, disputes, chargebacks, complaints to regulators. When you communicate clearly, you signal that you will accept a reasonable resolution and close the case. The implication is that clarity is not only persuasive; it is economical for the organisation.

Another escalation tool is the pause-and-return. Many people think escalation must happen immediately, in the same call, in the same emotional temperature. That is often a mistake. People say things they regret when they feel cornered, and regretful words are bridge-burners. A pause is not surrender. It is a choice to return with better evidence, better timing, and a calmer voice. "Thanks for clarifying. I'd like to review the policy wording and come back—what's the best channel for follow-up?" That line does two things: it ends the current dead-end without hostility, and it prepares a second attempt with better footing. The concept is *strategic delay*. The implication is that you can protect the relationship and improve your odds by refusing to fight in the worst moment.

There is also the question of escalation etiquette: how to ask for a supervisor without implying the agent is incompetent. Many customers say, "Can I speak to someone who knows what they're doing?" and then wonder why the agent becomes icy. A more intelligent phrasing is procedural: "Could you transfer me to a supervisor or the team that handles exceptions?" The phrase "handles exceptions" is important because it frames the escalation as functional, not insulting. It acknowledges the possibility that the agent simply lacks authority. The implication is that respectful escalation language helps the agent remain cooperative, which is often the difference between a smooth transfer and a prolonged standoff.

A credible counter-example is necessary. Sometimes escalation is genuinely pointless because the policy is fixed and the organisation is consistent. In those cases, escalation can waste time and raise stress without changing the outcome. The reconciliation is to treat escalation as a measured step, not as a reflex. If you have read the policy and can see no seam, or if the agent has already checked and the boundaries are clearly fixed, then the best escalation may be external—switching provider, leaving a review, or using a formal complaints process where appropriate. The key is to avoid escalating simply to discharge emotion. Emotion is real, but escalation is a tool. Tools should be used when they can do work.

What does "firm yet respectful" look like in practice? It looks like refusing to accept a first no as final when you have reason to believe flexibility exists, without turning that refusal into an attack. It looks like repeating your request in slightly different terms: factual, brief, anchored. It looks like asking, "Could you point me to the relevant policy clause?" because that question forces specificity and sometimes reveals that the policy is not as absolute as it sounded. It looks like stating your preference—refund, waiver, adjustment—while remaining open to alternative remedies that still resolve the problem. And it looks like keeping your voice steady, because a steady voice is harder to dismiss as unreasonable.

The motif here is the ladder. Escalation is not a battering ram; it is climbing. You move up one rung: supervisor, specialist team, written complaint, formal review. Each rung should have a purpose. Each rung should be taken without kicking the rung beneath you. The agent you speak to first may become the person who notes your account, who passes along your summary, who chooses whether to help you frame the issue for the next tier. If you humiliate them, you remove that help. If you respect them, you often keep it.

The forward test is a diagnostic question you can hold in the moment you feel the heat rise: is this "no" the end of the road, or simply the end of this person's authority—and can you ask for the next rung with enough composure that the bridge behind you remains intact even as you insist on moving forward?

Chapter 6
Travel, Hotels and Flights

On 15 April 2010, ash from Iceland's Eyjafjallajökull volcano drifted into European airspace, and airports across the continent became impromptu waiting rooms for stranded plans. In Heathrow's terminals, and in hotel lobbies from Glasgow to Barcelona, people learned a strange lesson: the travel industry is not a smooth conveyor belt but a living system, prone to bottlenecks, improvisations, and small acts of discretion. Suitcases thudded, tannoy announcements crackled, queues grew, and the most decisive travellers were not always the loudest. They were the ones who could ask a clear question at the right moment and accept an imperfect answer without turning it into theatre.

Travel is negotiation under time pressure.

That is why it feels different from negotiating bills at home. At home, you can spread papers on a table, gather evidence, choose your hour. Travel compresses everything into short encounters with strangers who are managing dozens of competing needs at once. You are tired, often hungry, sometimes anxious. The staff member is fielding delays, overbookings, complaints, and policy. Small requests can feel either trivial or impossible. Yet travel is full of natural negotiation windows precisely because it is so operational. Rooms can be reassigned. Seats can be swapped. Fees can be waived. Vouchers can appear. Late check-outs can be granted. Most of these outcomes are not guaranteed, and that is the point: when the system is fluid, timing and tone matter more than they do in stable contexts.

The first skill in travel negotiation is noticing the window. Windows appear at check-in, when allocations are still flexible; during delays, when the system must re-route people; when overbooking forces the airline or hotel to find volunteers or alternatives; and when small problems arise—noise, a broken key card, a seat that does not recline, a missed connection—that can be resolved cheaply if addressed early. Many travellers miss these windows because they either stay silent, hoping the problem will fade, or they erupt only when the issue has hardened into a formal complaint. The difference between a quiet fix and a prolonged dispute is often a five-minute timing gap.

"Reasonable" becomes the second skill, because entitlement is the quickest way to poison a travel conversation. Hotels and airlines operate under constraints: inventory, safety rules, crew hours, weather, maintenance, and the simple mathematics of too many people wanting the same thing. A request that is specific, proportionate, and easy to grant is more likely to succeed than a vague demand for "something to make up for it". This chapter teaches the difference between preferences and problems. A preference is wanting a higher floor. A problem is a room next to a construction site at 6 a.m. A preference is wanting to board early. A problem is a missed connection caused by a delay. Preferences can sometimes be accommodated; problems often require remedy. Mixing them up confuses the interaction and makes you sound either demanding or incoherent.

There is a surprisingly philosophical thread beneath all this. Travel makes visible the difference between what is promised and what is possible. You buy a ticket, a room, a schedule—a tidy future. Then reality intrudes. When reality intrudes, the question becomes: how do you reclaim agency without pretending you control the weather, the runway, or the hotel's occupancy? The answer is not to fight the system. The answer is to learn its levers. Some levers are procedural: knowing what the company is currently offering, asking what options exist, and choosing one without delay. Some levers are social: the calm, curious tone that keeps staff willing to help. Some levers are structural: understanding that different roles have different powers, and that telling your whole story to the wrong person is often wasted effort.

Upgrades and perks sit at the glamorous edge of this chapter, but the focus is not glamour. It is practicality: the quieter room, the later check-out, the seat change, the fee waived, the small concession that turns a rough journey into a tolerable one. The key is specificity. "Can you do anything for me?" is a question that forces the other person to invent your needs under pressure. "Is there a room away from the lift?" is a question that is easy to answer. "If there's any flexibility, could I have a late check-out tomorrow?" is a clear, bounded request. This is micro-negotiation at its cleanest: small, situational, polite, and anchored in what is actually possible.

Disruptions—delays, cancellations, lost luggage—are where many people either freeze or vent. Freezing leaves you last in line for solutions. Venting may feel satisfying but rarely improves your options. A calmer path begins with clarity: what exactly has happened, what is the company currently offering, and where is there flexibility? This is not a denial of frustration. It is a method for converting frustration into action. When you ask, "What are you offering passengers right now?" you prompt the staff member to state the menu. Once the menu is visible, you can choose, adjust, or ask for a reasonable variation. The emotional energy goes into decision rather than accusation.

Then there is the human complexity of travel staff. Call-centre agents, gate staff, and front-desk teams operate within different systems, and they are authorised to do different things. A gate agent may be able to move you to another flight but not issue certain reimbursements. A front-desk clerk may be able to change your room but not adjust the rate. A call-centre agent may be able to rebook you but not provide a physical voucher. Understanding this prevents a common waste: giving a long, heartfelt explanation to someone who cannot fix the core issue. A short, targeted question—"Are you able to change rooms?" "Are you able to rebook me?" "Who handles compensation?"—is often the most respectful thing you can do, because it honours everyone's time.

Modern relevance is woven through this because travel has become both more accessible and more operationally stretched. More people fly. More people book online. More systems are automated, which means that when something goes wrong, the human channels become crowded. Automation has also changed expectations: people are used to instant confirmations and perfect itineraries, so disruption feels like betrayal rather than as the normal turbulence of moving bodies through infrastructure. The result is a culture of heightened complaint, where travellers oscillate between passivity and outrage. This chapter offers a third posture: attentive opportunism. Not predatory. Not entitled. Simply awake to the small moments when asking a clear question can shift your experience.

The motifs from earlier chapters return in travel's own vocabulary. The hinge is the check-in desk moment, when a room assignment is still soft. The gate is the queue during disruption, when options are being allocated. The seam is the policy wording about late check-outs, baggage fees, or rebooking rules. The pause is the breath you take before speaking to someone who is already dealing with ten angry people. The aim is not to become a travel "hacker" in the shallow sense. The aim is to be the person who can move through travel's friction with more dignity and less waste.

The payoff is not only financial, though travel is full of avoidable fees and compensations people never claim. The payoff is psychological: fewer silent resentments, fewer avoidable discomforts, fewer moments of helplessness. This chapter is a guide to small, humane interventions—your own—during a process that can otherwise make you feel like baggage rather than a person.

The question that carries you into the chapter is diagnostic and immediate. Next time you are at a hotel desk, a gate, or a call queue with a disruption unfolding, will you wait for the system to decide your experience for you—or will you notice the window, choose a specific request, and speak in a way that invites a quiet fix before the problem hardens into "policy"?

Spotting Moments to Ask

On 11 September 2001, the United States closed its airspace; the ripple reached Heathrow and Gatwick within hours, and the modern travel system revealed itself as a tightly coupled machine that can seize without warning. That day is an extreme example, but it points to a quieter truth that holds even on ordinary Tuesdays: travel is not a single promise, it is a chain of handovers. Tickets become queues, queues become allocations, allocations become rooms and seats and baggage tags. At each handover, decisions are made quickly, often by people with limited time and partial authority. If you understand when those decisions are still soft, you can ask for small changes that materially improve your trip.

Timing is the hidden passport.

Most travellers assume negotiation in travel is a matter of charm or status. Charm helps. Status helps. Yet the most reliable factor is structural: whether the thing you want is still adjustable at the point you ask. A room assignment is easiest to change before you have taken the key. A seat is easiest to change before boarding closes. A fee is easiest to waive before it is charged. A disruption is easiest to manage before options are exhausted. None of this is romantic. It is operational. To negotiate well in travel, you do not need to become pushy. You need to become attentive to the moment a decision is being made.

The first principle is to distinguish *windows* from *walls*. A window is a moment when the system still has slack—unassigned rooms, flexible seating, unallocated upgrades, open rebooking options. A wall is a moment when the system has hardened—no inventory, closed boarding, policy enforced by automation, time-stamped cut-offs. People often waste energy arguing at walls. They also miss windows because they do not recognise them as such. The concept here is *system softness*: the degree to which an allocation can be changed without cost. The implication is that the same request can be granted easily at one moment and denied firmly ten minutes later, not because anyone has become mean, but because the system has set.

Check-in is the clearest window, and it is often squandered. Hotel arrivals are full of small, quiet opportunities: a room on a higher floor, a room away from a lift, a room not facing the road, a room ready early, a late check-out noted in advance. None is guaranteed. What matters is that at check-in the hotel is actively allocating inventory and that allocation is a human act. Human acts contain discretion. By the time you have gone upstairs, dropped your bags, and discovered that your room faces the loading bay, the cost of switching is higher: keys must be reissued, housekeeping schedules adjusted, availability rechecked. The hotel may still help, but the request now competes with logistics. The concept is *allocation friction.* The implication is that asking early reduces the cost of saying yes.

A short scene shows how this works without turning into a performance. A guest arrives for one night, tired, with an early meeting the next day. They check in and say, calmly, "If there's any chance, could I have a room away from the lift? I'm a light sleeper." That is a preference, not a complaint. The request is specific and easy to test: the clerk can see room locations. If the answer is yes, the adjustment is invisible but valuable. If the answer is no, nothing is lost. The point is not entitlement; it is using the window.

Late check-out is a particularly good example because it forces you to think about reasonableness. A late check-out is not a right in most hotels; it is a negotiation with housekeeping schedules and occupancy. The guest who asks for a late check-out at the moment they are already late and scrambling is asking at a wall. The guest who asks at check-in is asking at a window. The most reasonable request is also a specific one: not "Can I check out late?" but "Could I check out at 1 p.m. instead of 11, if possible?" Specificity allows the staff member to compare your request to the day's constraints. The concept is *precision reduces ambiguity*. The implication is that an exact request makes the staff member's decision easier and makes you sound like someone who will accept a clear yes or no without drama.

Airports create different kinds of windows. Seat changes, for example, are easiest when there is still time to reassign and still open seats to assign. The natural window is when a boarding pass is first issued or reissued—at online check-in, at bag drop, at the gate before boarding begins. A traveller who notices the opportunity early might say, "If there's a window seat available, could you move me? I'm happy to take any row." That last sentence is important: flexibility is a form of value. It reduces the cost of accommodating you. The concept is *flexibility as currency*. The implication is that travel negotiation often rewards the person who is specific about what they want but flexible about how it is achieved.

Delays and disruptions create windows that are easy to misunderstand. Many people treat a delay as an injustice and respond with anger. Anger is understandable. It is also strategically clumsy. In a delay, the airline's system is actively re-routing passengers, allocating seats on alternative flights, issuing vouchers, and managing crew constraints. That means the system is soft in some areas and hard in others, and the softness changes minute by minute. The first useful act is to clarify what is happening: is the flight delayed, cancelled, or awaiting a decision? The second act is to ask what is currently being offered. That question is not submissive. It is information gathering. It reveals the menu at that moment. Once you know the menu, you can decide quickly. The concept is *option visibility*. The implication is that calm questions can turn a chaotic delay into a sequence of manageable choices.

Overbooking is an especially pure negotiation window because it creates an explicit problem for the airline: too many passengers for too few seats. In such moments, the system becomes unusually open to bargains because the airline must find volunteers or reassignments. A passenger's "yes" has a measurable value. This is one of the rare times when the traveller's flexibility can be traded for tangible benefits. Yet the same rule applies: timing and clarity matter. The passenger who asks early, before the gate descends into panic, is more likely to be heard than the one who speaks after tempers rise. The concept is *market creation*: overbooking creates a temporary market for solutions. The implication is that the best moment to ask is when the airline is still assembling options, not when it is announcing final calls.

Minor issues in rooms and seats are also windows, but they require a distinction that many people avoid making: preference versus genuine problem. A preference is a desire: a view, a higher floor, a window seat, a quieter corner. A genuine problem is something that materially degrades the service promised: a room that smells of smoke in a non-smoking hotel, a broken air-conditioning unit, a seat that is unusable, a safety issue, a mis-sold product. This distinction matters because it affects both your tone and your ask. Preferences are best approached as light requests with flexibility. Problems should be described factually and promptly, because they often trigger remedies. The concept is *severity calibration*. The implication is that you gain credibility when you reserve complaint language for actual failures, and that credibility makes your smaller preferences easier to grant later.

An online travel ecosystem complicates this because many interactions now happen through platforms rather than directly with airlines or hotels. The platform might have one set of policies; the provider might have another. Yet the operational windows still exist. A room can be changed by a hotel regardless of where it was booked, but the price adjustment might be controlled by the booking channel. A flight can be rebooked by an airline, but compensation might require a separate claim. The traveller who understands this does not pour their whole story into the first person they reach. They ask a routing question: "Are you able to change my room allocation?" "Are you able to rebook me?" "Who handles refunds for this booking?" Routing questions preserve time. They also preserve dignity, because they avoid forcing a staff member to say no repeatedly.

There is a counter-example that must be faced: some moments are not negotiable because the constraints are real. A full hotel cannot invent a quiet room if every room is occupied. An aircraft cannot conjure an empty row if the flight is full. A storm cannot be argued with. Recognising this is not resignation; it is skill. It prevents you from wasting energy at walls and encourages you to focus on what can move: a different time, a different arrangement, a credit, a partial remedy. The reconciliation is to treat denial as a map. A denial tells you where the system is hard. You then look for the nearby soft point.

The deepest reason to learn this is not to extract perks. It is to reduce helplessness. Travel makes adults feel strangely childlike: waiting, being told where to stand, being moved like pieces. When things go wrong, that childlike feeling can become anger or passivity. Spotting moments to ask restores agency in a humane way. It is a quiet refusal to be carried along by default, and it does not require bravado. It requires attention.

The motif to carry through this chapter is the window itself: a brief opening before the glass slides shut. The traveller who notices the window does not shout through it. They speak clearly, briefly, and early. They ask for one thing at a time. They accept no without sulking. They keep moving.

The forward test is immediate. On your next trip, when you approach a desk or a gate and feel the familiar impulse to endure quietly or complain loudly, will you pause long enough to ask a different question—*is this a window or a wall*—and then choose your request accordingly?

Upgrades, Perks and Quiet Fixes

In February 2013, Marriott International bought the boutique brand and management company Gaylord Hotels, a deal noted in industry press because it reflected a broader truth about modern hospitality: large hotel groups increasingly treat the guest journey as a series of controllable touchpoints, each one capable of being tuned—room type, late check-out, lounge access, upgrade eligibility, service recovery. That corporate fact becomes personal at a front desk in Edinburgh on a wet evening: the soft clack of a keyboard, the faint scent of lobby citrus, the glance at a screen that decides whether your room faces a courtyard or a road. The guest stands there with a small, ordinary power: the ability to ask.

The ask should be small.

Travel perks are often discussed as if they belong to a secret class system: status cards, elite tiers, insider hacks. That worldview flatters the initiated and discourages everyone else. The reality is more mundane and, for that reason, more useful. Many upgrades and small fixes are not reserved for an aristocracy. They are operational adjustments that staff can sometimes make when the request is easy, reasonable, and timed well. The skill is not charm. It is clarity plus empathy. Clarity tells the staff member what you want. Empathy tells them you understand their constraints. Together, they create the conditions for a "quiet yes".

A quiet fix is different from a dramatic concession. A quiet fix solves a problem before it becomes a complaint. It is the room moved away from the lift before you spend a sleepless night. It is the seat reassigned before boarding begins, not after you have wedged yourself in and begun to seethe. It is the luggage fee waived at check-in because the circumstances make the rule feel unnecessarily harsh, not after you have paid and sworn vengeance. Quiet fixes are invisible to other passengers. They do not require a manager's grand gesture. They are precisely the sort of small adjustments that systems can make without much cost, which is why they are often possible.

The first claim is simple: specific requests are easier to grant than vague hopes. "Is there any chance of an upgrade?" is a vague hope. It forces the staff member to interpret what "upgrade" means—bigger bed, better view, higher floor, club access—and to decide whether you are asking for something expensive. Vague hopes also sound like fishing, which makes staff cautious. Compare that to a specific request: "If you have a room away from the road, I'd be grateful." Or: "If there's any chance of a seat on the aisle, I'd prefer that." Or: "Could you waive the baggage fee this time? My bag is within the weight limit, and I'm connecting to a short domestic flight." These requests are concrete. Concrete requests can be checked quickly. The concept is *checkability*. The implication is that the more quickly a staff member can check whether your request is feasible, the more likely they are to try.

The second claim is that empathy is not decoration; it is a mechanism that increases discretionary effort. Staff in travel settings spend their days absorbing other people's stress. A guest who acknowledges that fact—briefly, without performing sympathy—reduces the emotional labour of the interaction. This matters because discretionary effort is often what produces upgrades and fixes. A staff member may need to click into another screen, check a different inventory bucket, speak to a colleague, or bend a minor rule within permitted discretion. They are more likely to do that for a guest who treats them as a person rather than as a vending machine for perks. The concept is *discretionary effort*. The implication is that empathy can convert a neutral interaction into one where the staff member is willing to look a little harder.

Empathy, however, must not become apology for existing. There is a common mistake among polite people: they speak so softly and so tentatively that the staff member cannot hear the request, only the anxiety. "Sorry, I don't want to be a bother, but I was wondering if maybe..." is not empathy. It is self-erasure. Self-erasure often produces a muddled ask, and muddled asks are easy to decline. The useful form of empathy is clean: "I know you're busy; could I ask a quick favour?" Then the favour is stated plainly. The concept is *clean courtesy*. The implication is that you can be warm without being vague.

A hotel example shows how upgrades and quiet fixes differ. Suppose you arrive and want a quieter room. If you say, "Can you give me something better?" you invite a status contest: what counts as better, and why do you deserve it? If you say, "If you have a room away from the lift or ice machine, I'd appreciate it; I'm a light sleeper," you are not claiming superiority. You are stating a practical need. The staff member can check the map. If the hotel is full, they may not help. If there is availability, they can. The concept is *need framing*. The implication is that requests framed around practical comfort rather than entitlement often feel easier for staff to grant.

Consider the same approach with late check-out. Asking for a "late check-out" is vague. Asking for a specific time signals restraint and gives staff a real constraint to work with. "Could I check out at 1 p.m. tomorrow, if possible?" is a bounded request. It also gives the hotel the option to negotiate: perhaps they can offer noon, or perhaps they can offer luggage storage and lounge access instead. You are not demanding a perfect outcome. You are inviting an adjustment. The concept is *bounded flexibility*. The implication is that you can improve your outcome even when you do not get exactly what you asked for.

Seat changes on flights work similarly, but the windows and constraints differ. Seat allocation is a live system with safety rules, weight distribution considerations, and operational constraints. Yet within those constraints, there is often room to adjust. The most effective seat-change requests are both specific and flexible: "If there's an aisle seat anywhere, I'm happy to move. I don't mind the back." That sentence signals that you are not insisting on a premium seat. You are seeking a functional improvement. It reduces the staff member's cost of helping. It also makes you easier to accommodate because you have widened the set of possible solutions. The concept is *solution space expansion*. The implication is that being flexible about location while being clear about the feature you need often produces the result.

Now take the waived luggage fee, a request that can easily drift into entitlement if mishandled. Fees exist for reasons: revenue, fairness, operational constraints, discouraging overpacking. Staff often have limited authority to waive them, and airlines guard fee policies carefully. That said, there are circumstances where a waiver is plausible: a minor discrepancy, a genuine confusion caused by a booking channel, a loyalty status, an equipment issue, a connection problem, or an operational disruption where goodwill is being offered. The point is not to "game" the system but to recognise when the system itself has created a problem or when the cost of strict enforcement exceeds the benefit. The concept is *goodwill economics*. The implication is that a calm, fact-based request can sometimes trigger an exception, especially when the airline wants to keep the interaction smooth.

This is where scripts matter—not as lines to recite, but as shapes that keep your request clear under stress. A useful shape is: greeting, constraint acknowledgement, specific ask, flexibility signal, thanks. "Hello—thanks for your help. I know baggage rules are strict. My bag is just over by a small amount; is there any flexibility today, or should I repack? I'm happy to step aside if needed. Thank you." This is not manipulative. It gives the staff member options: waive, suggest repacking, offer a different approach. It also signals that you will cooperate. Cooperation is the currency that makes discretionary help feel safe.

A second named, checkable example can anchor how systems sometimes offer structured perks during disruption. On 15 April 2010, after Eyjafjallajökull's eruption disrupted flights, airlines and hotels across Europe faced a mass reallocation problem. In such disruptions, "perks" often appear not as generosity but as operational necessity: vouchers, rebookings, hotel rooms, meal allowances. The lesson is not that chaos produces freebies. The lesson is that when systems are under strain, they rely on standard menus of remedies. If you can ask what the menu is, you can choose promptly. Prompt choice matters because inventories—hotel rooms, seats on alternative flights—get allocated fast. The concept is *remedy menu*. The implication is that your ability to ask clear questions early can convert disruption into a better set of options.

It is also important to address the credible limitation: sometimes the answer is no, and no amount of elegance changes that. A full hotel cannot move you to a quieter room if the only available rooms are near the lift. A full flight cannot create an aisle seat if every seat is assigned and boarding is closed. Some staff roles have no authority to waive fees, regardless of circumstance. The reconciliation is that the skill is not in forcing yes; it is in asking in a way that keeps no from becoming hostile. A well-handled no preserves your ability to ask a different question: "Is there any other option?" "Could you note this for next time?" "Is there a quieter floor?" "Could I be moved if something opens up?" The implication is that graceful asking keeps the conversation alive rather than collapsing into resentment.

The deeper ethical point matters because travel is a temptation for entitlement. People are tired, delayed, stressed, and far from home; they can begin to treat staff as obstacles rather than as humans. Entitlement also has a practical cost: it makes staff less willing to help. Staff can often sense when a customer is asking for a "perk" as a trophy rather than for comfort or fairness. Trophy-seeking creates adversarial dynamics. Comfort-seeking is easier to sympathise with. Fairness-seeking is easier to justify. The aim of a light, opportunistic style is not to become calculating. It is to remain human while being alert.

This is why "quiet fixes" are the core. A quiet fix is not a prize. It is a small, friction-reducing adjustment that preserves goodwill on both sides. It also aligns with the reality that staff have limited time. A guest who asks for one clear improvement and accepts the answer, rather than spinning a web of demands, stands out for the right reasons. That kind of guest becomes easier to help because they are not a risk. The concept is *low-friction requesting*. The implication is that asking for less—more precisely—often yields more.

The motif threading through this subchapter is the keycard. It is a small object that grants access, and it can be reissued, changed, corrected. It symbolises how much of travel is contingent on quiet administrative acts. Your goal is to prompt those acts at the right moment, with the right clarity, so that the trip you actually experience is closer to the trip you intended.

The forward test is an internal diagnostic you can carry to the next desk or gate. When you feel the impulse to ask for "something", can you translate that impulse into one specific, checkable request—quiet room, seat feature, time-bound check-out, fee review—and deliver it with enough warmth that the person on the other side can help without feeling they are rewarding entitlement?

Handling Delays and Disruptions

On 15 April 2010, Eyjafjallajökull's ash cloud pushed airlines and airports across Europe into a kind of choreographed failure: cancellations, rebookings, packed terminals, hotel shortages, and a public lesson in how quickly "normal" travel dissolves. In Manchester Airport that week, the soundscape was a constant loop of tannoy announcements and suitcase wheels, and the emotional atmosphere was a mixture of bafflement and anger—people staring at departure boards as if the pixels could be argued into a different future. What separated the travellers who found a workable path from those who simply endured was rarely status. It was sequence: the ability to ask the right question in the right order.

Chaos rewards the calm.

Delays and disruptions provoke two instinctive responses. One is freezing: waiting for information, waiting for a miracle, waiting for the queue to move, hoping someone else will solve it. The other is venting: turning frustration into accusations, demanding justice, trying to make the company feel the pain. Both responses are natural. Neither is a reliable route to resolution. A delay is not a moral debate; it is an operational problem. The traveller who treats it as an operational problem gains a form of agency that does not depend on the company's benevolence. They focus on next steps.

The first move is clarification, and it is deceptively powerful. "Delayed" can mean ten minutes. It can mean cancelled in all but name. It can mean waiting for a crew, waiting for a slot, waiting for weather to clear. The difference matters because each scenario triggers different options. A delay with a known departure time invites one set of decisions. An indefinite delay invites another. A cancellation triggers rebooking rules, vouchers, and sometimes accommodation. The concept here is *state diagnosis*: identifying what kind of failure you are actually experiencing. The implication is that you can make better decisions, and ask better questions, once you know whether you are in a delay, a cancellation, or a holding pattern.

Clarification also protects you from a common trap: investing emotionally in the original plan long after it has become unlikely. People cling to the first itinerary because it is theirs; letting it go feels like surrender. Yet in disruptions, the "original plan" often becomes a sunk cost. The departure board does not care that you booked months ago. A calm question can save hours of false hope: "Is this still expected to depart today?" Another: "Has a new crew been assigned?" These questions are not aggressive. They are diagnostic. The concept is *reality checking*. The implication is that you can pivot sooner, which often improves your options.

The second move is to ask what the company is currently offering. This shifts you from speculation to menu. Many travellers ask, "What are my rights?" or "What are you going to do about this?" Those questions can be reasonable, but they also invite defensiveness, especially if the staff member has limited authority.

"What are you offering passengers right now?" is different. It invites the staff member to state the set of available remedies without debating blame. It also reveals whether the company has already activated its disruption protocols: rebooking options, meal vouchers, hotel accommodation, refunds, baggage arrangements. The concept is *menu visibility*. The implication is that once you can see the menu, you can choose quickly rather than being swept along by the crowd.

Choice speed matters because disruptions produce scarcity. Seats on the next flight are limited. Hotel rooms near the airport are limited. Staff time is limited. The queue is not merely a line; it is a rationing mechanism. The traveller who waits too long to decide may lose options not because they were unreasonable, but because the inventory has been allocated. This is why calmness is not just a personality trait in disruptions; it is a practical advantage. Calmness keeps your cognitive resources available for decision-making. The concept is *cognitive bandwidth*. The implication is that emotional venting can cost you options.

The third move is to explore flexibility. Flexibility is not the same as demanding special treatment. It is asking whether the menu can be adjusted within reason. "If I'm rebooked, could you put me on the earlier connection rather than the later one?" "If there's a flight tomorrow morning, could you move me to that instead of the evening?" "If the next available flight is from another airport, is there any support for getting there?" These questions acknowledge the constraints while searching for a better fit. They are also easiest to answer when you are specific. Specificity reduces the staff member's labour. The concept is *bounded variation*. The implication is that a good flexibility question does not ask for miracles; it asks for a different configuration of existing options.

A weather delay illustrates why blame is a dead end. Weather is the purest external constraint. The airline cannot negotiate with cloud. The traveller who shouts about incompetence is arguing with physics. Yet even in weather disruptions, the operational choices remain: rebook, reroute, wait, refund. The calm traveller focuses on what can be moved. They clarify whether the delay is due to local weather at departure, weather at destination, or air traffic control restrictions. Those distinctions affect what happens next. They ask what the airline is offering. They decide whether to accept a rebooking, pursue an alternative route, or postpone travel. The concept is *constraint acceptance*. The implication is that accepting the constraint frees you to act within it.

Lost luggage is a different kind of disruption because it combines operational complexity with emotional vulnerability. Luggage is personal. It contains clothes, medication, gifts, sentimental items. When it goes missing, people feel exposed. That exposure often produces anger. Anger again is understandable. But lost luggage is a tracing problem, and tracing problems respond best to clear data: baggage tag number, flight details, description of the bag, contact information, destination address. The traveller who provides those data points quickly improves the likelihood of recovery, and also improves the quality of any interim support offered. Here, "risk" is visible in the airline's fear of fraudulent claims and in the practical difficulty of locating a bag in a vast system. The concept is *traceability*. The implication is that the more traceable you make your bag, the easier it is for the system to help you.

An online purchase analogy is useful because both contexts involve a system processing exceptions at scale. In a disruption, staff and systems look for patterns: "rebookable", "cancelled", "misconnected", "bag delayed", "bag lost". Each pattern triggers a protocol. The traveller's job is to place themselves in the right pattern quickly. This is not about gaming; it is about being legible. A legible case is easier to resolve. The concept is *case legibility*. The implication is that you can shorten your disruption by learning how the system classifies problems.

The best disruption conversations therefore have a particular shape. They begin with a calm statement of facts. They include one question at a time. They avoid long narratives, because long narratives are hard to process in a noisy airport or a crowded desk. They end with a clear next step: a rebooking confirmation, a voucher, a reference number, a written summary, a time to call back. Even when the outcome is imperfect, the traveller leaves with something concrete. Concrete beats vague hope. The concept is *closure objects*: reference numbers, confirmations, receipts. The implication is that you protect yourself by turning spoken promises into checkable artefacts.

There is also a social reality that many travellers dislike acknowledging: staff are more likely to help someone who is composed. This is not because staff are petty. It is because a composed customer is safer. Safety here means less risk of escalation, less risk of abuse, less risk of the interaction consuming time. In a disruption, time is scarce. The customer who is calm signals that the interaction will remain manageable. The concept is *interactional safety*. The implication is that composure can function as a quiet advantage without requiring charm or manipulation.

A credible counter-example must be admitted. Sometimes there is simply no flexibility. Weather can shut down an airport. Mechanical issues can ground a fleet. A strike can paralyse a route network. In those cases, your questions may yield little beyond confirmation of scarcity. The reconciliation is that clarity still helps. It helps you decide whether to stay in the queue, find accommodation, book an alternative route, or postpone. It reduces the time spent in limbo. It also reduces the likelihood that you will miss a rare opening—an extra flight, a newly available seat—because you were too busy arguing to notice. The implication is that even when you cannot improve the system's capacity, you can improve your own decisions.

The motif threading through this subchapter is the departure board. It looks authoritative. It is often provisional. Travellers treat it like scripture and are then betrayed when it changes. The skilled traveller treats it like a signal, not a promise. They update their plan as the signal updates. They ask questions that convert uncertain pixels into actionable choices.

The forward test is stark and practical. When your next journey breaks—delay, cancellation, missing bag—will you spend your limited energy litigating blame, or will you move through the calmer sequence: diagnose the state, ask for the current menu, probe for bounded flexibility, and leave each interaction holding something verifiable that moves you towards a workable next step?

Talking to Agents and Front Desks

On 14 September 1999, British Airways and American Airlines launched a new phase of their alliance cooperation, part of the wider consolidation that made modern air travel a web of shared codes, shared inventories, and shared responsibility that is never quite shared when something goes wrong. The traveller standing at Gate A12 in Heathrow hears one airline's name on the boarding pass and another on the screen, while a third appears on the email confirmation. The gate area smells faintly of coffee and disinfectant. A voice announces a delay. A queue forms. The person at the front of the queue begins telling their whole story to the first staff member they reach, as if the story itself will generate authority.

Authority does not work that way.

Travel negotiation is often mis-taught as persuasion: be charming, be firm, be persistent. Those traits matter, but they are secondary to a more structural skill—speaking to the right person in the right way. Different travel roles have different powers, different systems, and different risks. A call-centre agent may be able to rebook you but cannot hand you a meal voucher at the airport. A gate agent may be able to move you to a different flight but cannot change how a third-party booking site processes refunds. A hotel front desk can move rooms, extend check-out, and issue small service recovery gestures, yet might not be authorised to discount a prepaid rate set by a corporate contract. If you treat every staff member as interchangeable, you will waste time and, worse, you will generate friction by asking people to do what they cannot do.

This is why the first question is often not the request itself, but a *routing question.* "Are you able to rebook me?" "Are you able to change my seat?" "Are you the right team to handle compensation?" Routing questions are not bureaucratic fuss. They are respect in action. They prevent you from unloading a long narrative onto someone who will end up saying, "I can't do that." They also reduce your own fatigue: repeating your story is a tax. The concept here is *authority mapping.* The implication is that you can improve outcomes by locating the right locus of control before you spend your emotional energy.

Authority mapping begins with recognising that travel organisations are layered like a ship. The person you see is often not steering; they are managing a local section of the deck. A gate agent manages boarding and real-time passenger movement. They are in the business of speed and safety. A call-centre agent manages bookings and policy compliance. They are in the business of records and rules. A hotel front desk manages inventory and guest satisfaction. They are in the business of comfort and problem prevention. Each role has a different incentive structure, which shapes how they respond to you. When you align your request with their incentive structure, your odds improve without any need for theatrical persuasion.

Consider a simple example: a missed connection because of a delayed inbound flight. The traveller's instinct may be to rush to the gate and plead. Pleading can work, but it is clumsy because it assumes the gate agent has the right tools. Sometimes they do. Sometimes rebooking is handled elsewhere. A routing question cuts through: "Can you rebook missed connections at this gate, or should I go to customer service?" If the gate agent says customer service, you have saved five minutes of pleading in the wrong place. If they say yes, you have permission to proceed. The concept is *permission gating.* The implication is that asking for permission to pursue a remedy in a specific channel makes the interaction smoother and faster.

Brevity is the companion skill, and it is frequently misunderstood. People think brevity means being cold. It does not. Brevity means being legible. In travel settings, staff are processing multiple queues: physical queues and digital queues. They also work with constrained attention in noisy environments. A long story is hard to parse. It increases the chance that the staff member will latch onto the wrong detail and make a wrong decision—or simply tune out. The most helpful travel narratives are small: a timeline, a request, a constraint. When you compress your story into a few checkable facts, you reduce the staff member's cognitive load and make it easier for them to act.

A compare-and-contrast scene shows this sharply. A traveller approaches the hotel front desk at 9 p.m. "I've had a terrible day, the flight was late, the taxi took forever, and I'm exhausted, and my room is right by the lift and I really can't sleep with noise, and I booked weeks ago and—" The clerk, already handling three arrivals, hears distress but not a clear request. Now compare: "Hello—could you help me with a quick room change? I'm in 214 next to the lift and it's very noisy. If there's any room away from the lift, I'd be grateful." The second version is not unkind. It is simply clear. The concept is *request compression.* The implication is that staff can help you faster when you present the situation as a solvable unit rather than as a life story.

The same applies at the gate during disruptions, where emotions run hottest. Gate staff are often dealing with safety-critical tasks, time pressure, and a crowd. They are not equipped to listen to ten minutes of moral argument. Yet they can sometimes make decisive changes—seat swaps, rebooking, volunteer compensation offers, standby allocation. A short, respectful approach works best: "Hi—my flight has been cancelled. Are you able to rebook me from here, or should I use the app or call support?" If the staff member says,

"Use the app," that is not dismissal; it is routing. If the app fails, you return with a new, specific fact: "The app is showing no options; can you rebook me to the 10:40 tomorrow?" Specificity again. The concept is *channel escalation.* The implication is that you can move between channels without antagonism when you treat each refusal as information rather than insult.

Call-centre agents are different. Their world is quiet, scripted, and recorded. They have time, but they also have process. They can see your booking, note your account, and apply policy. They may be able to waive certain fees, reissue tickets, or explain entitlements. They may also be constrained by what is documented and what is authorised. When speaking to call-centre agents, a slightly longer explanation can help, but it should remain structured: reference number, problem, desired outcome, constraints. What matters is that you do not bury the desired outcome in the middle of a narrative. The agent needs to know what you want before they choose a path through their system. The concept is *front-loading the ask.* The implication is that you can make phone interactions more productive by stating the request early and then supplying supporting facts.

There is also a subtle psychological element: different staff roles face different forms of personal risk. A hotel front desk clerk may fear giving away too many upgrades and being reprimanded for lost revenue. A gate agent may fear making a change that causes a boarding error. A call-centre agent may fear violating policy and having it audited. Fear produces conservatism. Conservatism produces no. Your job is not to eliminate fear. Your job is to reduce perceived risk by being precise, cooperative, and aligned with policy where possible. Risk becomes visible here as behaviour: you provide the booking reference, accept process, and avoid asking for something that sounds like a precedent. The concept is *risk-limiting communication.* The implication is that the more safely a staff member can justify helping you, the more likely they are to do it.

A second named, checkable example anchors why roles have become so segmented. In April 2010, the Eyjafjallajökull disruption forced airlines and airports into mass rebooking and service recovery at scale, and the industry's response over the following years included more automation, more channel separation, and more reliance on apps and centralised systems. Again, this is context, not a claim of simple progress. The point is that segmentation is now built into the architecture: self-service handles the routine, humans handle exceptions, and within humans, roles handle slices of exceptions. The implication is that your micro-negotiation skill is partly a navigation skill—knowing where to direct your request so it lands in a system that can act on it.

None of this should be confused with treating staff as mere conduits. The human relationship still matters. Courtesy is not optional because you want to be a decent person, but also because courtesy keeps the interaction from becoming defensive. Yet courtesy should not dilute firmness. Firmness is simply clarity about what you are asking for and what you will do next if it cannot be resolved in that channel. "If you can't do that here, could you tell me who can?" is firm. It is also respectful. It keeps the ladder intact. It avoids the corrosive implication that the staff member is refusing out of spite.

A credible limitation remains: sometimes no one can do what you want. The flight network may be full. The hotel may be sold out. The booking channel may have locked the rate. The staff member may genuinely have no tools. The reconciliation is to treat such moments as a search for the nearest alternative remedy. If you cannot change the room, can you be moved tomorrow? If you cannot get the seat, can you be put on standby for a swap? If you cannot get a fee waived, can it be credited later? If you cannot be rebooked, can you get a clear reference number for a claim? These are not consolation prizes; they are ways of preserving agency when the main outcome is unavailable.

The motif here is the switchboard. Modern travel is a switchboard of channels and roles, and your experience depends on which wire your problem is plugged into. Plug it into the wrong socket and nothing happens, no matter how eloquent your story. Plug it into the right one and a small change can occur quickly, almost invisibly.

The forward test is blunt. Next time something goes wrong on a trip, will you tell your entire story to the first person you reach, hoping sympathy becomes authority—or will you begin with a routing question, compress your request into a few checkable facts, and move deliberately to the channel that can actually change the outcome?

Chapter 7
Repairs, Tradespeople and Quotes

In June 2017, the Grenfell Tower fire in London forced the country to look hard at buildings, maintenance, and the often invisible chain of decisions that sit behind "work done". Most domestic repairs are not matters of life and death, yet they live in the same moral neighbourhood: materials chosen, corners cut or not cut, scope understood or misunderstood, responsibilities assigned or shrugged off. The modern home is a dense machine—boilers, electrics, roofs, pipes—and when one part fails it demands a negotiation with someone who has skills you do not. The smell of damp plaster, the rattle of a radiator, the sudden silence of a dead boiler on a winter morning: these are not merely inconveniences. They are moments when ordinary people discover how quickly money moves when urgency is in the room.

Urgency is expensive.

Repairs are where micro-negotiation becomes most emotionally charged because the stakes are rarely just financial. They are practical and intimate. Your home is the place you rest, work, and recover; when it breaks, you feel exposed. That exposure makes people do odd things. Some become passive, nodding along as if they have no right to ask questions. Others become combative, treating every tradesperson as a potential trickster. Both reactions are understandable. Both are costly. The wiser posture is neither deference nor suspicion, but structured clarity: the ability to ask for comparable quotes, to define scope, to discuss price in plain terms, and to handle surprises without turning the relationship toxic.

This chapter is built around a blunt truth: most disputes with tradespeople do not begin with greed. They begin with ambiguity. A "quote" that is really an estimate. A conversation that is really a contract. A vague agreement about what is included, which becomes a fight about what was assumed. A job that expands because the underlying problem was worse than anyone could see, and the invoice grows without the client having consented to the expansion. The tragedy is that many of these conflicts are avoidable with a few short questions asked at the right time. The questions are not clever. They are simply the questions that turn hidden assumptions into explicit agreements.

Comparable quotes are the first rung because comparison is how fairness becomes visible. People collect two or three numbers and assume they have done due diligence. Yet numbers are meaningless without common scope. One quote may include parts, disposal, VAT, and follow-up testing; another may not. One may assume scaffolding; another may not. One may price for a full day; another for a half. If you compare totals without comparing what sits inside them, you are not negotiating; you are gambling. The skill here is to request quotes that can actually be lined up, item by item, without forcing tradespeople into bureaucratic paperwork. Clarity protects both sides: you avoid overpaying for ambiguity, and the tradesperson avoids being blamed for expectations you never articulated.

Scope is where most domestic negotiations quietly fail, because scope is boring until it is not. "Fix the leak" sounds simple until the leak is inside a wall. "Replace the boiler" sounds straightforward until the flue needs upgrading, the controls need modernising, and the old pipework reveals its age. Scope confusion is not a sign that someone is dishonest; it is a sign that the work touches reality, and reality has layers. The question is whether those layers are discussed before work starts, and whether changes are agreed when they arise. A five-minute conversation at the start of a job can prevent weeks of resentment later. The chapter will show how to ask what is included, what is excluded, what might change, and what happens if it does.

Price negotiation in repairs often feels awkward because it brushes against pride. Tradespeople know their value and are tired of being treated as interchangeable. Clients know their budgets and are tired of being surprised. The aim is not to squeeze someone unfairly. It is to make price transparent and terms workable. Once scope is clear, price becomes a conversation about options: fixed price versus day rate, staged payments, timing flexibility, materials choices, and scheduling. The best negotiation in this context often looks like collaboration: finding the arrangement that keeps the work viable for the tradesperson while keeping the cost predictable for you. A gentle reference to another quote can be part of this, but only when done with respect and without the theatre of "pitting" people against each other.

Then comes the moment that tests character: surprises and extras. Work rarely goes exactly to plan, and pretending otherwise leads to conflict. A roof reveals rotten battens. A boiler installation reveals a problem with ventilation. A bathroom refit reveals damp. At that point, you have a choice. You can accept the extra work and cost without question because you feel trapped, or you can accuse the tradesperson of inventing problems to inflate the bill. Both choices corrode trust. The better approach is to pause the work, clarify the new issue, and agree the changed scope and price before proceeding. Pausing is not hostility. It is consent. It is how you keep the relationship workable even when reality becomes complicated.

Modern relevance runs through this chapter because home repairs now sit at the intersection of tight household budgets, rising labour costs, complex building standards, and a market shaped by online reviews and lead-generation platforms. People can summon quotes via apps, yet still struggle to compare them. They can message tradespeople instantly, yet still fail to put agreements in writing. They can watch a five-minute video on boiler maintenance and feel falsely confident, or falsely suspicious. This chapter offers something more durable than tips: an approach to communicating with skilled people in a way that respects their craft while protecting your own interests.

There is also a quiet philosophical dignity in learning this. Being an adult involves maintaining the systems that keep life habitable: heat, water, shelter. Outsourcing the work does not mean outsourcing responsibility for the agreement. Micro-negotiation in repairs is not about becoming a quasi-expert in plumbing or electrics. It is about being the client who can define what they want, ask for clarity, and make decisions without panic. Panic is the real enemy here. Panic makes you accept vague promises. Panic makes you sign off on scope you do not understand. Panic makes you postpone necessary work until it becomes urgent and expensive.

The motifs from earlier chapters return, but they take on the texture of the home. The seam is the line between "included" and "excluded" in a quote. The hinge is the point at which a job expands. The pause is the moment you decide not to authorise extras until you understand them. The ledger is the written record—a message, an email, a quote—that transforms a friendly conversation into a shared reference when memory becomes unreliable. These are not bureaucratic burdens. They are the tools that allow trust to exist without naivety.

The emotional payoff of this chapter is relief: the sense that you can face repairs without either shrinking or snarling. The intellectual payoff is a clearer model of how work is priced, how scope is defined, and how agreements can be made fair without turning them cold. The practical payoff is the money you do not lose to ambiguity and the time you do not spend in conflict.

The question that carries you forward is simple but sharp. The next time your home needs work and urgency tries to rush you into acceptance, will you treat the quote as a number to endure—or as the beginning of an agreement you can shape, by asking the few precise questions that turn a stressful repair into a controlled decision?

Getting Comparable Repair Quotes

In March 2022, the UK Government's Boiler Upgrade Scheme opened for applications in England and Wales, a policy nudge designed to steer households towards lower-carbon heating. The scheme is public, searchable, and tied to clear technical eligibility rules. Yet for many households it surfaced a more basic, older problem: not how to choose a technology, but how to compare the quotes that arrive when you invite tradespeople into your home. A boiler replacement in Bristol might generate three numbers that look like three answers. In reality they are three different questions. One includes a power flush and new controls; another quietly assumes existing pipework is sound; a third prices for a different boiler size altogether. The homeowner reads the totals and feels either suspicious or defeated.

Comparison fails quietly.

People believe they are comparing quotes when they compare totals. That is the domestic version of comparing books by weighing them rather than reading the spines. A quote is not simply a price; it is a proposed description of work, a schedule, a risk allocation, and a set of assumptions. If those assumptions differ, the totals cannot be meaningfully compared. The result is a familiar frustration: the cheapest quote feels too cheap to trust, the most expensive feels like a tax on ignorance, and the "middle" feels like a superstition masquerading as judgement. Comparable quotes replace superstition with structure.

A comparable quote begins before anyone quotes. It begins with the information you provide upfront. Tradespeople cannot price accurately without a shared picture of the job. When the picture is vague, they fill in the gaps with their own assumptions. Assumptions are where quotes diverge. The concept here is *assumption drift.* The implication is that your first message or call—the "job brief"—determines whether you receive three comparable proposals or three incompatible guesses.

There is a temptation to send almost no information, hoping to keep things simple. "Need a new boiler, please quote" or "Roof leaking, how much?" seems efficient. It is not. It forces each tradesperson to decide what you mean. One person imagines a straightforward swap. Another imagines a complex system upgrade. A third imagines a full re-roof because they have seen too many rotten battens. Each may be acting in good faith. Yet their quotes will not match because they are pricing different realities. Efficiency, in this context, means spending two extra minutes upfront to reduce hours of confusion later.

The most useful upfront details are those that reduce uncertainty without turning you into an amateur surveyor. For a boiler replacement, this might include the make and model of the current boiler, its approximate age if known, whether it is combi or system, where it is located, and any specific issues that prompted replacement. For a roof repair, it might include the type of roof (flat, pitched), the rough location of the leak, whether it occurs only in heavy rain, and whether there has been previous work. These are not technical diagnoses; they are observable facts. They allow tradespeople to frame the job similarly. The concept is *shared baseline.* The implication is that you improve fairness for both sides by reducing the need for guesswork.

Fairness matters here in a way that people do not always admit. A trade quote is not a battle between a clever customer and a gullible contractor. It is a negotiation between two people who both carry risk. The homeowner risks overpaying or getting poor work. The tradesperson risks underpricing the job and absorbing extra hours, or entering a home where expectations are unspoken and later weaponised. Comparable quotes reduce risk on both sides because they make the work visible and the assumptions explicit. Trust becomes a set of behaviours: clear description, written scope, itemised costs, and agreed exclusions.

The next step is to ask for quotes in writing that include the same categories of information. "In writing" is not about being formal. It is about making the ledger legible. A written quote can be read, compared, and referred back to when memories diverge. It also discourages casual optimism. Spoken numbers are often rounded, softened, and ambiguous. Written numbers tend to come with qualifiers, which is exactly what you need. The concept is *record anchoring*. The implication is that written quotes create a stable reference that supports later negotiation without turning it hostile.

The written quote should make clear what is included and what is excluded. Included means materials, labour, disposal of old parts, scaffolding if relevant, testing and commissioning, and any follow-up. Excluded means anything that could later appear as an "extra": repairing plaster after pipework changes, replacing rotten timbers discovered mid-job, upgrading electrics to meet current standards, redecorating, moving furniture, or dealing with asbestos. Exclusions are not always a sign of trickery; they are often a sign of honesty. They indicate the tradesperson has noticed uncertainty and is refusing to pretend it is certainty. The concept is *uncertainty disclosure*. The implication is that the best quotes often feel slightly less comforting because they are realistic.

A roof repair illustrates this vividly. One roofer looks at a leak and says, "Two hundred quid, mate." Another says, "It depends; I need to check the flashing, the tiles, and the underlay." The first number might be right. It might also be fantasy. The second roofer is naming uncertainty. If they then provide a written quote that specifies "Replace damaged tiles in area X; re-dress flashing around chimney; dispose of waste; includes materials; excludes replacement of rotten battens if discovered," you now have something to compare. You can ask the first roofer to quote on the same basis. The goal is not to shame the casual quoter. The goal is to bring all quotes into the same frame so you can make a decision based on substance rather than mood.

This is where the show–name–explain engine becomes practical. Show: three quotes arrive for a boiler swap, and the prices vary wildly. Name: *scope mismatch*. Explain: one quote includes a magnetic filter and new thermostat, another reuses existing controls, another includes a power flush and condensate pipe reroute to meet current best practice. Implication: the totals are not comparable until you align the scope categories. The customer who spots this can ask a simple question that forces alignment: "Does your quote include a flush and new controls? Does it include disposal? Does it include commissioning and certification?" Those questions are not antagonistic. They are comparative.

A second named, checkable reference helps keep the standards grounded. In the UK, Gas Safe Register is the official gas registration body, and work on gas appliances must be carried out by appropriately registered engineers. This is not a quirk; it is a safety regime. When comparing boiler quotes, therefore, one element you can compare is not a perk but a compliance marker: whether commissioning and required certification are included. The visible behaviour is listing it explicitly. The concept is *compliance transparency*. The implication is that a cheaper quote that omits compliance steps is not cheaper in a meaningful sense; it is incomplete.

Comparable quotes also require you to specify the decision unit. Are you comparing fixed-price quotes, or day rates? Day rates can be sensible when uncertainty is high, but they complicate comparison because the total becomes a function of time. Fixed prices simplify comparison but may include a risk premium if the job has unknowns. Neither is inherently better. What matters is that you compare like with like, or at least understand what is being priced: certainty or flexibility. The concept is *risk pricing*. The implication is that you can choose consciously rather than stumbling into a risk you did not mean to take.

There is a credible counter-example: some jobs cannot be quoted precisely in advance without invasive inspection. A hidden leak, structural rot, electrical faults behind walls—these can only be revealed once work begins. In such cases, insisting on a fully fixed quote may either be refused or result in an inflated price that protects the contractor from surprises. The reconciliation is to aim for comparability of *framework* rather than comparability of exact totals. You can compare how each tradesperson handles uncertainty: do they propose a diagnostic phase, do they define how extras will be approved, do they set clear hourly rates for unforeseen work, do they commit to pausing before proceeding? These elements can be compared even when the final cost cannot. The implication is that a quote is sometimes less about the number and more about the method of managing what cannot yet be seen.

The homeowner's role, then, is to shape the quote request so that it elicits comparable information without becoming burdensome. A short message can achieve this when it includes observable details and a request for written scope. For example: "Boiler replacement: current unit is a Worcester Bosch Greenstar (model on label), installed roughly 2012, located in kitchen cupboard. Hot water intermittently drops; engineer advised replacement. Please quote in writing and confirm what's included (removal/disposal, any system flush, controls/thermostat, commissioning/certification) and any exclusions." That message is not an instruction manual. It is a frame. The concept is *quote framing*. The implication is that framing encourages tradespeople to quote on the same categories, which makes your later negotiation fairer and faster.

Notice that this approach also respects the tradesperson's time. It reduces back-and-forth. It signals that you are organised and serious. It discourages opportunists who thrive on vague jobs and desperate customers. It attracts competent professionals who prefer clear briefs because clear briefs reduce disputes. Competence is not merely skill with tools; it is skill with agreements. The concept is *professional signalling*. The implication is that your clarity can change who responds and how they respond.

The motif for this subchapter is the measuring tape. It is a humble object, used quietly, often unnoticed. Yet it represents the shift from impression to measurement, from "about this much" to "this exact length". Comparable quotes are measuring tape for agreements.

They turn hand-waving into shared dimensions. They allow you to compare without cynicism.

The forward test is deliberately practical. The next time you need a repair, will you accept three totals as three answers—or will you treat the quoting stage as the first negotiation, shaping your request so that each tradesperson prices the same work, states the same assumptions, and gives you a decision you can make with your eyes open?

Clarifying Scope and Expectations

In October 2000, the Millennium Bridge in London—designed by Foster + Partners and opened with public fanfare—was abruptly closed two days after opening because it developed an unexpected lateral wobble under pedestrian load. The engineering response was not to argue about intentions. It was to clarify behaviour, model forces, and modify the structure until it matched reality. Domestic repairs are not high-profile infrastructure, but the pattern is the same: most conflict begins when what was imagined fails to match what happens. A handyman arrives in Sheffield on a grey morning, tool bag on the step, and the client says, "Just fix it, please." The request is heartfelt. It is also vague.

Vagueness is a hidden invoice.

Scope is the boundary of an agreement: what will be done, to what standard, by when, and what sits outside the boundary. People avoid scope conversations because they feel awkward, nit-picky, or distrustful. They also avoid them because they assume scope is obvious. It rarely is. In repairs, what seems obvious to a homeowner is often invisible to a tradesperson, and what seems obvious to a tradesperson is often unspoken to a homeowner. The result is a predictable cycle: the job begins under a haze of assumptions, the work expands or diverges, and the invoice becomes the first time both sides discover they were imagining different jobs. The conflict is not merely about money. It is about dignity—no one likes to feel fooled, and no one likes to feel accused.

Scope clarification is therefore not a "negotiation trick". It is a respect practice. It respects your budget and your time. It respects the tradesperson's time and their need to avoid unpaid extras. It also respects the future relationship, because most disputes become personal only after they have become expensive. The earlier you set boundaries, the less likely you are to need hard confrontation later.

A short story makes this concrete. A client hires a handyman to "sort the bathroom door" because it sticks and scrapes the floor. The handyman arrives, planes the door, refits it, and the door swings freely. The client is relieved, until they notice the door now has an exposed strip of bare wood at the bottom and the trim looks scuffed. They assumed "sort the door" included repainting and making it look as it did before. The handyman assumed the job was functional: make the door work. Neither assumption is immoral. Both are costly when they collide. Five minutes at the start would have surfaced it. "When you fix the door, will it need repainting? If so, is that included?" That is not a challenge. It is a scope question.

The show–name–explain engine begins here. Show: a job described in general terms leads to surprise about finishes. Name: *scope ambiguity*. Explain: repairs have multiple dimensions—function, appearance, durability, and compliance—and different people prioritise different dimensions unless they are named. Implication: without explicit scope, you can end up with work that is "done" in one sense and "unfinished" in another, and the cost of aligning those senses arrives later as friction or extra payment.

The most useful scope questions are simple. They are not technical, and they do not require you to sound like a project manager. They ask about inclusion, exclusion, and change. Inclusion: "What exactly is included in the price?" Exclusion: "What is not included that people often assume is?" Change: "If you find something unexpected, how will we handle it before you do extra work?" These questions feel almost too obvious, which is why people skip them. Yet their power is precisely in their obviousness. They prevent both sides from hiding behind ambiguity later.

Because the audience here includes shy or conflict-averse people, it matters to notice that scope questions can be delivered as curiosity, not accusation. Tone shapes the response. "I'm just making sure I understand" is not weakness; it is a framing that makes it easier for the tradesperson to answer without feeling suspected. You are not asking, "Are you going to rip me off?" You are asking, "What are we agreeing?" The concept is *curiosity framing*. The implication is that a curious tone keeps scope conversations collaborative, which is essential when you need the other person's expertise and goodwill.

Written follow-up is the second half of scope clarification. Many domestic agreements happen in kitchens and hallways, in hurried conversations. Memory is unreliable, especially under stress. Written summaries turn memory into a shared reference. A message that says, "Just confirming: you'll replace the tap and check for leaks under the sink; you'll supply the tap; disposal is included; any pipework beyond the immediate connection would be discussed first," is not legalistic. It is humane. It prevents both sides from later saying, honestly, "I thought you meant…" The concept is *shared ledger*. The implication is that written clarity reduces future conflict by creating a neutral artefact both sides can point to.

A second named, checkable example shows how professionals treat scope when stakes are higher. The Royal Institute of British Architects (RIBA) Plan of Work, widely used in UK construction projects, breaks projects into stages precisely to manage scope, deliverables, and changes. Home repairs are smaller, but the underlying reason is the same: work expands unless boundaries are defined. The point is not to import professional bureaucracy into your kitchen. The point is to borrow the spirit: stage the work mentally, and ensure you know what "done" looks like for this stage. "Done" is not a feeling. It is an observable condition.

Observable conditions are the antidote to abstraction. "Make it safe" can mean different things. "Stop the leak" can mean it does not drip today, or it has been pressure tested, or it has been replaced. "Fix the roof" can mean patching one tile, or redoing an entire section of flashing. Abstractions like "safe" and "fixed" are emotionally satisfying but operationally vague. Pair them with visible criteria. "No water ingress during heavy rain" is still not a guarantee, but it is a clearer target. "Boiler runs without error codes and produces hot water consistently" is a clearer target. The concept is *success criteria.* The implication is that when you define what success looks like in observable terms, both parties can agree when the job is complete and avoid disputes about whether it "counts".

Scope also involves time and access. Tradespeople often plan days tightly. Clients often have unspoken constraints: school runs, work calls, noise restrictions, neighbour sensitivities. If these constraints are not discussed, they become friction mid-job. A simple question—"How long do you expect this to take, and will you need access to any other areas?"—prevents surprises. It also supports fairness: if a job is likely to take longer because of access issues, that is part of the price conversation. The concept is *constraint disclosure.* The implication is that sharing constraints early allows the work to be priced and planned realistically rather than turning delays into blame.

Change management is where scope becomes most emotionally charged. Many jobs reveal hidden problems. A tradesperson discovers rotten joists beneath a bathroom floor. An electrician discovers unsafe wiring. A plumber discovers corroded pipes. These discoveries are real, but they also create a negotiation moment: what happens next, and who pays? The worst pattern is when the tradesperson proceeds without explicit agreement, and the client is then presented with an expanded invoice. The second-worst pattern is when the client assumes the tradesperson is inventing extras to inflate the bill. Both patterns corrode trust. The better pattern is a pause, a brief explanation of the new issue, and an explicit decision about whether to proceed and at what cost. The concept is *pause protocol.* The implication is that agreeing to a pause protocol in advance makes it easier to execute calmly when surprises emerge.

A credible limitation must be acknowledged. Not all tradespeople provide beautifully itemised scope statements for small jobs. Some work by experience and habit. Some are excellent with tools and less comfortable with paperwork. If you insist on a level of documentation that is disproportionate to the job, you may alienate good workers or simply waste time. The reconciliation is proportion. For a £100 job, a brief text confirmation may be enough. For a £5,000 job, a written quote with inclusions and exclusions is reasonable. The skill is to match the level of scope formality to the stakes. The implication is that scope is not a binary of "formal contract" versus "handshake"; it is a spectrum, and you can choose the point on that spectrum that fits the situation.

The motif for this subchapter is the line on a builder's chalk: a boundary drawn before cutting, so that the cut is deliberate rather than accidental. Scope questions are chalk lines for agreements. They are drawn before the work begins, when the material is still intact and changes are still cheap. Drawn later, they become arguments about damage already done.

The forward test is a decision you can make in the doorway, before tools come out. The next time you hire someone for a repair, will you let "just sort it" stand as your entire scope—or will you take five minutes to draw the chalk line, asking what is included, what is excluded, and what happens if the job changes once reality reveals itself?

Negotiating Price and Payment Terms

In June 2020, the UK Government's "Build Back Better" slogan arrived alongside a practical attempt to stimulate home improvement through schemes such as the Green Homes Grant in England. The policy itself changed course later, but the moment captured something lasting: when homes become workplaces and refuges, repairs and upgrades stop being occasional chores and become strategic decisions. In a terraced house in Birmingham, a kitchen table turns into a bidding desk. Three quotes sit beside a mug of cooling tea. One is a fixed sum. One is a day rate. One is a fixed sum with a suspiciously vague line called "extras as required". The homeowner feels the old tension: wanting to be fair, wanting not to be taken for a ride, wanting the work done well.

Money is never just money.

Once scope is clear, price becomes discussable in a way it is not when the work is still hazy. Scope clarity does something psychological: it removes the fear that you are haggling blindly. When you know what is being done, you can talk about what it costs without feeling you are insulting someone's craft. The conversation shifts from "Are you expensive?" to "How is the price structured, and can the structure fit us both?" That shift is the heart of negotiating price and payment terms in repairs. It is not about squeezing. It is about making the agreement durable.

The first claim is that price is often less flexible than terms, and terms are where fairness hides. Many clients focus narrowly on reducing the headline number because it is the easiest thing to compare. Yet tradespeople often have limited room on the number because it reflects labour, materials, overhead, and the risk premium of uncertainty. They may, however, have room to adjust *how* the number is paid, *when* the work is scheduled, and *what* is included. Payment terms can reduce risk for one side and therefore reduce cost pressure. Timing flexibility can reduce disruption to the tradesperson and therefore invite a small discount. Staged payments can protect the client while keeping cashflow workable for the tradesperson. The concept here is *term elasticity*. The implication is that a fairer deal often comes from reshaping terms rather than trying to bludgeon the price downward.

Fixed price versus day rate is the first structural choice because it tells you who carries uncertainty. A fixed price shifts more risk to the tradesperson: if the job takes longer than expected, they absorb the cost. A day rate shifts more risk to the client: if the job runs long, you pay more. Neither is morally superior. Each suits different kinds of work. A boiler swap with known conditions may suit a fixed price because uncertainty is low. A job involving hidden damage—rot behind plaster, unknown pipework—may suit a day rate or a hybrid because the true scope cannot be fully known in advance. The concept is *risk allocation*. The implication is that you can choose a pricing structure that matches the uncertainty of the job instead of pretending uncertainty does not exist.

Hybrid structures are common in practice, even when people do not name them. A tradesperson might quote a fixed price for the known work and a defined hourly rate for genuinely unforeseen extras, with a commitment to pause before proceeding. That pause is not a bureaucratic nicety; it is how consent survives contact with reality. If you accept a day rate, the fairness hinge becomes time transparency: how time will be recorded, what counts as billable hours, how travel time is treated, how materials are charged. If you accept a fixed price, the hinge becomes scope clarity and exclusion clarity: what might trigger a variation and how variations are priced. In both cases, the conversation is about control, not distrust. Control here means knowing what you are agreeing to and what you will owe.

Payment terms are the second lever because they change the risk profile of the job. Tradespeople dislike being paid late or chased for money; clients dislike paying too much upfront and losing leverage if the work slips. A staged payment plan is a compromise built around milestones—observable points at which value has been delivered. Milestones might be "materials delivered", "old boiler removed", "new boiler installed", "commissioning completed", "site left clean". The details vary. What matters is that payment aligns with progress. The concept is *progress-linked payment*. The implication is that you can reduce conflict by ensuring money moves in step with visible completion rather than in advance of it.

This is also where the word "deposit" needs calm scrutiny. Deposits can be reasonable, especially when materials must be ordered. They can also be used to lock clients in. The ethical centre is proportionality. A modest deposit that covers materials is different from a large upfront payment that covers labour not yet performed. The point is not to declare one universally right. The point is to notice what the deposit is doing: funding materials, securing a slot, or shifting all risk onto you. Risk again becomes visible as a decision: how much you pay before you see work. The concept is *front-loaded risk*. The implication is that payment structure can matter as much as total cost in determining whether the deal feels fair at the end.

Timing flexibility is the third lever, and it is often overlooked because it feels like a nuisance rather than a bargaining chip. Tradespeople have schedules, cancellations, and awkward gaps. A client who can accept a job in a quieter period, or who can be flexible about start dates, can sometimes be cheaper to serve. The savings may not be dramatic, and they should not be assumed. Yet it is a legitimate question: "If I can be flexible on timing, is there any difference in price?" This does not demean the work. It recognises scheduling as a cost. The concept is *schedule value*. The implication is that flexibility can create a fair exchange: you accommodate their calendar; they may accommodate your budget.

Now to the delicate matter of referencing other quotes without turning it into a crude auction. Many people either avoid mentioning other quotes because they fear seeming rude, or they mention them in a hostile way—"I've got someone cheaper; match it or I'm gone." That style can backfire because it insults the tradesperson's judgement and encourages them to cut corners to hit a number. It also assumes prices are interchangeable. They often are not, because scope and quality vary. A gentler reference is more truthful: "I've had another quote that's lower, but I'm comparing like-for-like and

I prefer your approach. Could we look at whether there's any way to bring yours closer—perhaps by adjusting timing or the specification?" This line does several things. It acknowledges the other quote as a data point, not a threat. It signals preference, which respects the tradesperson. It invites a conversation about structure rather than a demand for a discount. The concept is *comparative transparency*. The implication is that you can be honest about alternatives without weaponising them.

A concrete example helps. Suppose you have two quotes for a bathroom refit. One is £6,500 fixed price including disposal, waterproofing, and a mid-range suite. Another is £5,400 with a day rate component and less detail. You prefer the first tradesperson because their quote is clearer and they seem organised. You could simply accept the higher quote. You could also ask whether there is any flexibility: perhaps you can supply the suite yourself, or accept a slightly later start date, or stage payments differently. You are not asking them to work for less than their worth; you are asking whether the shape of the job can be modified to reduce cost without reducing quality. The concept is *specification tuning*. The implication is that the price conversation becomes collaborative and practical rather than adversarial.

The moral danger here is pretending that all costs are "negotiable" in a way that implies tradespeople should absorb your budget constraints. That is not fair. Yet it is equally unfair to treat the first quoted price as a sacred number immune to discussion, especially when quotes often include contingency, scheduling assumptions, and choices of materials that can vary. The mature stance is to treat price as a proposed structure open to refinement, within bounds that respect labour and expertise. Respect is visible in how you ask: you focus on options and constraints rather than on accusations.

A second named, checkable anchor can ground the principle that contracts about services are not merely social; they have legal and regulatory context. In the UK, the Consumer Rights Act 2015 sets expectations that services will be carried out with reasonable care and skill. This is not legal advice; it is a reminder that workmanship standards exist beyond private sentiment. In practical terms, it means that "cheaper" is not always cheaper if it means poorer work that must be redone. When negotiating, therefore, the quality baseline should be non-negotiable, even if materials and timing can move. The concept is *quality floor.* The implication is that a fair negotiation keeps the work's standard intact while adjusting terms around it.

A credible limitation must be admitted. Some tradespeople will not negotiate at all, especially when demand is high or when they have abundant work. Others will negotiate, but only within tight margins. Some will view negotiation as a red flag, fearing future conflict. The reconciliation is that negotiation in this context is best framed as clarity and fit rather than as haggling. If a tradesperson reacts badly to a polite inquiry about terms, that reaction itself is information about how future disagreements might go. This is not a prediction. It is a signal. The implication is that the negotiation conversation can also serve as a test of professionalism and communication, not merely of price.

The motif for this subchapter is the invoice line. A line is either itemised or it is not. When it is itemised, you can discuss it: materials, labour, disposal, testing, contingency. When it is a single lump, discussion becomes emotionally loaded because any reduction feels like an attack on the person rather than an adjustment to a component. Itemisation turns money into parts. Parts can be reshaped. The invoice line is therefore a tool of civility: it allows negotiation without insult.

The forward test is a choice you will face the next time a quote arrives and your stomach tightens. Will you treat price as a verdict you must accept or reject—yes or no—or will you treat it as a structure you can discuss, asking about fixed versus day rate, about staged payments, about timing flexibility, and about specification options, so that the final agreement is not simply cheaper or dearer but more transparent, more balanced, and more likely to hold when reality interferes?

Dealing with Surprises and Extras

In June 2017, Grenfell Tower in London burned with an awful speed that forced the UK to confront the consequences of hidden decisions in buildings—materials chosen, corners cut, risks misunderstood. Domestic repairs are smaller and quieter, but they share one stubborn feature with all work on real structures: you never see everything until you open it up. A plumber in Leeds removes a bath panel and a stale, earthy smell rises from the cavity; damp has been sitting there for longer than anyone guessed. A roofer in Cardiff lifts a few tiles and finds the felt torn and the battens soft. The client hears a new sentence—"There's more going on here"—and feels their chest tighten. This is the moment when trust can grow or curdle.

Pause. Then decide.

Surprises and extras are the point at which many repair relationships break. Not because one side is necessarily dishonest, but because uncertainty collides with money. The client hears "extra" and suspects opportunism. The tradesperson hears "why?" and suspects they are being accused of making things up. Both reactions are human. Both are combustible. The skill in micro-negotiation here is to create a small procedural bridge between discovery and agreement: a way to acknowledge new information without immediately agreeing to new cost, and without humiliating the person who brought the information.

The first claim is that surprises are inevitable and therefore should be treated as a normal phase of work, not as a moral scandal. Buildings hide their history. Pipes corrode behind walls. Roofs are patched repeatedly. Wiring is altered by previous occupants. Even a conscientious inspection cannot reveal everything without dismantling. This is why the best tradespeople often speak cautiously at the start: they are not being evasive; they are respecting uncertainty. When a surprise appears, the question becomes not "How dare this happen?" but "How do we decide what to do next?" The concept here is *uncertainty realism*. The implication is that if you accept surprises as a category, you can focus your energy on managing them rather than denying them.

Management begins with language. The difference between a workable conversation and a fight is often a few sentences. A client who says, "You're adding extras," frames the situation as a wrongdoing. A client who says, "Can we pause and talk through what you've found and what it changes?" frames it as a joint problem. The second sentence does not concede anything. It simply opens a decision space. The concept is *decision framing*. The implication is that you can keep the relationship intact while still protecting your budget and your right to consent.

Consent is the core. Many clients feel trapped mid-job: the house is half dismantled, the tradesperson is already on site, and saying no feels impossible. That trapped feeling often leads to silent agreement followed by resentment. Resentment then erupts at invoice stage, when it is least useful. The healthier approach is to treat mid-job discovery as a formal pause point. Work stops briefly. The issue is described. Options are outlined. Costs and time impacts are stated. Then a decision is made. This is not bureaucracy. It is adult consent applied to physical reality. The concept is *pause protocol*. The implication is that a short pause now prevents a long argument later.

A short story shows how this works in practice. A handyman is fitting shelves in a living room. The client asked for "three shelves on that wall". Midway through, the handyman says the wall is not solid brick as expected; it is plasterboard with studs, and the shelves will need different fixings and perhaps a timber batten for strength. The client hears "different fixings" and imagines a cash grab. The handyman hears the client's silence and worries about being blamed later if the shelves sag. A five-minute conversation prevents the blow-up. “Could you show me what you mean? If we do it properly, what changes in cost and time? And if we keep it as originally planned, what’s the risk?” That is calm. It is curious. It produces a decision based on visible facts: what the wall is, what the shelves will hold, what the fixings cost, what the time impact is. The extra cost, if any, becomes understandable rather than mysterious.

That sequence—show, name, explain, implication—works here almost mechanically. Show: the tradesperson points to the damp patch, the corroded pipe, the rotten timber, the unsafe cable. Name: this is a hidden defect, not part of the original scope. Explain: it changes the work required and therefore the cost and time. Implication: you either accept a variation, choose a workaround, or defer the extra work with a known risk. The key is that the decision is explicit. Explicit decisions reduce later moral drama because both sides can point to what was agreed.

Two named, checkable examples help anchor how systems treat variation when stakes are higher. In construction, variation orders are standard practice—written changes to scope and price when conditions differ from the plan. The language varies by contract, but the principle is widespread precisely because real-world work surprises. Similarly, the RIBA Plan of Work, used in UK building projects, treats design development and site realities as stages where change is expected, not scandalous. The point is not to mimic a commercial contract in your kitchen. The point is to adopt the professional habit: changes are documented and agreed. The concept is *variation discipline.* The implication is that you can borrow a professional norm—document changes—without importing professional bureaucracy.

Documentation in a domestic context can be light. A text message or email is often enough: “Confirmed: additional work to replace rotten battens in area X; £Y extra; adds half a day; approved before proceeding.” That line is not aggressive. It protects both sides. It also prevents the common invoice surprise where an “extra” appears as a fait accompli. Written confirmation turns "I told you" into "we agreed". The concept is *ledger reinforcement.* The implication is that small written notes preserve trust by reducing reliance on memory.

The second claim is that extras on invoices should be treated as requests for consent after the fact, and that is a risky position for both sides. When an invoice arrives with unexplained additions, the client feels ambushed. The tradesperson may feel they did necessary work and deserve payment. The disagreement often becomes personal because it touches fairness. The most productive first response is neither immediate refusal nor immediate payment. It is a clarification request: "Could you break down these extras and tell me when they were agreed?" That question is not an accusation. It is a request for traceability. The concept is *invoice traceability.* The implication is that you can challenge surprises without hostility by asking for the decision trail.

Traceability has a moral dimension. If the tradesperson can point to a message, a call, a photo sent mid-job, and a stated cost, the extra becomes legitimate even if it is inconvenient. If they cannot, the extra becomes questionable even if the work was real. The aim is not to "catch" anyone. The aim is to align payment with agreement. Payment without agreement is where trust collapses. Agreement without payment is also where trust collapses. The only stable arrangement is agreement followed by payment. The concept is *sequence integrity.* The implication is that preserving the correct sequence—agree, then pay—protects both parties.

A credible limitation must be admitted: sometimes work must proceed immediately for safety or to prevent damage. A major leak cannot always wait for a leisurely discussion. An electrical hazard may require swift action. A roof opening in heavy rain may need emergency covering. In these moments, strict pause protocols can be impractical. The reconciliation is to distinguish emergency stabilisation from elective improvement. Stabilisation is immediate work to stop harm. Improvement can be discussed. If stabilisation requires extra cost, it should still be communicated as soon as possible, with the smallest possible decision: "I need to do X now to prevent damage; it will cost roughly Y; I'll confirm details once things are stable." This is not advice; it is a description of how competent people tend to manage emergencies: act to prevent harm, then document. The implication is that even in urgency, communication can preserve consent as much as conditions allow.

Another limitation is psychological: many clients struggle to ask questions mid-job because they fear appearing ignorant or distrustful. That fear is expensive. Ignorance is not shameful in repairs; it is the default. Tradespeople are paid to know things you do not. The shame should attach only to pretending you understand when you do not and then resenting the consequences. A simple phrase defuses this: "I'm not an expert—could you explain what you're seeing and what my options are?" That sentence is honest. It signals respect for expertise and a need for clarity. The concept is *competence humility*. The implication is that admitting ignorance can actually increase your control because it invites explanation rather than leaving you to guess.

This is also where calm curiosity beats accusation as a method. Accusation tends to produce defensive, terse answers. Curiosity tends to produce information. Information allows decision. Decision reduces conflict. The pattern is almost scientific: ask for evidence, ask for options, ask for costs, decide. Your tone does not need to be saccharine. It needs to be steady. The aim is not to be liked. It is to keep the conversation within the realm of facts and choices rather than motives and character.

The motif for this subchapter is the lifted floorboard. It symbolises both the inevitability of hidden realities and the moment of exposure when new decisions must be made. Once the floorboard is up, you cannot pretend the problem is not there. You can, however, decide how to handle it—now, later, properly, minimally—if you keep the decision process clear.

The forward test is a trade-off you will almost certainly face. When a tradesperson says, mid-job, "We've found something else," will you react as if you are being tricked—or will you pause, ask to see the evidence, ask what changes in scope, time and cost, and decide explicitly before any extra work continues, preserving both your budget and the working relationship?

Chapter 8
Clarifying Scope and Extras

In April 1970, after the Apollo 13 explosion, NASA engineers on the ground faced a problem that was not merely technical but linguistic: how to describe, precisely and quickly, what could be done with what was available. The spacecraft had limited power, limited oxygen, limited time. Vague intentions were useless. Only clear constraints and explicit choices mattered. Most of life is not a damaged spacecraft hurtling around the Moon, but the underlying pattern is closer than we like to admit. We all live inside limits—hours, attention, money, goodwill—and we often behave as if those limits are negotiable only at crisis point. Scope creep is the slow, everyday version of an oxygen leak.

It does not arrive with drama.

Scope creep rarely looks like a single outrageous demand. It looks like a small add-on that feels rude to refuse. It looks like a "quick question" that becomes an afternoon. It looks like a favour that turns into a role. It looks like a project that starts with one deliverable and quietly acquires four more because nobody wanted to be difficult. People tend to imagine scope creep as a workplace phenomenon, an affliction of consultants and contractors, but it thrives in the softer spaces of life: friendships, families, volunteer committees, group chats, and the shadowy zone of informal labour that keeps organisations and households afloat.

The reason it spreads is not that others are always selfish. It spreads because vague agreements invite interpretation, and interpretation tends to drift towards whatever is convenient for the person asking. A colleague says, "Could you have a look at this document?" and you assume a quick skim. They assume a full rewrite. A friend says, "Can you help me move?" and you imagine an hour with a few boxes. They imagine a day, a van, and your emotional labour as well as your arms. Nobody states the terms, so the terms expand until they hit resistance. If you do not provide resistance, they expand until they hit your exhaustion. The moral sting comes later: you feel used; the other person feels surprised by your resentment. Both reactions can be sincere.

This chapter sits at a hinge in the book's arc, because by now it is clear that micro-negotiation is not chiefly about saving money, though it often does. It is about making the invisible visible. In repairs, scope creep appears as extras on an invoice. In travel, it appears as a delay that steals hours because you did not ask the right questions early. In relationships and work, it appears as time that disappears into obligations you never consciously accepted. The same mechanism runs through all of it: agreements without boundaries. Boundaries are not walls; they are maps. Without them, you are wandering.

Modern life makes this worse in two particular ways. First, communication has become frictionless. Messages arrive at all hours, requests can be forwarded instantly, tasks can be dropped into your lap without the social awkwardness of asking face-to-face. Second, work has become less bounded for many people: hybrid schedules, remote teams, side projects, informal collaborations. The old cues that signalled "this is work time" versus "this is personal time" have blurred. In that blur, requests multiply because it is easier to ask than to plan. The cost is paid in attention and fatigue. Fatigue then erodes judgement, which makes it harder to set boundaries, which invites more scope creep. It is a loop.

The chapter's core proposition is simple but not easy: clarity is kinder than compliance. Many people equate kindness with saying yes, especially in the small moments where refusal feels socially dangerous. Yet compliance without clarity often becomes a delayed cruelty. It leads to missed deadlines, quiet resentment, passive aggression, or abrupt withdrawal. Clarity, delivered early, allows others to adjust. It respects their planning. It respects your limits. It keeps relationships honest. The person who asks for boundaries is often perceived as "difficult" only by those who benefit from your vagueness.

Scope creep also reveals something philosophical about identity. People often accept extra tasks not because they have time, but because the task touches their self-image: dependable colleague, loyal friend, helpful sibling, "the one who can be relied upon". That self-image can become a trap. You begin to confuse your value as a person with your willingness to absorb unpriced labour. The chapter will confront that confusion gently but firmly. You are not your availability. Your worth is not measured in how quickly you reply or how often you rescue others from their poor planning.

There is a practical reason to address this now, after the material on repairs and invoices. In repairs, the line between scope and extras is visible in paperwork. In social and professional life, the line is invisible, which makes it more dangerous. You cannot point to a quote and say, "That wasn't included." You can only point to a conversation, and conversations are notoriously elastic. This is why writing simple scope messages matters. A short message can function as a miniature contract without the coldness of legal language. It can be warm and still be precise. It can say, in plain terms, what you will do, what you will not do, and what will happen if circumstances change.

The chapter will also take on the most emotionally loaded skill in the book: saying no. Many people fear no because they fear conflict, and they fear conflict because they fear rejection. They imagine that refusing a request is the same as rejecting the person. It is not. Refusing a task is a statement about capacity and priorities, not about affection or respect. Yet in practice, no must be delivered with care, because people do sometimes take it personally. The goal is not to become blunt or hardened. It is to learn a form of refusal that is bounded, calm, and collaborative—one that offers alternatives when appropriate, and that does not invite negotiation when negotiation would be unhealthy.

Renegotiation is the final piece, because life changes. Deadlines move. Budgets tighten. A child becomes ill. A parent needs care. A project expands beyond its original shape. The adult skill is not to cling to the original agreement out of pride, but to reopen the conversation before the agreement breaks. That reopening can be done without drama: stating what has changed, explaining the impact, proposing options. It is a way of treating agreements as living things rather than as traps. It is also a way of preserving trust, because trust is not built by never changing your mind; it is built by changing your mind openly rather than silently failing.

A quiet motif threads through this chapter: the margin. In books, margins are where notes are made and where meaning accumulates. In life, margins are the leftover minutes, the unclaimed energy, the small spaces that make work and care possible. Scope creep eats margins first. It does not announce itself; it nibbles. When your margins vanish, you lose not only rest but also the ability to negotiate at all, because negotiation requires a small surplus of attention. The person with no margin says yes by default and resents it later. The person with a margin can pause, clarify, and choose.

The emotional payoff of this chapter is not a new assertiveness persona. It is relief: the sense that you can remain generous without becoming overextended, and that you can be dependable without being endlessly available. The intellectual payoff is a clearer model of how agreements expand and how written clarity and bounded refusal can prevent that expansion from turning corrosive. The practical payoff is time—time you keep because you learned to define scope in friendships and offices as carefully as you would define it with a roofer.

The question that should tug you forward is uncomfortable in the way useful questions often are. When the next "quick favour" arrives, will you let it slide into your schedule as an undefined obligation—or will you claim the right to a margin, by clarifying what "help" means, writing it down in a sentence, and choosing your yes or no with enough precision that nobody has to guess what you owe?

Why Scope Creeps Quietly

In November 1988, at CERN in Geneva, Tim Berners-Lee wrote a proposal titled "Information Management: A Proposal" that would later be recognised as a seed of the World Wide Web. The document is modest in tone. It does not declare a revolution. It describes a practical problem—people could not easily keep track of complex, shifting relationships between projects and documents—and suggests a system to reduce confusion. That impulse, to turn messy reality into something navigable, sits behind every well-run agreement. Yet most agreements in ordinary life do the opposite. They begin as a neat sentence—"Could you help with this?"—and then silently acquire footnotes, dependencies, and hidden deliverables until the original sentence is no longer recognisable.

Scope creeps because nobody names the footnotes.

Scope creep is not primarily a failure of willpower. People imagine it as a personal flaw: the inability to say no, the inability to set boundaries, the inability to "manage time". That story is too simple and therefore unhelpful. Scope creep is, in large part, a failure of definition. It thrives where agreements are vague, where roles are informal, and where social pressure rewards compliance more than clarity. When scope is undefined, it expands towards the needs of whoever is asking and towards the convenience of the system the request is embedded in. That is not cynicism. It is an observation about how humans and organisations behave when terms are left elastic.

A small office scene makes it visible. A manager asks a colleague to "pull together a quick slide for Friday". The colleague hears "one slide". The manager imagines a deck, a narrative, and an appendix of numbers, because that is what the meeting usually requires. The colleague spends an hour producing a slide. On Thursday afternoon, the manager says, "This is a great start—can you add a few more to make it coherent?" Friday morning arrives with the email, "Could you also present it?" The colleague does not want to be difficult, so they comply. The work balloons from one hour to a day, and the colleague is left resentful, not because any single request was outrageous, but because the boundary between "a quick slide" and "a whole deliverable" was never drawn.

This is not merely an office pathology. It appears in volunteer work, friendships, and family life precisely because those relationships feel too precious to risk with blunt negotiation. A friend asks, "Can you help me move on Saturday?" The person asked imagines a couple of hours. The friend imagines the whole day, plus lunch, plus borrowing your car, plus emotional reassurance, plus the after-lift cleanup. The friend's imagination may not be selfish; it may simply be incomplete. When we are stressed, we underestimate the burden we impose on others. The person asked, meanwhile, imagines that saying no—or even clarifying the terms—will read as a lack of care. So they say yes, and then they pay for the yes with their weekend.

The show–name–explain engine is useful here because it reveals why the expansion happens. Show: vague requests generate mismatched assumptions. Name: *interpretation drift*. Explain: when terms are not specified, both parties fill the gap with their own default model of what "help" means, and the requester's model tends to expand as new needs become visible. Implication: the cost of scope creep is often paid in time, attention, and relationship friction, and that cost is preventable with early definition.

Interpretation drift has a cognitive basis. Humans are poor at forecasting effort, especially for complex tasks that involve coordination, feedback, and revision. Psychologists Daniel Kahneman and Amos Tversky described patterns of overconfidence and misestimation that have become widely discussed as the planning fallacy, later developed in research by others: we tend to underestimate how long tasks will take even when we have experience. This matters because many requests begin as optimistic fantasies. The requester genuinely believes it will be quick. The receiver, if they accept without clarifying, inherits the fantasy. The concept here is *effort misforecasting*. The implication is that scope creep is often the collision between an optimistic forecast and the real labour required.

Yet scope creep is not only about misforecasting. It is also about social economics. In many groups, saying yes confers status. The helpful person becomes central, trusted, relied upon. That reliance can feel like love. It can also be a trap. The more you say yes, the more you become the default solution to other people's problems. Your reliability becomes a resource others plan around. Planning around you increases requests. Requests increase your workload. Your workload reduces your capacity to refuse gracefully. The loop tightens. The concept is *reliability taxation*. The implication is that unbounded helpfulness can turn into a system that extracts your margins without anyone consciously intending harm.

There is also an institutional form of this in workplaces. Organisations often reward those who absorb ambiguity. The person who "just gets it done" becomes indispensable. Indispensable people are often praised, but they are also often exploited—not necessarily by malicious individuals, but by the structural incentives of a system that always has more work than capacity. When a project has unclear ownership, it tends to drift towards the person who will pick it up. That person may feel proud of being capable. They may also feel secretly furious. The concept is *ownership vacuum*. The implication is that scope creep is sometimes a symptom of organisational design: unclear roles and unclear boundaries push work onto the most conscientious.

A second example, named and checkable, shows how this plays out outside the office. In 2020, mutual aid groups across the UK expanded rapidly during COVID-19 lockdowns, organising food deliveries, prescriptions, and support for neighbours. Many were impressive, humane, and necessary. They also revealed how quickly volunteer scope expands when need is urgent and boundaries are soft. Volunteers who began with one task—drop groceries to an elderly neighbour—found themselves coordinating WhatsApp groups, sourcing supplies, mediating conflicts, and providing emotional support. Again, the expansion was not immoral. It was emergent. The need was real. The boundaries were not. The implication is not that volunteering is bad; it is that even good work can devour you if you do not define scope.

Scope creep also feeds on what might be called politeness ambiguity. English social life, especially in professional contexts, often uses vague phrasing to avoid awkwardness: "Could you just…", "Would you mind…", "When you have a moment…". These phrases lubricate social interaction. They also conceal urgency and effort. "When you have a moment" can mean "this week" or "in the next hour". "Just" can mean "one small task" or "a chain of work that will take all day". The listener, wanting to be cooperative, often interprets the phrase in the way that seems most generous. The requester, under pressure, often interprets the phrase in the way that seems most urgent. The result is predictable disappointment. The concept is *polite vagueness*. The implication is that cultural norms of softness can unintentionally create hard conflicts later.

There is a deeper reason scope creeps quietly: the line between generosity and obligation is often not drawn until it breaks. People do not want to negotiate intimacy. They want friendship to feel effortless. They want family care to feel natural. They want teamwork to feel fluid. Negotiation sounds clinical. Yet the absence of negotiation does not produce purity; it produces hidden accounting. You keep track, even if you pretend not to. Humans are exquisitely sensitive to fairness. When you feel you are giving more than you receive, your body often knows before your mind does: fatigue, irritability, a tightening in the chest when a message arrives. Those are signals that your internal ledger is filling with unpaid invoices.

The practical manifestation of trust in this chapter is not blind giving. It is clarity. Trust is visible when you can say, early, what you can do and what you cannot. It is visible when you ask, without hostility, "What does 'help' look like to you?" It is visible when you confirm timelines and outputs in a sentence. Those behaviours reduce the risk of later rupture. They also allow generosity to be sustained. Generosity that burns you out is not a virtue; it is a short-lived performance.

A credible limitation must be faced. Some scope creep is unavoidable because life changes. A project genuinely expands due to new information. A family member's needs intensify unexpectedly. A friend's crisis deepens. In these situations, insisting on rigid boundaries can be cruel. The reconciliation is that boundaries are not primarily about refusal; they are about renegotiation. When circumstances change, the agreement should change. The problem is not change itself. The problem is silent change—when the scope expands without being named, and the receiver is expected to absorb it by default. The implication is that flexibility and boundaries are not opposites; boundaries make flexibility possible because they allow change to be discussed rather than smuggled in.

The motif for this subchapter is the small word *just.* It is a harmless-looking word that often precedes the theft of an afternoon. "Could you just have a look?" "Can you just jump on a call?" "Would you just mind proofreading?" *Just* acts like a tranquilliser. It tells the listener, "This won't cost much." Often it is wrong. Not maliciously. Wrong nonetheless. Noticing *just* is a way of noticing scope creep at the moment it begins rather than at the moment you break.

The forward test is a question you can ask yourself the next time a request arrives wrapped in vagueness. Is this truly small—or is it simply unspecified? If it is unspecified, will you accept it as a blank cheque, or will you do the quieter, braver thing: define the scope while you still have margin, before "just" becomes the first word in a story you resent telling later?

Writing Simple Scope Messages

In July 1971, the first email was sent by Ray Tomlinson, working at BBN in Cambridge, Massachusetts. It was a small technical act—choosing the "@" symbol to route messages between computers—that quietly changed how agreements are made. Email did not merely speed up communication; it created a permanent, searchable trace of what was said, when, and by whom. That trace is why modern misunderstandings often feel so bitter: the evidence exists, yet the meaning still slips. A colleague in Manchester leaves a meeting thinking you agreed to "support the rollout". You leave thinking you agreed to "review the draft". Two days later, an email arrives asking for a presentation, a briefing note, and attendance at a steering call. You scroll, and there it is: no explicit boundary. Only friendly noise.

Write it down. Kindly.

A scope message is a short written summary that turns conversational mist into something you can see. It does not need to sound like a contract. In fact, it should not. Legalistic language can provoke defensiveness and suggests distrust. The power of a good scope message is that it feels ordinary and human—one person ensuring that another person has the same picture in mind. The concept here is *shared picture*. The implication is that written clarity protects relationships precisely because it prevents later accusations about who "promised" what.

The reason scope messages work is not magical. It is structural. Humans misremember, misinterpret, and fill gaps. We do it with innocence and confidence. Conversation encourages this because it is fast and social. People nod, laugh, agree, and move on. They assume alignment because the social ritual of agreement has happened. A scope message is a gentle interruption of that ritual. It says: before we proceed, let's confirm what we mean. That confirmation is not an expression of doubt; it is an expression of respect for reality. The concept is *reality anchoring*. The implication is that a single short message can prevent hours of correction, rework, and emotional friction.

Scope messages are particularly valuable when tasks involve revision, coordination, or reputational exposure—anything where "help" can expand. A "quick review" becomes a rewrite. "Support" becomes ownership. "Can you handle the comms?" becomes a full stakeholder programme. The message works by naming deliverables, time boundaries, and exclusions in plain language. Deliverables are what will be produced. Time boundaries are when it will be produced and how much time you can commit. Exclusions are what you are not doing, especially the things that might otherwise be assumed. These three elements form a tiny scaffold strong enough to hold an agreement without turning it into a bureaucratic exercise.

Show–name–explain makes the mechanism clear. Show: a meeting ends with vague agreement and later one party feels abandoned. Name: *implicit contract*. Explain: the mind treats nods and friendly language as commitments, even when commitments were never specified. Implication: without written clarification, both sides believe they are right, and the relationship pays the price. The scope message breaks the implicit contract and replaces it with an explicit one.

A scope message can be sent before work begins or after a conversation. The difference is timing, not function. Before work, it sets expectations. After a conversation, it confirms them. Both are useful. Before-work messages are especially valuable when the requester is emotionally invested, because emotional investment tends to inflate expectations. After-conversation messages are valuable when the conversation was rushed, because rushed conversations produce hazy agreements. In both cases, the message should be short enough to be read. A scope message that requires a scroll is already failing. The aim is not completeness. It is alignment.

Alignment depends on language choices. The best scope messages use concrete verbs rather than soft abstractions. “Draft”, “review”, “summarise”, “send”, “attend”, “introduce”, “check”, “compile”. Concrete verbs are measurable. They can be compared against what happened. “Support” and “help” are not measurable; they invite interpretation. It is not that “support” is a bad word. It is that it hides work. Where possible, replace “support” with a specific action. If you cannot, define what “support” means in this case. The concept is *verb specificity*. The implication is that when you use concrete verbs, you reduce the room in which scope creep breeds.

A brief email example shows how this looks in real life, without becoming a template that sounds like a machine wrote it. Imagine a colleague asks you, after a chat, to help with a funding application. The scope message might read like this: “Thanks for the chat today. Just to confirm my part: I’ll review the draft narrative and send comments by Thursday 3 p.m. I can also check the budget table for obvious inconsistencies. I won’t be able to rewrite the narrative or join the call with the funder, but if you’d like, I can suggest two questions to raise on that call.” This kind of message does several things at once. It commits to a deliverable and a time. It defines the type of effort. It states an exclusion. It offers a bounded alternative. Most importantly, it makes the implicit explicit.

Notice the emotional tone. It is cooperative. It does not apologise excessively. It does not sound resentful. It does not frame exclusions as punishments. This matters. People often sabotage their own scope messages by making them either too cold (“Per our discussion, I will deliver…”) or too apologetic (“Sorry, I’m terrible, I can’t do much…”). Coldness invites confrontation; excessive apology invites negotiation of your limits. A simple, warm, factual tone tends to land well because it feels like competent adulthood. The concept is *tone stability*. The implication is that the way you phrase boundaries can determine whether the message prevents conflict or triggers it.

Scope messages also operate as quiet social technology. They teach others how to request help from you. When you consistently clarify scope, people begin to ask more precisely. They stop sending vague requests because they know you will turn them into explicit agreements. This is not because you have become feared. It is because you have become reliable in a deeper sense: reliable about what you will and will not do. The unreliable person is not always the one who misses deadlines; it is also the one who says yes vaguely and later fails silently. The scope message prevents silent failure by making the boundaries visible from the start.

It also supports renegotiation later. When circumstances change, the scope message becomes a reference point. Instead of arguing about what was "meant", you can point to what was written and discuss how to adjust. Written clarity makes renegotiation feel less personal because it shifts the conversation from character to contract. Not a legal contract—a human contract. "We agreed X; now Y has changed; how do we adjust?" That is a problem-solving tone. The concept is *renegotiation footing.* The implication is that scope messages do not lock you in; they create a platform from which you can change terms without chaos.

A second named, checkable reference helps illustrate how normal written confirmations are in professional practice. In medicine, aviation, and other safety-critical fields, checklists and written protocols exist because memory and improvisation are unreliable under pressure. Atul Gawande's work on checklists, including his 2009 book *The Checklist Manifesto*, popularised this idea for a general audience: simple written prompts prevent avoidable errors in complex environments. Again, this is not an argument that your email is surgery. It is an argument that human cognition is consistent across domains. We forget. We assume. We mishear. A short written note reduces error. The implication is that scope messages are cognitive safety equipment for everyday agreements.

A credible limitation must be acknowledged. Some relationships are too delicate for overt boundary writing, at least at first glance. A grieving friend asks for help, and a formal-sounding scope message might feel cruel. A family member asks for care, and writing down boundaries can feel transactional. The reconciliation is that scope messages are not inherently transactional; they can be adapted to emotional contexts. The core is still clarity, but the tone shifts. "I can come on Tuesday evening for two hours, and I can bring food. I can't stay overnight, but I can help you arrange someone for that." This is a scope message. It is also care. Clarity does not cancel tenderness; it makes tenderness sustainable.

Another limitation is that some requesters will resist specificity because vagueness benefits them. Vague requests allow them to adjust expectations later without explicitly asking for more. When you clarify, they may respond with, "Let's just see how it goes," or "Don't worry about it." This is where clarity becomes a quiet test of respect. If the person refuses to specify, they may be trying to keep a blank cheque. Your response can remain calm: "Happy to help—what would be most useful for me to deliver, and by when?" You are not refusing. You are asking for the minimum structure required to proceed. The concept is *minimum viable agreement*. The implication is that you can protect yourself without becoming combative by insisting on a few concrete details before you commit.

The motif for this subchapter is the margin note. In the margin of a page, a brief annotation can change how the whole text is read. Scope messages are margin notes for your life. They are short, easy to overlook, and disproportionately powerful. They prevent the main text—your week, your energy, your relationships—from being overwritten by other people's assumptions.

The forward test arrives the next time you walk out of a conversation with a pleasant sense of having agreed to something. Will you let that pleasant sense stand in for a shared understanding, hoping it holds—or will you take sixty seconds to write the margin note, clarifying what you will do, what you will not do, and what happens if the work changes once reality arrives?

Saying No Without Drama

In May 1536, in the Tower of London, Thomas More was executed after refusing to swear an oath that would have affirmed Henry VIII's supremacy over the Church in England. The scene has been retold so often it risks becoming a moral postcard, but its hard fact remains: More's "no" was not a tantrum. It was a refusal anchored to an internal boundary, delivered in the language of conscience and law, and it carried consequences. Most refusals in modern life are not matters of state and life, yet the emotional physics can feel strangely similar. A request arrives, and a person hears not merely "will you do this?" but "are you the kind of person who helps?" The stakes inflate. The word *no* sticks in the throat.

Five words can change everything.

"No, not this week, sorry."

That sentence is short, human, and often sufficient. The drama that follows, when it follows, is usually not created by the word no itself but by the stories people attach to it. Many people believe refusal must be justified until it becomes acceptable. They believe they must offer a detailed explanation, a convincing excuse, a full autobiography of commitments, and perhaps a small ritual of self-blame. They do this to soften the other person's disappointment, but they also do it to protect their own self-image: if I explain well enough, I am not selfish. The result is that the refusal becomes a negotiation, because the more reasons you offer, the more the other person can counter them. The clean no becomes a messy debate.

A non-dramatic no is not a performance of hardness. It is a form of clarity. It says, in effect, that your time and attention have limits, and that those limits are not an insult to the requester. The skill is to separate the request from your identity. You are not your availability.

You are not your capacity to rescue. You are a person with finite hours. When you say no to a task, you are not saying no to the person's worth, and you are not saying yes to conflict. You are stating a boundary so that the relationship can remain honest.

The show–name–explain engine helps here because refusal is often treated as a moral act when it is more accurately a logistical one. Show: a colleague asks for "just a quick review" late on Thursday, and you say yes even though you are already overloaded. By Sunday you are exhausted and resentful; the review is rushed; the colleague is disappointed. Name: *false yes*. Explain: you agreed to protect social harmony in the moment, but the hidden cost emerged later as poor work and bad feeling. Implication: saying yes when you cannot deliver is not kindness; it is a delayed form of unreliability. A non-dramatic no is sometimes the more respectful act because it prevents false promises.

Why do false yeses happen so reliably? Partly because of immediate social pressure. A request, especially in person or in a work chat, arrives with an implied time limit: answer now. That pressure collapses your ability to think. It invites a reflex. Humans are social creatures; we dislike being the person who disrupts flow. In offices, the person who slows things down can be labelled obstructive. In families, refusal can be read as disloyalty. In friendships, it can be read as distance. These interpretations are not always fair, but they are emotionally plausible, which is why people comply. The concept here is *immediacy bias*. The implication is that many yeses are not decisions at all; they are reflexes under social time pressure.

Non-dramatic refusal begins by reclaiming time. Not hours. Sometimes seconds are enough. A small pause changes everything because it breaks the reflex. The pause can be silent, or it can be verbal—"Let me check my week" or "I need to think about that". These phrases are not evasive when used honestly; they are an assertion that your agreement has value and should not be extracted under pressure. The visible behaviour is delaying commitment long enough to assess capacity. The concept is *decision latency*. The implication is that refusing drama often requires refusing speed.

Once you have time, the next task is to choose the shape of your no. A no can be absolute or bounded, immediate or deferred, direct or accompanied by an alternative. The mistake people make is thinking there is only one kind of no—harsh, final, relationship-damaging. That is a myth. In practice, many noes are better understood as boundary statements: "I can do X, not Y." "I can help for 30 minutes, not three hours." "I can do it next week, not this week." The point is not to turn every no into a yes-in-disguise; it is to offer what you genuinely can, without being manoeuvred into more. The concept is *bounded yes*. The implication is that you can remain collaborative without becoming absorbent.

This is where phrases matter, not as scripts to parrot but as structures that make boundaries legible. A good refusal phrase tends to include one of three elements: a clear negative, a brief reason that does not invite debate, and—sometimes—an alternative that you can actually deliver. The reason should be simple and non-defensive. "I don't have capacity" is often better than a detailed story. Detailed stories invite cross-examination. Simple reasons tend to be accepted because they respect the other person's time and your own privacy. The visible behaviour is resisting the urge to over-explain. The concept is *explanation restraint*. The implication is that the more you justify, the more you teach people that your boundaries are negotiable.

A workplace example shows the contrast. A colleague says, "Can you join this call at 5?" A dramatic refusal might involve apology, guilt, or a long explanation: "I'm so sorry, I'd love to help but I've had such a crazy day and I'm behind on everything and I have to cook and I'm exhausted…" This invites the colleague to reply, "It's only 15 minutes," or "We really need you." A calmer refusal might be: "I can't make 5. If you send the questions, I can reply by midday tomorrow." The second response states a boundary and offers a specific, bounded alternative. It does not invite a debate about how tired you are. It offers a path forward. The goal is not to appear robotic. It is to be clear enough that the other person can plan.

Friendship offers a different challenge because alternatives can be emotionally loaded. A friend asks for help moving. You cannot. The drama arises because refusal feels like a comment on the friendship. Here, the non-dramatic no must carry warmth as well as clarity: "I can't do the move on Saturday. I do want you to be sorted—if it helps, I can come by Friday evening to pack for an hour, or I can order the van for you." The warmth is not manipulation. It is truthful: you care, but you have limits. The visible behaviour is distinguishing between caring and complying. The concept is *care–task separation.* The implication is that relationships survive refusal more easily when care is communicated without surrendering boundaries.

There is also the family version, which often arrives with unspoken history. A sibling asks you to "pop round" to help with a parent. The request may carry years of perceived imbalance. A no here can trigger old stories. Yet the same principles hold: pause, clarify, bound. "I can come on Tuesday and Thursday after work. I can't do every evening. Let's work out a rota." Notice the move: it turns a vague, morally charged request into a schedule. Schedules are not cold; they are how care becomes sustainable. The concept is *sustainable commitment.* The implication is that refusal can be a step towards fairer distribution rather than a withdrawal of love.

Two named, checkable references can add intellectual backbone without turning the piece into a bibliography. In 1960, psychologist Stanley Milgram began the obedience experiments at Yale University, exploring how social pressure and authority influence behaviour. The experiments are controversial for ethical reasons, but they remain a landmark in demonstrating that ordinary people can be pushed into actions they would not choose alone. Requests in daily life are not shocks in a lab, but the lesson about pressure is relevant: context can override judgement. A second reference is the sociologist Erving Goffman's work on social interaction—*The Presentation of Self in Everyday Life* (1956)—which describes how people manage impressions in social settings. Refusal threatens the image of being agreeable, so people avoid it. The implication is not that we are doomed to perform. It is that we can notice the performance impulse and choose differently.

A credible counter-example must be faced: sometimes saying no does cause real consequences. It can damage a relationship. It can cost you an opportunity. It can invite retaliation in unhealthy workplaces. In some environments, boundaries are punished. Pretending otherwise would be dishonest. The reconciliation is that the chapter's aim is not to promise safety; it is to help you choose consciously. There are times when you may decide to say yes for strategic reasons, even when you would prefer not to. The difference is that a strategic yes is owned; a false yes is resented. The implication is that the true opposite of no is not yes—it is consent.

Consent, in this context, includes accepting that the other person may be disappointed. People often try to eliminate disappointment by sacrificing themselves. That is an impossible project. Disappointment is part of adult life. A non-dramatic no does not aim to prevent disappointment; it aims to prevent dishonesty. It allows the other person to feel what they feel without forcing you to pay for their feelings with your time. This is subtle and difficult because many of us were trained to manage other people's emotions as a form of politeness. Yet politeness that requires self-erasure is a fragile virtue.

The motif threading this subchapter is the door. Not the slammed door of caricature, but the quietly closed door that keeps a room usable. A door is not an insult to the corridor. It is a boundary that allows different activities to exist without chaos. Saying no is closing a door on a task so that you can keep other doors open—work you already promised, rest you require, relationships you want to maintain without bitterness. When you never close doors, your life becomes a drafty hallway.

The forward test is sharp because it touches identity. The next time a request lands and you feel the reflex to comply, will you treat the reflex as evidence of your goodness—or will you pause long enough to choose, offering a clear no or a bounded yes, accepting the discomfort of someone else's disappointment so that you do not become the person who says yes in the moment and disappears in the aftermath?

Renegotiating When Things Change

In September 2008, as Lehman Brothers collapsed in New York and the shock rippled across markets, countless agreements quietly broke—not because people became immoral overnight, but because the assumptions underneath the agreements evaporated. Budgets vanished. Credit tightened. Jobs disappeared. "We'll renew" became "we can't." "We can deliver by December" became "we're freezing spend." The crisis is a named historical moment precisely because it made visible a truth that is usually hidden: agreements are built on conditions, and conditions change. Even when the stakes are smaller—an office deadline, a family commitment, a volunteer role—the logic is the same. An agreement made under one set of conditions can become untrue under another.

Reality moves. So must terms.

Renegotiation is the adult alternative to two common failures: silent suffering and sudden collapse. Silent suffering is when you keep the promise outwardly while your internal capacity fractures—late nights, irritability, corners cut, a growing resentment that poisons the relationship. Sudden collapse is when you finally cannot cope and you drop the commitment with little warning, leaving others scrambling. Both failures feel personal, but they are often procedural. They happen when people treat agreements as fixed objects rather than as living arrangements that require maintenance.

Renegotiation is that maintenance, and it can be done without drama or guilt if you understand what it really is: an update to shared reality.

The show–name–explain engine clarifies why renegotiation matters. Show: a team member agrees to lead a workstream, then a caregiving situation emerges at home and their availability halves. They try to keep up, miss messages, deliver late, and feel ashamed. The team begins to doubt them. The relationship strains. Name: *capacity shift.* Explain: the original agreement assumed a certain level of time and attention that no longer exists. Implication: the longer the shift is unspoken, the more the eventual renegotiation will feel like failure rather than foresight. Renegotiation is not a confession. It is an early-warning system.

Many people resist renegotiation because they mistake it for backtracking. They imagine a promise as a moral bond that must be honoured even at great personal cost. That belief can be admirable in the abstract and corrosive in practice. The best agreements are not those that never change; they are those that adapt before they break. Adaptation is not weakness. It is competence. Consider how good engineering works: when loads change, designs are adjusted. When new information emerges, plans are revised. A fixed plan in a changing world is not integrity; it is denial.

To renegotiate well, you need a structure that is simple enough to use under pressure. The most reliable structure is three moves: state the change, share the impact, propose options. Each move matters because it prevents a different failure. Stating the change prevents ambiguity. Sharing the impact prevents the other person from having to guess what this means for them. Proposing options prevents the conversation from becoming a complaint rather than a negotiation. This is not a script; it is a logic. It keeps the conversation in the realm of facts and choices instead of shame and blame.

Stating the change should be concrete and time-stamped where possible, because vagueness invites anxiety. "Things are a bit hectic" is not helpful. "From next week, I'll be caring for my mum three evenings a week" is clearer. "Our budget has been reduced for Q2" is clearer. "The supplier has delayed delivery by two weeks" is clearer. Notice how these statements name what changed and when. They make reality visible. The concept is *change declaration.* The implication is that when you name the change plainly, you reduce the space for misunderstanding and speculation.

Sharing the impact is where many people either over-apologise or under-communicate. Over-apologising makes the other person your emotional caretaker; they end up reassuring you rather than solving the problem. Under-communicating leaves them blindsided when consequences appear. Impact should be stated as a practical constraint: "That means I can't meet the Thursday deadline," or "That means I can attend one call a week, not three," or "That means the scope we discussed won't fit within the revised budget." This is not self-pity. It is a boundary derived from conditions. The concept is *impact articulation.* The implication is that you give the other person the information they need to plan, rather than forcing them to infer it from your stress.

Proposing options is the moment where renegotiation becomes collaborative rather than confessional. Options can include reducing scope, extending timeline, shifting ownership, or changing the form of delivery. The crucial thing is that options are specific enough to evaluate. "We'll have to figure it out" is not an option. "I can deliver the analysis but not the slides; someone else could present," is an option. "We can keep the full scope if we move the deadline two weeks," is an option. "If the budget is fixed, we can drop feature X and still deliver Y," is an option. The concept is *option framing.* The implication is that the person you are renegotiating with can choose rather than react.

A caregiving example shows how this can be done with honesty and without guilt. Imagine someone has agreed to coordinate a volunteer rota for a community group. The work is not enormous, but it is constant: messages, reminders, last-minute swaps. Then a parent becomes ill and care demands increase. The coordinator feels torn: stepping back feels like abandoning the group; staying in feels impossible. The renegotiation begins with a simple message: "From next week I'll be taking my dad to appointments twice a week, so I can't keep coordinating the rota at the same level. I can keep doing the Sunday schedule update, but I can't handle daily swaps. If someone else can take swaps, I can hand over the WhatsApp admin; if not, we may need to simplify the rota for a month." This message does not dramatise. It does not plead. It states change, impact, options. It also respects the group by giving them time and choices rather than a sudden disappearance.

A workload example shows the same logic in professional context. A project lead agrees to deliver a report by a certain date. Midway through, a new priority arrives—an urgent client issue, a production incident, an internal audit. The lead realises the report will slip or suffer. A poor response is silent struggle, followed by a rushed report and a late-night apology. A better response is early renegotiation: "We've had an urgent client escalation that will take most of my next two days. That means the report won't be ready by Friday if I keep the current scope. Options: I can deliver a shorter version on Friday with the key findings and send the full appendix next week, or we can move the full delivery to Wednesday." Again: change, impact, options. The aim is not to avoid responsibility. It is to manage it intelligently.

Two named, checkable references can add weight without pretending that negotiation is a laboratory science. In 1976, Albert O. Hirschman published *The Passions and the Interests*, exploring how societies have historically tried to channel human behaviour through incentives and institutions. One of his enduring insights is that systems shape what people do, not merely individual character. In renegotiation, the "system" is your set of commitments and constraints. When constraints change, behaviour must change or something breaks. A second reference is the widespread concept of "change control" in project management and engineering—formal processes exist because uncontrolled change leads to failure. The domestic version is informal, but the principle holds: changes need naming and agreement. The implication is that renegotiation is not personal weakness; it is a practice that serious systems adopt because reality is not static.

A credible counter-example must be faced. Sometimes renegotiation is used as a cover for poor planning or for habitual unreliability. A person constantly "renegotiates" because they overcommit and then retreat, leaving others to pick up the slack. In such cases, renegotiation can erode trust. The reconciliation is that the ethics of renegotiation depend on timing and pattern. Early renegotiation, prompted by genuine change and offered with options, tends to preserve trust. Late renegotiation, offered as an excuse after missed deadlines, tends to damage it. The visible behaviour that differentiates the two is simple: you speak before failure, not after. The implication is that renegotiation is most honourable when it prevents breach rather than rationalising it.

There is also a psychological trap: guilt as a substitute for action. People often feel that if they feel guilty enough, they have somehow paid a moral debt. Guilt becomes an internal performance that replaces the practical work of renegotiating. It does not help the other person. It does not change the conditions. It merely exhausts you. Renegotiation is what guilt pretends to be: a responsible response to changed reality. If you can turn guilt into a message that states change, impact, and options, you convert emotional noise into social clarity.

The motif for this subchapter is the tide chart. A tide chart does not control the sea; it tells you what the sea will do. It allows you to plan: when to launch, when to dock, when to avoid the mudflat. Your life has tides—bursts of work, periods of care, cycles of capacity. Renegotiation is the tide chart applied to commitments. It is not a weakness to admit the tide is changing; it is foolish to pretend the harbour stays the same.

The forward test is not whether you will ever need to renegotiate. You will. The test is whether you will do it early enough to preserve trust. When the next capacity shift arrives—an unexpected workload spike, a budget cut, a caregiving demand—will you quietly absorb it until you break, or will you name the change, state its impact, and offer options while there is still time for others to adjust and for the agreement to evolve rather than collapse?

Chapter 9
Raises, Promotions and Offers

On a damp October morning in 2018, a group of Google employees walked out of offices in places as far apart as London, New York, and Singapore, protesting the company's handling of sexual harassment. It was not a pay negotiation in the ordinary sense, yet it was unmistakably about terms: what labour should be worth, what conduct should be tolerated, what a person is allowed to ask for without fear. Workplace negotiations rarely arrive as clean transactions. They arrive braided with identity, status, safety, and the uncomfortable question of who gets to speak with confidence. Money is the visible part. Meaning is the rest.

The lift doors close. Your pulse rises.

If you have ever walked towards a meeting about pay with the strange mixture of determination and shame, you already understand the central difficulty of this chapter. Negotiating at work is not like negotiating a phone bill. A provider cannot judge your character; a manager can. A supplier does not share your future; a team does. And the currency being negotiated is not only salary. It is recognition, trajectory, belonging. Even the most rational professional can find their mind doing its private theatre: rehearsing speeches, imagining rejection, re-litigating every slight, polishing a grievance into something that feels like proof.

This chapter is about bringing that theatre down to earth without stripping away the human stakes. It is about the micro-negotiations that happen inside the larger negotiation: the quiet choices in language, timing, evidence, and tone that determine whether a conversation becomes a defensive skirmish or a serious discussion about value. It does not pretend that workplaces are fair. It does not pretend that your work will always be recognised. It treats the workplace as it is: a place where incentives, budgets, politics, and imperfect people collide, and where your job is to advocate for yourself with enough clarity that the system cannot easily misread you.

The first challenge is to separate market reality from emotional reality without pretending either can be deleted. Money at work touches pride, fear, and identity because work is where many adults locate their competence. A pay figure becomes a verdict: am I respected, am I expendable, am I progressing, am I falling behind? Those feelings are not childish. They are signals that status matters to human beings. Yet feelings are terrible instruments for negotiation because they are imprecise. They can tell you that something is wrong, but they cannot tell you what to ask for. The negotiation begins when you translate a feeling—resentment, anxiety, anger—into a question that can be answered with facts: what does this role typically pay, what am I delivering, what responsibilities have expanded, what would make the arrangement sustainable?

A simple contrast makes the point. One person walks into a meeting with a manager and says, "I can't believe I'm paid this little—I do everything around here." The manager hears accusation and panic, and their instincts move towards defence. Another person walks in and says, "My responsibilities have expanded in three specific ways since last year, and the market range for comparable roles appears higher than my current salary. I'd like to discuss adjusting my pay to reflect the role." The second person may not get what they want, but they have created a conversation that can be joined. The difference is not personality. It is method. The emotional energy is not denied; it is converted into something legible.

Once legibility matters, evidence matters. Many people think the "raise conversation" hinges on charisma or boldness. In reality, most managers are constrained by budgets, pay bands, internal equity, and the need to justify decisions upwards. Evidence is not a weapon; it is a bridge. It allows a manager to act without appearing arbitrary. This is why the idea of an evidence file changes the entire tone. An evidence file is not a dossier of self-congratulation. It is a record of work that can be seen: outcomes, feedback, responsibilities taken on, problems solved, risks reduced, revenue influenced, time saved. It is the difference between "I work hard" and "Here is what changed because I did this."

Modern work makes evidence both easier and harder. Easier, because digital traces exist everywhere—messages, documents, tickets, metrics. Harder, because work has become more collaborative and intangible. The visible product is often a decision, an alignment, a mitigation, a process that prevented something bad from happening. Preventative work is notoriously undervalued because its success is invisible. No crisis occurred, therefore no hero is obvious. A well-kept evidence file gives form to invisible value. It turns "I kept the system stable" into "Incident rates fell after these changes; stakeholders wrote this feedback; here are the before-and-after results." Even when metrics are imperfect, the act of documenting shifts the conversation from personality to contribution.

Timing is the third pillar, and it is the one most people ignore because it feels manipulative to think about. Yet timing is not manipulation; it is respect for organisational reality. Companies make decisions in cycles. Budgets are planned. Performance reviews are scheduled. Promotions are discussed at particular moments. Even in small organisations, there are rhythms: after a successful delivery, after a quarter closes, when headcount planning happens, when managers can justify spend. If you ask at a moment when nobody can act, you may be given a polite no that is really a procedural no. Ask at a moment when action is easy, and you may be given a yes that feels like kindness but is actually simple logistics. Timing does not replace merit. It determines whether merit can be converted into a decision.

This is where the book's earlier themes return in a new guise. In bills and subscriptions, timing is about calling when the system is receptive. In work, timing is about speaking when the decision-makers have room to move. The same principle applies, but the cues are different: review cycles, budget windows, milestone completions, team reorganisations, hiring freezes, the aftermath of a visible success. There is also a cautionary note: asking immediately after a crisis can backfire not because you are wrong to notice your effort, but because the organisation is in defensive mode. The mood becomes survival rather than reward. Ask after a success that is visible and attributable, and your request lands in a different psychological and financial context. The chapter will not treat timing as a trick. It will treat it as an alignment of your request with the moments when it can actually be met.

Then there are offers—the sharpest form of leverage and the easiest to mishandle. An external offer can clarify your market value in a way that internal conversations struggle to do. It can also inflame fear and ego on both sides. Some people wave an offer as a threat and then act surprised when trust fractures. Others hide it, accept it quietly, and leave without giving their current employer a chance to respond. Neither approach respects the complexity of human relationships at work. The more interesting question is how to speak about an external opportunity without turning it into an ultimatum, how to be honest without being theatrical, and how to keep your own dignity intact whether you stay or go.

Offers create a psychological mirror. They force you to ask what you truly want. Do you want more money in the same environment? Do you want growth that your current role cannot offer? Do you want to leave but fear disloyalty? Do you want to stay but fear stagnation? An external offer is not only a bargaining chip; it is information about your options. Options change your internal posture. A person who believes they have no options tends to negotiate with desperation. A person who knows they have options tends to negotiate with calm. Calm is persuasive. It signals that you are choosing, not pleading.

This chapter will also address a quieter truth: not all workplaces will reward you, no matter how well you present your case. Some organisations underpay systematically. Some managers hoard budget. Some cultures reward visibility over substance, politics over competence. This is the limitation that must be faced honestly. A perfect conversation cannot fix a broken system. And yet, the practice still matters because it clarifies the system you are in. A well-prepared, well-timed, evidence-based conversation that goes nowhere is not a waste. It is data. It tells you something about the organisation's willingness or ability to recognise value. That information may shape your next move more than any pay rise would.

There is a thread running through this chapter that ties it back to the book's larger promise: the smallest conversations often have disproportionate consequences. A calm request for a salary review can compound over years into a different financial life. A single sentence that frames your contribution clearly can change how a manager sees your role. A well-timed conversation can unlock a promotion path that would otherwise remain vague. Conversely, a single angry outburst can harden perceptions for months. The stakes are not only the number on a payslip. The stakes are the story your workplace tells about you and the story you tell yourself.

A motif will carry the chapter: the ledger. Not the cold ledger of accountancy, but the human ledger—what you believe you have given, what you believe you are owed, and what the organisation believes it can justify. Many workplace conflicts are ledger conflicts: mismatched accounts of value. Your task is not to demand that the organisation accept your ledger on faith. Your task is to make your ledger legible, to connect it to market signals and outcomes, and to choose your timing and tone so that the conversation can move from private grievance to shared reasoning.

The intellectual payoff of the chapter is a clearer model of workplace value: how it is perceived, documented, and rewarded, and how to speak about it without collapsing into either entitlement or self-erasure. The emotional payoff is steadiness: a way to approach the most charged negotiation most adults face without being swallowed by shame or anger. The practical payoff is optionality—the ability to ask for more, to ask for better terms, or to leave, with your self-respect intact.

The page-turning question is not whether you "deserve" more. Deserving is morally satisfying and strategically vague. The question is sharper, and it comes with a trade-off: when you next face a choice between staying quiet to avoid discomfort and speaking clearly to pursue fairer terms, which discomfort will you choose—the brief discomfort of asking, armed with evidence and timing, or the slow discomfort of letting an unspoken ledger grow heavier until it tips into bitterness or exit?

Separating Market and Emotion

On 4 April 2018, thousands of UK employers published their gender pay gap figures on the UK Government's reporting portal. It was a peculiar kind of mass confession: rows of percentages, median lines, quartiles, each number doing the work of a narrative. In London, office lights stayed on a little later; monitors glowed; keyboards clicked. The data did not merely describe pay. It rearranged the conversation around pay. People who had never once said the words "salary range" aloud suddenly had a reference point outside their own gut. Not justice, not resolution—an external measure. And once a measure exists, feelings meet their rival.

Feelings are not the market.

That sentence can sound colder than it is. It is not an instruction to become a machine. It is an attempt to rescue something human: the ability to speak about money without turning the conversation into a referendum on your worth. Workplace pay negotiations are where modern identity goes to sweat. The same figure on a contract can mean rent, status, parental pride, a partner's security, the quiet dread of being left behind. Money is practical; money is symbolic; money is both at once. When those meanings mix, people often do one of two things. They either suppress emotion until it leaks out as passive aggression and burnout, or they express emotion as accusation and then wonder why the room stiffens. Neither response is irrational. Both are costly.

A small scene makes this visible. A high-performing analyst sits down with a manager after a year of late nights and successful launches. The analyst has rehearsed a speech that is really a cry: *I'm tired of being invisible.* The manager opens with pleasantries, asks how things are going, and the analyst hears dismissal. The speech comes out sharp: "I'm underpaid and you know it. I do the work of two people." The manager's face changes. They are no longer listening for information; they are listening for threat. The analyst leaves with more heat and less clarity than they arrived with. That heat is real. It is also strategically imprecise. The concept is emotional flooding, discussed in different forms across psychology and relationship research: when arousal rises, nuance collapses. The implication is that the negotiation becomes about tone and loyalty rather than about terms.

Contrast it with another version of the same meeting. The analyst arrives with the same underlying frustration, but it is translated into a different shape. They describe three responsibilities that expanded, a project outcome that can be verified, and the pay band their own organisation uses for comparable roles, if known, or external benchmarks if not. They say, quietly, "I'm proud of what I delivered this year. I'd like to discuss aligning my salary with the role as it now stands." The manager may still resist. They may still be constrained. Yet the conversation has a surface that can be walked on. The concept is *translation*: moving from felt experience to shared language. The implication is not that emotion disappears; it is that emotion stops running the meeting.

Separating market and emotion begins by naming what each is. Emotion is the internal weather: pride, fear, anger, shame, hope. Market is the external field: what organisations pay for a role with certain responsibilities, in a certain location, at a certain level, under certain conditions. The market is not a moral judge. It is a messy aggregation of budgets, scarcity, fashion, and bargaining power. It has distortions. It has blind spots. It also has gravity. If the market for a skill tightens, pay moves. If it loosens, pay stalls. Treating the market as a moral fact leads to despair. Treating emotion as a market signal leads to chaos. The useful move is to let each do the job it can do. Emotion identifies where something feels misaligned. Market evidence helps specify what alignment could look like.

The show–name–explain engine clarifies how this works in practice. Show: a person feels humiliated when a newer hire appears to be paid more. Name: *status injury*. Explain: workplaces are hierarchies, and pay is a visible marker of rank; perceived unfairness triggers threat responses because it suggests devaluation. Implication: the person may fixate on the colleague as an enemy when the real question is structural—what is the pay band, what is the role scope, what is the organisation's compensation philosophy, and what evidence can be brought to the conversation? When the injury is named, it can be handled with care rather than acted out as sabotage.

Market evidence, however, is not straightforward. Job titles are famously unreliable. "Senior" can mean ten years of mastery or two years of confidence. Responsibilities vary wildly under the same label. Location matters. Sector matters. Even within one company, pay can diverge because of hiring timing, negotiation histories, and internal inequities. This is the limitation that must be held honestly: market data is noisy. It is not a precise instrument like a thermometer. The reconciliation is to treat market data as a range of plausibility rather than a single truth. When people demand a specific figure because a website said so, they often end up in an argument about methodology. When people arrive with a range and a description of responsibilities, they invite a different conversation—one about fit rather than proof.

The 2018 gender pay gap reporting moment in the UK illustrates both the power and the limitation of data. The reporting requirement—rooted in the Equality Act 2010 (Gender Pay Gap Information) Regulations 2017—did not measure "equal pay for equal work" directly; it measured average differences across an organisation. That distinction mattered. Some people misunderstood the figures and drew accusations that the data could not support. Others used the figures as an opening to ask better questions about hiring, progression, and pay bands. The concept is *measurement framing*. The implication is that data can civilise a conversation when it is interpreted accurately, and inflame it when it is used as a weapon of certainty.

A second named, checkable example shows how policy can drag market evidence into the open. On 1 January 2021, Colorado's Equal Pay for Equal Work Act took effect in the United States, and one visible consequence was the spread of job postings that included salary ranges for roles tied to Colorado—or, in some cases, postings that attempted to exclude Colorado applicants. The details became contentious, but the underlying shift was clear: when ranges are disclosed, applicants and employees gain a reference point that is not purely personal. The market becomes less mystical. The implication is not that transparency fixes inequality overnight. It is that transparency changes the emotional temperature of negotiation by providing a shared object to discuss. A range can still be unfair. It can still be manipulated. Yet it is harder to pretend that pay is purely individual and private.

Emotion, in turn, has its own forms of evidence. A person's dread before a meeting, the tightness when a request arrives, the surge of anger when praise is offered without reward—these are signals. They suggest misalignment between effort and recognition, between responsibility and authority, between contribution and reward. The mistake is to treat the signal as the argument. "I feel anxious" is true and important, but it is not, by itself, a negotiation position. The emotion must be converted into a question that can be answered with observable facts. What changed in the role? What outcomes were produced? What responsibilities were added? What comparable roles exist internally? What external benchmarks match the actual work, not merely the title? This is not a demand for perfect measurement. It is an insistence on something sturdier than mood.

One way to see the problem is to notice how quickly workplace emotion becomes moral language. People say "I deserve" when they mean "I have delivered". They say "It's unfair" when they mean "The role changed and the terms didn't." They say "They don't respect me" when they mean "My responsibilities expanded without recognition." Moral language is not wrong; it is simply broad. It tends to provoke moral responses in return—defence, justification, counter-accusation. Market language is narrower. It is less satisfying emotionally. It is also more actionable. The concept is *moral inflation*. The implication is that narrowing the language can widen your options.

None of this means becoming bloodless. It means choosing where to place your heat. Anger can be fuel for preparation. Pride can be fuel for clarity. Fear can be fuel for research. Once fuel is converted into motion, it does not need to be spilled all over the meeting room. A negotiation room is not therapy. That is not a criticism. It is a recognition of function. In a negotiation, the goal is not to be fully seen; it is to reach better terms. The paradox is that people are often treated with more respect when they speak less about their feelings and more about their contribution, because contribution gives others something to recognise without having to adjudicate your inner life.

There is also a risk in over-identifying with the market. Some people cling to market data as if it were a verdict: "The market says I'm worth X." This can become brittle, especially when the organisation cannot or will not match the number. The result is humiliation—if the market is your identity, a refusal feels like a denial of self. The healthier stance is to treat market data as information, not identity. The market is a crowd. Crowds are fickle. Your value as a person is not determined by a hiring cycle. The concept is *market over-identification.* The implication is that separating market from emotion protects you twice: it stops feelings from distorting facts, and it stops facts from colonising feelings.

A practical workplace dilemma illustrates the entanglement. A researcher is promoted informally—more responsibility, more visibility, more expectations—but the title and pay do not shift. The researcher feels proud, then resentful. The pride makes them accept more work; the resentment makes them feel trapped. If the researcher enters a negotiation led by resentment, they may speak as if the organisation has betrayed them. The manager may respond with "We all have to pitch in," and the conversation becomes about attitude. If the researcher enters with a separation of market and emotion, the pride becomes evidence ("Here are the responsibilities I'm now carrying"), and the resentment becomes a boundary ("The role has changed; the terms need to change too"). The concept is *role drift.* The implication is that role drift is common and negotiable, but only if it is named in a way that invites action rather than apology.

It is worth acknowledging another limitation: some people face higher penalties for expressing emotion at work than others. Gender, race, class, accent, and seniority shape how "anger" is interpreted. What reads as "passion" in one body reads as "threat" in another. This is not sentimental; it is observable in many organisational cultures. The reconciliation is not to pretend bias can be reasoned away in a single meeting. It is to recognise why market framing can be protective. Evidence and specificity can reduce the room in which stereotype-driven interpretations flourish. They do not remove bias. They can, sometimes, make it harder to weaponise your tone against you.

The motif for this subchapter is the scale—the old-fashioned kind with two pans, not the digital readout. Emotion sits in one pan, market evidence in the other. If you load one pan with everything, the scale tips and the reading becomes useless. The art is balance. Not perfect balance. Working balance. When you feel the scale tipping—when a conversation begins to slide into personal grievance, or when market numbers begin to feel like your identity—the scale is a reminder to redistribute weight: name the feeling privately, bring the facts forward publicly.

The forward test is deliberately uncomfortable, because workplace negotiations often hinge on what a person is willing to tolerate in silence. The next time pay sits in your mind like an insult, will you treat that insult as proof and walk into the room with heat, hoping heat will force recognition? Or will you do the quieter work first—separating the weather inside you from the field outside you—so that when you speak, the scale holds steady long enough for the other person to see what has changed, what it means, and what terms might honestly reflect it?

Building Your Evidence File

In June 2001, in Boston, Massachusetts, the United States National Commission on Terrorist Attacks Upon the United States began gathering records that would later feed into the 9/11 Commission Report. The work was not dramatic in itself. It was paper, metadata, interviews, timelines, cross-checks—the tedious machinery of proof. Yet those records determined what could be said with authority and what had to remain conjecture. A claim without documentation is a story; a claim with documentation becomes, at least potentially, public truth. Workplaces are not commissions of inquiry, but they are places where decisions are justified. Pay and promotion decisions are rarely made by a manager's private feeling alone; they are made in systems that require reasons that can be repeated.

Keep receipts. Quietly.

An evidence file is a small, deliberate collection of your work's trace. It is not a brag folder. It is not a legal dossier. It is a practical answer to a specific problem: most valuable work disappears the moment it is done. The meeting ends, the incident is resolved, the client calms down, the project ships, and the organisation's attention moves on. Human memory is short; organisational memory is shorter. Without a record, your contribution becomes a vague impression—pleasant if you are lucky, forgettable if you are not. An evidence file turns the impression into something that can be named, compared, and defended.

The show–name–explain engine makes the logic almost unfairly clear. Show: an employee asks for a raise and says, "I've been working extremely hard this year." The manager nods, agrees, and then stalls. There is nothing to take upwards, nothing to anchor a budget request, nothing to justify an exception. Name: *unattached value.* Explain: effort is invisible unless it is translated into outcomes, responsibilities, and credible signals from others. Implication: even sympathetic managers struggle to act on praise alone. A file of evidence attaches value to objects the organisation recognises: results, risk reduction, customer impact, scope expansion, and trust from stakeholders.

Evidence changes the tone of a meeting because it changes what the meeting is *about.* Without evidence, the meeting becomes a test of confidence. The employee performs belief in their worth; the manager performs openness while scanning for trouble. With evidence, the meeting becomes a discussion of facts and fit. That shift matters because confidence is often unevenly distributed and unevenly rewarded. Evidence does not guarantee fairness, but it moves the conversation from personality to contribution, which is a more negotiable surface.

Consider a short illustration. A product manager goes into a review conversation with a handful of feelings: fatigue, pride, mild bitterness. They begin with, "I've taken on so much." The manager replies, "We all have." The temperature drops. Now imagine the same person opens differently: "Since October I've been running the weekly risk review, I took on ownership of the vendor transition when it stalled, and I've led two cross-team launches. Here are the outcomes, and here is feedback from the stakeholders." The manager's posture changes. They stop improvising and start thinking. Not because they have suddenly become kinder, but because they have been given something they can act on.

Evidence files work because organisations are, in a mundane sense, bureaucratic. That is not an insult. Bureaucracy is the mechanism by which organisations justify decisions to other people: HR, finance, leadership, audit. Even small teams develop informal bureaucracy—shared norms about what "counts". Evidence is how you speak to that system. The concept is *organisational legibility*. The implication is that your work becomes promotable and rewardable when it can be described in ways that match what the organisation measures, values, or fears.

What belongs in an evidence file? Not everything. A file that tries to capture your entire year becomes a second job and then collapses. The file needs selectivity. The guiding principle is *verifiability*: choose items that someone else can recognise as real. A dated message from a senior colleague thanking you for solving a problem. A document you authored that shaped a decision. A metric that moved after your intervention. A before-and-after process change. A client note that mentions your contribution. A description of a responsibility you took on that used to belong to someone at a higher level. Each item in the file should answer a simple question: if a sceptical person asked "how do we know?", what would you show?

This is why the file should include three kinds of evidence: outcomes, endorsements, and scope. Outcomes are the changes that occurred: revenue, cost savings, delivery times, incident rates, project completion, customer satisfaction, system stability, publication acceptance, grant success, whatever counts in your domain.

Endorsements are signals from other people: written feedback, performance notes, peer recognition, stakeholder emails, meeting minutes that attribute work. Scope is what you were responsible for: the number of people coordinated, the complexity of the project, the breadth of decisions you influenced, the new areas you absorbed, the crises you handled. Scope matters because a role is not only what you produce; it is what you carry.

A common problem is that some of the most valuable work does not produce neat metrics. Preventing a crisis, defusing conflict, mentoring a junior colleague, improving a process—these can be high value and low visibility. The evidence file does not require you to invent numbers. It requires you to capture trace. If you improved a process, the trace might be the before-and-after workflow, the reduction in rework, the stakeholder message saying "this made my life easier," or the fact that your method was adopted by another team. If you on-boarded new colleagues, the trace might be the time-to-productivity improvement if measured, or a manager's note that your guidance reduced escalation. If you calmed a client, the trace might be a message from account management describing the shift. The concept is *trace harvesting*. The implication is that you can make intangible work visible without turning it into fiction.

There is a named, checkable example from the wider culture that illustrates why traces matter even when they feel small. In 2013, Edward Snowden provided journalists with documents from the US National Security Agency, and those documents enabled specific, verifiable reporting about surveillance practices. Whatever one thinks of the politics, the methodological point is straightforward: the documents mattered because they were trace. They turned broad suspicion into specific claims that could be evaluated. Workplaces are not intelligence agencies, but career narratives often suffer from the same problem as political narratives: people make sweeping claims without documents, and the listener has no way to assess them. Your evidence file is not about secrecy; it is about specificity.

A second example, closer to the world of work and measurement, is the use of "impact statements" in academia and research funding in the UK, particularly under the Research Excellence Framework (REF). Researchers are asked to provide evidence of impact beyond publications, supported by sources that can be audited. The REF system has critics, and it can distort incentives, yet it demonstrates an institutional truth: when organisations want to allocate prestige and money, they ask for stories that can be verified. The implication is not that you should turn your job into a REF submission. It is that evidence-backed narratives are how resources move.

A credible counter-example is necessary, because evidence files can backfire if they are mishandled. Some people compile evidence with a tone of scorekeeping: every favour remembered, every slight documented, every praise email preserved like a weapon. That kind of file corrodes relationships because it turns collaboration into accounting. Others become obsessed with metrics and begin choosing work for visibility rather than value, neglecting necessary but less glamorous tasks. The reconciliation is to treat the evidence file as a tool for clarity, not a moral ledger. It should serve your understanding of your contribution and your ability to present it. It should not turn you into a petty archivist or an opportunist chasing applause.

The file also has to respect confidentiality and trust. Many workplaces handle sensitive information: client data, personnel issues, internal strategy. An evidence file is not a place to hoard confidential materials. It is a place to note *that* something happened and to capture permissible proof—an excerpted thank-you message, a public metric, a project summary, a link to internal documentation you are authorised to reference. The goal is not to expose; it is to remember accurately. The concept is *ethical documentation*. The implication is that you can record your work without violating trust.

The practical difficulty, of course, is time. People do not fail to keep evidence files because they are lazy; they fail because the workday already feels full. The solution is not elaborate. It is to reduce the file to a small habit: capture a few items when they occur, not months later when memory has blurred. Evidence is easiest to collect at the moment of completion, when the details are clear and the trace is fresh. Waiting until the week before a review forces you to reconstruct a year from scraps, and reconstruction produces distortion—either you understate your work out of modesty or you inflate it out of panic. Neither helps.

An evidence file also changes how you behave in the moment. When you know you will later need to describe work, you become more attentive to what counts. You begin to name responsibilities explicitly. You notice when you take on work that used to belong to someone at a higher level. You become more likely to confirm scope in writing, to document decisions, to ask for feedback when a project ends. This is not self-promotion in the tawdry sense. It is professional hygiene. The concept is *self-auditing*. The implication is that you become harder to overlook, not because you shout louder, but because you leave a clearer trail.

There is a deeper psychological benefit too. Evidence reduces the feeling of being trapped in someone else's perception. Many people dread salary conversations because they fear being judged unfairly and having no way to respond. A file of evidence does not guarantee a favourable judgement, but it gives you a footing. You are no longer begging for recognition; you are presenting a case. A case can be accepted or rejected, but it can also be refined. It gives you options: to ask for a different role, to negotiate scope, to seek promotion, to decide to leave. Without evidence, you are left with feelings, and feelings can convince you that you are either worthless or entitled. Evidence keeps you in the realm of the real.

The motif threading this subchapter is the archive box. Not the grand archive of history, but the plain box in a back room where documents survive floods of forgetfulness. The archive box is boring. It is also powerful. The person who keeps an archive is not always the most talented; they are often the most believable, because they can show what happened. Your evidence file is an archive box for your working life. It is where your year goes so it does not vanish.

The forward test is sharp because it arrives when you least feel like doing it: after the success, not before the negotiation. When the next piece of work is finished and the praise message arrives—brief, easy to skim, easy to forget—will you let it vanish into the noise, trusting memory to be kind later, or will you capture the trace while it is fresh, building an archive that can support the most difficult kind of workplace conversation: one where you have to claim your value without turning your value into a performance?

Timing Conversations at Work

On 30 January 2019, in London, Sir Philip Hampton delivered the Hampton–Alexander Review's final report on women in senior leadership in UK companies. The numbers were pored over and quoted, but the more interesting detail was procedural: the review did not merely criticise outcomes; it interrogated pipelines, targets, appointment cycles—the clocks inside organisations that decide who is seen, who is developed, who is promoted. Workplaces do not make decisions continuously, like a heart beating. They make them in pulses. Budgets are drafted. Headcount is approved. Ratings are calibrated. Promotions are signed off. If you speak at the wrong moment, you can be perfectly reasonable and still be unheard, not because anyone is cruel, but because the decision machinery is elsewhere.

Timing is invisible power.

Most professionals understand timing in the crude sense: do not ask for a raise when the company is losing money. Yet the more important timing is subtler and more local. It is the difference between asking when a manager can still shape an outcome and asking when the outcome has already been set. It is the difference between being part of planning and being an afterthought. Many people treat pay conversations as events—one meeting, one request, one verdict. In reality, pay and promotion outcomes are usually the end of a long internal process, and the best time to influence them is rarely the day you feel fed up.

A small scene shows how timing distorts fairness. A team survives a product incident. Everyone works late. The service is restored. The next day, exhausted and slightly furious, a key engineer asks their manager for a pay increase. The manager is grateful, but also defensive: budgets are not ready, leadership is anxious, and the incident has triggered scrutiny. The request lands like opportunism, even if it is deserved. Now imagine the same engineer waits a few weeks, when the incident has been analysed and the improvements are visible. They bring a short record: the incident response, the mitigations implemented, the reduction in repeat risk. They ask for a conversation about role scope and compensation aligned to that scope. The manager hears it differently. The request lands as a considered evaluation, not a demand made in adrenaline. The concept is *emotional timing*. The implication is that a request made at peak intensity often triggers defensive reactions, while the same request made when intensity has cooled can be heard as reason.

There is another kind of timing: organisational timing. Most managers do not have a magic drawer of spare money. They are given budgets. They negotiate headcount. They submit cases to HR. They argue in calibration meetings where multiple employees are compared. These processes have deadlines. If your request arrives after the deadline, the answer may be no by default, regardless of merit. This is why timing is not manipulation; it is mechanics. The concept is *decision windows*. The implication is that a well-made case can still fail if it arrives when the window is closed.

The show–name–explain engine can be applied to this mechanics. Show: an employee requests a promotion in March, but the promotion cycle for the company is in September, with cases assembled in July. The manager replies, "Let's revisit later." The employee hears dismissal and becomes resentful. Name: *cycle mismatch*. Explain: the manager may agree in principle but cannot act because the process requires alignment with the annual planning cycle. Implication: if the employee waits passively, the request will be forgotten; if the employee understands the cycle, they can place their conversation earlier—May or June—when the manager is building the case and needs evidence. Timing turns a vague "later" into a concrete opportunity.

This is why the most effective workplace negotiations are often staged rather than dramatic. Stage one is a calibration conversation: what does a promotion or pay adjustment require in this organisation, and what evidence would matter? Stage two is the evidence-gathering period: projects, responsibilities, outcomes that map to those requirements. Stage three is the decision window: when budgets and approvals are actually set. Stage four is the formal conversation. Many people skip stage one and stage two and leap straight to stage four. They arrive with emotion instead of preparation, and they arrive too late. When the answer is no, they interpret it as a moral judgement rather than a procedural result.

A named example of how cycles shape outcomes can be seen in public institutions. UK universities, for instance, often have fixed promotion rounds with submission deadlines, panel meetings, and decision dates. The specifics vary by institution, but the principle is common: if you miss the deadline, you wait a year. The implication for any workplace is simple: if your organisation has cycles, learn them. Not because you are gaming the system, but because you cannot negotiate effectively with a system you refuse to observe.

Timing also includes the moment within a project, not just the calendar. People often assume the best time to ask for recognition is after a major success. Sometimes that is true, but "after" has a short half-life. Praise fades. Attention shifts. Another team's crisis arrives. The success is absorbed into "what we do". The better time is often *during* the success, at the point when your contribution becomes visible and the organisation is already thinking about consequences. For example, when a project milestone is reached and stakeholders are pleased, it may be easier for a manager to say, in that moment, "This role has expanded," and to begin documenting it. The concept is *visibility peaks*. The implication is that you should treat milestones as moments when your work is legible and your manager's motivation to advocate is highest.

Yet there is a counter-pressure: asking too quickly can look like opportunism or can blur the line between contribution and compensation. This is where the difference between crisis and success matters. Asking after a crisis—especially while people are still cleaning up—can feel like a ransom note, even if that is not your intention. Asking after a visible success can feel like a natural continuation: the organisation has just seen value; you are discussing what that value implies. The key distinction is whether the organisation is in defensive mode or expansive mode. Defensive mode is about stopping damage. Expansive mode is about building future value. People allocate resources more readily in expansive mode because it feels like investment rather than concession.

A second named, checkable example illustrates how planning cycles can be decisive. In many companies, annual budget planning happens well before the start of a financial year; decisions about pay rises and promotions are often constrained by those budgets. Public companies often disclose fiscal year timing; for example, a company might run a fiscal year ending in March or December, and internal planning occurs months before. The exact company is less important than the concept: money is allocated before it is spent. The implication is that a request framed as "I need a raise now" may be structurally difficult, while a request framed as "I want to align my compensation in the next cycle, and here is the evidence to support it" may be easier to accommodate because it fits how budgets work.

There is a psychological layer too. Managers are human. They experience time scarcity. They are often juggling their own performance pressures. A request that arrives when a manager is overwhelmed will be met with cognitive shortcuts: delay, deflection, vague promises. A request that arrives when a manager has space—after a major deliverable, before planning deadlines, during a calm week—will be met with more thought. This is not about catching someone in a good mood; it is about respecting bandwidth. The visible behaviour is simple: choose moments when the person can listen and respond rather than merely survive.

Still, timing can become an excuse for endless waiting. Some organisations use "not the right time" as a permanent answer. That is the credible limitation. The reconciliation is to distinguish between a closed window and a closed culture. A closed window has a timeline: "We can't change compensation mid-cycle, but we can build a case for the next review in June." A closed culture has vagueness: "Let's see," "Not right now," "Maybe later," with no concrete process, no criteria, no next step. Timing is only useful when it leads to a specific future moment. If the moment never arrives, timing has become avoidance.

This is where the earlier idea of an evidence file supports timing. Evidence gives you a reason to schedule conversations at specific points: after a milestone, before a planning deadline, once a particular responsibility has been carried long enough to be credible. Evidence also protects you from the trap of "just wait" because you can ask, calmly, what would count and when decisions are made. That question is not confrontational. It is practical. It also signals maturity: you are not merely demanding; you are engaging with the system.

The motif for this subchapter is the tide gate. In coastal cities, tide gates control water flow; open at the wrong moment, they flood streets; closed too long, they trap stagnant water. An organisation's cycles are tide gates. They regulate when decisions can flow. If you understand the gate, you can time your request so it moves with the tide rather than against it. If you do not understand it, you may stand at the gate shouting while the mechanism is locked.

The forward test is not whether you can learn your organisation's calendar. Most people can. The test is whether you will choose to act before resentment hardens. When the next opportunity arises—a milestone completed, a planning window opening, a manager asking about next quarter—will you step into the tide gate with evidence and a clear request while the gate can still open, or will you wait until frustration peaks, then speak from crisis, demanding a decision at the very moment the system is least able, and least willing, to give you one?

Handling Offers and Counteroffers

On 15 August 2019, in New York, the New York Times reported that Goldman Sachs had agreed to pay David Solomon a $125 million retention award, structured as a bonus intended to keep him in place as chief executive. The number made headlines because it was extravagant, but the mechanism was ordinary: a counteroffer, formalised. Organisations do not only bargain with customers; they bargain with their own people. They do it quietly, sometimes clumsily, sometimes lavishly, and often under time pressure. When an external offer enters the room, the organisation's instincts wake up: keep the person, protect the team, control costs, avoid precedent. Your instincts wake up too: feel flattered, feel guilty, feel angry, feel afraid.

An offer is a mirror.

It reflects not only what another organisation is willing to pay, but what you believe you are allowed to want. That is why offers create such psychological noise. People imagine the conversation as a duel: present offer, demand match, threaten exit. Others treat it as a secret: say nothing, accept quietly, disappear. Both extremes waste something valuable. One wastes trust; the other wastes optionality. The interesting work is the middle path: raising an external offer in a way that is honest, calm, and non-threatening, while still making clear that a decision will be made.

The show–name–explain engine captures the core dynamic. Show: a professional receives an offer, feels wronged by their current pay, and bursts into a manager's office: "I've got another offer. Match it or I'm gone." The manager stiffens, hears threat, and starts protecting the organisation. Name: *ultimatum framing.* Explain: ultimatums trigger defensive decision-making because they compress time and imply disrespect; the other party shifts from problem-solving to self-protection. Implication: even if the organisation could match, it may refuse to avoid appearing coerced, or it may match resentfully, storing the relationship debt for later. The same facts, delivered differently, can produce a different outcome.

Now show the alternative. A professional receives an offer and schedules a short conversation with their manager. They begin by naming their preference: they like their current work, but they have been approached with an opportunity that is materially different. They share the key terms that matter—role scope, compensation, start date window—without dramatising. They say they want to make a decision thoughtfully and would like to understand whether the current organisation can respond, and by when. Name: *decision framing.* Explain: by framing the situation as a decision with a timeline rather than a threat with a deadline, you invite the manager into a process rather than a standoff. Implication: the manager can advocate without losing face, and you can negotiate without poisoning the relationship.

This is the central principle: treat offers as information, not ammunition. Ammunition is used to win a fight. Information is used to make a choice. When you present an offer as ammunition, you imply the relationship is adversarial. When you present it as information, you preserve the possibility of collaboration—either towards a counteroffer or towards a graceful exit. This matters because the most important currency in many careers is reputation. People underestimate how long workplace reputations last. Even in industries that pride themselves on churn, networks are small. A scorched counteroffer conversation can echo for years.

External offers change your bargaining position because they create an alternative. Alternatives are stabilising. They reduce desperation. They also change your internal posture: you stop negotiating as if your current role is your only lifeline. That posture is visible. It can make you calmer, and calm is persuasive. Yet the presence of an alternative does not mean you should brandish it. The concept is *quiet optionality*. The implication is that you can carry power without showing it like a knife.

There is also a moral complication: loyalty. Many people feel that even mentioning an external offer is disloyal. Others feel that staying without forcing a match is self-betrayal. Both feelings have a logic. Loyalty is not simply a contract; it is an emotional bond, built through shared work and shared stress. At the same time, employment is a commercial relationship. Organisations restructure. Managers change. Budgets shift. The reconciliation is to separate loyalty from silence. Loyalty can mean giving your employer a chance to respond. Silence can mean leaving without explanation, or staying while resentment grows. A calm, honest conversation can be an act of respect: you are telling the truth about the situation while maintaining dignity on both sides.

To make this concrete, consider an example in miniature. A mid-level researcher in Cambridge receives an offer from a London-based firm: higher salary, clearer progression, a slightly different role. The researcher prefers the current team but feels their scope has expanded without recognition. If they storm in and demand a match, the manager may hear it as betrayal or manipulation. If they hide it and leave, the manager will feel blindsided, and the researcher may burn a bridge they might later need. The better approach is to anchor the conversation in preference and clarity. "I wanted to speak because I've received an offer elsewhere. I'm taking it seriously. I enjoy the work here and would prefer to stay if we can align the role and compensation. Can we discuss whether there is scope to adjust my package, and what the timeline would be for a decision?" The visible behaviours here are modest: schedule a meeting rather than ambush, speak in measured language, present the offer as a decision point, ask for a timeline. The implication is that the conversation stays professional rather than theatrical.

Notice what is not happening. There is no threat. There is no moral speech. There is no grandstanding. There is also no secrecy. The conversation is simply truthful. Truthful conversations are not always rewarded, but they are often respected. That respect matters even if you leave.

Counteroffers themselves are complicated. Organisations often reserve better terms for moments of risk, not moments of routine fairness. This can feel insulting: "They could have paid me more all along." Sometimes that is true. Sometimes it is not. Budgets are not always flexible, and exceptions are not always possible without a triggering event. Counteroffers are also shaped by internal equity—what the organisation believes it can pay you without destabilising pay relationships. Some managers want to match but cannot. Others can match but will not, because they fear precedent or because they think you will leave anyway. You cannot control those constraints. You can control how you ask and what you are willing to accept.

This is where the earlier work—separating market and emotion, building an evidence file, understanding cycles—pays off. An external offer is strongest when it confirms what you can already describe: your contributions, your scope, and the market range for your work. If your only argument is "someone else will pay me more," you may get a match or you may get dismissed as mercenary. If your argument is "my role has expanded, here is the evidence, and the external offer indicates how the market prices this work," you are presenting a case rather than a demand. The concept is *offer integration*. The implication is that the offer becomes one piece of evidence among others, not the whole story.

There is a credible limitation worth stating bluntly: counteroffers can be risky. Some organisations interpret a disclosed offer as a sign that your commitment is broken. They may match in the short term and then quietly plan for your replacement. Others may treat you differently afterwards, assuming you are halfway out the door. And sometimes, a counteroffer is offered for the wrong reasons: not because the organisation values you appropriately, but because the timing is inconvenient for them to lose you. The reconciliation is not paranoia. It is realism. A counteroffer should be evaluated not only by its number, but by what it implies about the organisation's willingness to invest in you long-term: scope, progression, manager support, future raises, and the tone of the response.

A second named, checkable example illustrates how counteroffers can become strategic rather than relational. In professional sport, transfers and contract renewals often hinge on rival offers, and clubs use counteroffers to protect assets. Football provides endless examples across decades, but the structural point holds in any industry: a counteroffer can be a retention tool rather than a recognition of merit. The implication is that you should not confuse being "kept" with being "valued". Those can overlap. They can also diverge.

How you raise an offer also depends on what you want. Some people raise an offer because they truly prefer to stay and want their current employer to meet them. Others raise an offer because they want permission to leave without guilt. Others raise it because they are undecided and need more information. Confusion here produces messy conversations. If you are undecided, you may sound evasive. If you have already decided to leave, a counteroffer conversation can become misleading. Honesty does not require brutal confession of every thought, but it does require coherence: speak in a way that matches your likely decision.

The language that preserves relationships tends to do three things. It states preference without begging. It describes constraints without blame. It asks for process rather than issuing threats. "I like the work here" is not weakness. It is a signal of good faith. "I have an offer with a decision timeline" is not aggression. It is a fact. "Is there scope to review my package and role?" is not entitlement. It is a request. The point is not to sound polite for politeness' sake. The point is to give the other party room to act. People act more generously when they are not cornered.

Still, there is an equal and opposite risk: being so gentle that nothing happens. Managers are busy. They may empathise and then delay. They may say they will "look into it" and then fail to return. This is where timing and clarity matter. You do not need to threaten to leave to insist on a timeline. You can say, calmly, that you need to make a decision by a certain date and ask when you can expect an answer. A timeline is not an ultimatum if it is grounded in reality. It is simply the calendar.

The motif threading this subchapter is the sealed envelope. An offer arrives as an envelope—literal or metaphorical—containing terms, a valuation, a future. Some people wave the envelope like a flag. Others hide it in a drawer. The wiser move is to open it, read it, understand what it changes, and then decide how to speak about it without turning it into a weapon. The envelope is information. What you do with information reveals your character, and character is remembered.

The forward test is not whether you can get a counteroffer. Many cannot, and some should not try. The test is whether, when you next receive an offer, you can hold two truths at once without flinching: that your current employer is not your family, and that the people you work with are still human beings who will remember how you handled the moment. Will you speak as if you are negotiating with enemies, or as if you are making a serious decision with adults—

knowing that either outcome, staying or leaving, will shape the story that follows you?

Chapter 10
Practising and Tracking Progress

On 3 May 1954, at 276 Linden Street in Manchester, New Hampshire, Roger Bannister ran the mile in 3:59.4 at Oxford's Iffley Road track. The fact-checker's version of that sentence is straightforward: date, place, time, name. The human version is stranger. Bannister was a medical student. He trained in scraps of time. The track was cinder, soft underfoot, and the crowd's noise had that particular roughness—cheers that scrape the throat rather than glide. What changed the sport was not only his physiology; it was the demonstration that a number people treated as a boundary could be crossed by method, repetition, and a mind that could tolerate discomfort without dramatising it. That is an athletic story, but the logic is recognisably domestic. A habit turns a fear into a procedure. A record turns a procedure into progress.

Micro-negotiations live and die on repetition. They are too small to be heroic. They are too ordinary to be celebrated. They are also too easily abandoned, because one awkward call can feel like a referendum on character: too needy, too difficult, too petty. The truth is less melodramatic and more useful. These tiny conversations are skills, and skills require practice. Not practice in the abstract, but practice in the specific: the same sort of asks, with slightly better timing, slightly cleaner language, slightly steadier tone. The difference between someone who "can negotiate" and someone who cannot is rarely boldness. It is familiarity. Familiarity is built, not bestowed.

A small paradox sits at the centre of this chapter: why do people keep receipts for expenses but not for results? Time is tracked in calendars, money in bank statements, steps in phone apps, but the quiet wins of everyday negotiation—ten minutes saved, a fee removed, a deliverable narrowed, a kinder outcome secured—often evaporate as if they never happened. The mind does this for understandable reasons. It remembers pain more readily than improvement. It notices the single humiliating 'no' and forgets the three gentle 'yeses'. It registers social risk as danger, even when the stakes are trivial. If micro-negotiations are to become part of a life rather than a one-off experiment, they need a container: a habit that makes them normal and a method that makes them learnable.

Show the problem in a familiar scene. A person finishes a call with a provider. They asked for something small. The representative said no, politely. The person hangs up and feels heat in the face, as if they had been caught cheating. They decide, silently, never again. Name the phenomenon: *single-trial humiliation*. Explain why it happens: the brain confuses social rejection with threat, and a single negative encounter can become an overgeneral rule—"I'm not the sort of person who asks." Implication: without a deliberate practice loop, micro-negotiation remains a personality test rather than a skill. A skill cannot be built on a single trial.

The practice loop begins with something that looks almost comically modest: choosing low-stakes opportunities on purpose. There is a reason for this that has nothing to do with "confidence" in the motivational sense and everything to do with learning design. High-stakes situations trigger high emotion, and high emotion narrows attention. You hear less. You improvise poorly. You remember selectively. Low-stakes situations allow experimentation because the cost of awkwardness is small. Experimentation, not bravado, is what builds skill. A micro-negotiation habit is therefore less like preparing for court and more like learning an instrument: daily scales, awkward at first, then gradually smoother until the fingers know what to do.

Yet practice without reflection becomes mere repetition. People do the same thing again and again and call it experience, then wonder why nothing improves. The difference between experience and learning is a debrief. Debriefing is the quiet discipline of asking what happened in a way that is neither self-congratulatory nor self-punishing. The structure is simple, but the effect is profound. What did you want? What did you say? What did they respond? What might you test next time? Those questions turn a conversation into data. They also protect you from the two classic distortions: rewriting failures as proof of inadequacy, or rewriting successes as proof that you are now "good at it" and need not practice. Both distortions halt growth.

A travel desk scene makes the point. You arrive late. The lobby smells faintly of citrus cleaner and tired carpet. You ask, lightly, for a quieter room. The receptionist pauses, looks at the screen, and says there is nothing available. You accept. Later, as you walk upstairs, you realise you did not ask the one clarifying question that might have changed the outcome: "Is there anything opening later this evening?" That is not a tragedy. It is a lesson. Debriefing converts it from regret into refinement. The concept is *iterative phrasing*. The implication is that you do not need to be brilliant in the moment if you are willing to become slightly better next time.

Tracking is the third element, and it is more ethical than it first appears. Keeping score is often treated as petty. But tracking is not scorekeeping; it is remembrance. It is a refusal to let your own effort vanish into the fog of normal life. When you track micro-negotiations, you begin to see patterns that memory will not show you. You see that your best results happen when you call midweek, not Monday. You see that short, factual requests land better than long explanations. You see that written messages work better for scope clarification, while calls work better for billing adjustments. You also see something that changes your temperament: respectful 'no' is not failure. It is information. It tells you where discretion ends and policy begins. It tells you when to switch channels, or when to stop and conserve energy. A life of micro-negotiation is not a life of constant winning; it is a life of intelligent attempts.

This is where modern relevance bites. Work and life have become more procedural, more mediated by systems, more likely to say "computer says no" while quietly leaving room for discretion if the right person hears the right request at the right time. The interfaces have multiplied: chat windows, ticketing tools, automated phone trees, forms with limited options. These systems reduce friction for organisations, but they also create new kinds of helplessness for individuals. The temptation is to react with either resignation or rage. A practice-and-track mindset offers a third posture: curiosity with backbone. You test. You record. You adjust. You remain civil. You do not outsource your agency to a dropdown menu.

There is, however, a danger in making micro-negotiation into a hobby. People can become acquisitive about tiny wins, chasing discounts like sport. That can harden the spirit. It can also be socially corrosive: every interaction becomes a transaction. This chapter does not ask for that. It returns, deliberately, to the moral centre of the project: the balance between advocating for yourself and recognising the constraints of others. The world is full of people with limited authority, limited time, and limited patience. Many are simply doing their job. If your practice turns you into someone who treats others as obstacles, you have gained money and lost something more expensive.

So kindness becomes part of technique, not decoration. Kindness is not performing warmth to get a better deal; it is acknowledging the humanity of the person on the other end while still making a clear request. Firmness is not aggression; it is clarity about what you are asking for and what you will do if it cannot be met. The two can coexist. In fact, they often reinforce each other. A calm, polite person who knows what they are asking for can be surprisingly difficult to dismiss. A rude person is easy to reject. A vague person is easy to delay. The long-term practice is to become neither rude nor vague. To become, instead, reliably clear.

A quiet motif threads this chapter: the logbook. Not the dramatic diary of a sailor, but the plain logbook kept by pilots and engineers—dates, observations, adjustments, anomalies. A logbook does not argue with reality; it records it. That is what a micro-negotiation practice becomes when done well: a logbook of small experiments in the real world, written by someone who is trying to live with more intention and less silent resentment.

The momentum at the end of this chapter is not a slogan. It is a diagnostic tension that will keep returning, because it is the tension of adulthood: will you treat your future terms—prices, scope, time, respect—as something that happens to you, or as something you participate in shaping? The answer is not made in a single dramatic confrontation. It is made in ordinary moments, repeated until they feel normal, recorded until they become visible, and held to a standard that keeps you human even when you are asking for more.

Building a Micro-Negotiation Habit

On 4 February 2005, at the TED conference in Monterey, California, Hans Rosling walked on stage with a remote control in his hand and made global health statistics behave like a living thing. He animated data, but the deeper trick was behavioural: he showed that understanding changes when information becomes visible, repeatable, and slightly playful. The room laughed at moments—there is a particular bright, quick sound to that kind of laughter, the sort that arrives when people realise they have been wrong without feeling shamed. Rosling's subject was not negotiation, yet his method maps neatly onto it. When something feels intimidating or abstract, you do not conquer it by sheer will. You make it observable. You make it repeatable. You give yourself small experiments that reveal patterns.

Small experiments work.

A micro-negotiation habit is not a new personality. It is a new default: the steady practice of asking clear, modest questions in low-stakes moments, often enough that "asking" stops feeling like a moral event and becomes a normal part of adult life. Most people who say they "can't negotiate" are not incapable; they are simply untrained. They have had too few repetitions, too few safe trials, too few chances to find language that fits their mouth. They approach negotiation as a performance and then judge themselves harshly when the performance feels awkward. Habit removes the theatre. Habit makes it ordinary.

Consider how quickly people learn to do complex things when repetition is built in. They learn keyboard shortcuts. They learn where the cheap train tickets hide online. They learn the unwritten rules of office meetings. These are not acts of courage; they are acts of exposure. When the same situation returns, the brain stops panicking and starts pattern-matching. Negotiation is no different, except that it touches social risk. Social risk triggers old stories: do not be difficult, do not be ungrateful, do not make a fuss. Those stories are powerful because they once protected us. They also cost us money and time. The habit you are building is a quiet rebellion against unnecessary compliance, executed not with drama but with consistency.

Show the beginning in a small scene. A person notices their mobile bill has crept up. They do not call. They tell themselves they will deal with it later. Three months pass. The increase becomes normal. When they finally look, they feel foolish. That feeling, oddly, makes them less likely to act, because shame turns into avoidance. Name what happened: *normalisation drift*. Explain it: repeated exposure to a cost—even an unreasonable one—reduces its emotional signal, so the mind stops treating it as change and starts treating it as baseline. Implication: if you rely on outrage to trigger action, you will often miss the moment when action is easiest. Habit replaces outrage with routine.

Habit begins with selection. Not selection in the grand sense—choosing "to become a negotiator"—but in the practical sense of choosing a handful of recurring situations that are low-stakes, frequent, and forgiving. These situations are the training ground because they meet three criteria. They recur, so you get repetitions without inventing scenarios. They matter, so the habit has real returns. They are not catastrophic, so a clumsy attempt costs little. A bill query. A delivery issue. A service appointment. A small scope clarification at work. These are not glamorous. That is their advantage.

There is a reason low-stakes repetition is superior to high-stakes heroics. High stakes narrow attention. They make people rush, over-explain, or freeze. Low stakes invite curiosity. Curiosity is the engine of improvement. When you are curious, you listen better. You notice what language changes the other person's tone. You hear where the policy is rigid and where discretion exists. You see which requests land and which ones slide off the conversation like rain off a coat. The concept is *practice bandwidth*. The implication is that the best way to become competent in hard conversations is to start with conversations that feel almost too small to count.

A micro-negotiation habit also depends on how you define success. Many people define success as getting a "yes". That makes them fragile, because a single "no" feels like failure. A practice mindset uses a broader metric: did you ask cleanly, did you learn something, did you keep the relationship intact, did you make the next attempt easier? These are visible outcomes, not abstractions. You can measure whether you asked. You can measure whether you stayed calm. You can measure whether you clarified a policy. You can measure whether you uncovered options. The concept is *process wins*. The implication is that you can improve even when the answer is no, because you are training the skill, not gambling on a result.

Still, there is a credible limitation: habit can become mechanical. People can turn micro-negotiations into scripts and then sound artificial. They can also become indiscriminate, asking for concessions even when the situation does not warrant it. That corrodes relationships and, ironically, reduces future goodwill. The reconciliation is to treat habit as disciplined attentiveness rather than compulsive asking. A habit is not "always negotiate". It is "notice when terms are not fixed, and test politely when a test is reasonable". Habit is discernment, repeated.

To build discernment, it helps to see micro-negotiations as small scientific trials. You have a hypothesis: a modest request, delivered calmly, at a reasonable time, may improve terms. You test it. You observe the response. You refine. This framing matters because it changes the emotional meaning of awkwardness. Awkwardness becomes data. It is no longer evidence that you are socially inept; it is evidence that you are learning. Scientists do not interpret a failed experiment as a personal insult. They interpret it as information about the conditions. The concept is *experimental posture.* The implication is that you can stay steady, because you are not begging for approval; you are gathering evidence about how the world works.

Two named, checkable examples from outside negotiation make the power of repeated small trials obvious. In 1997, the British cycling team appointed Dave Brailsford as performance director, and he later popularised the idea of "marginal gains": small improvements across many areas that compound over time. The idea has been debated and sometimes mythologised, but the underlying principle is visible in any craft: repeated small improvements can outperform occasional dramatic efforts. In 2006, James Clear did not yet publish *Atomic Habits*—that came later—but the cultural fascination with tiny improvements was already building, in part because it matches how learning actually works. The implication for micro-negotiations is straightforward: one spectacular discount is nice, but a habit of modest improvements across recurring costs is transformative.

A second example is older and less fashionable. Benjamin Franklin, in his autobiography, describes a system of tracking virtues, marking daily failures on a chart. Franklin's moral project was idiosyncratic, and no one needs his particular list, but the method is instructive: he understood that intention is unreliable unless it is accompanied by observation. The implication is not that one should become a joyless self-auditor. It is that behavioural change often requires a record, even a small one, because memory flatters and deceives.

The motif for this subchapter is the lab notebook. Not the romantic leather-bound journal, but the plain notebook where someone records what they tried, what happened, and what they will test next. A micro-negotiation habit, done well, creates a life that is slightly more evidence-based. It is not cold. It is simply less foggy. You stop relying on vague impressions—"they never budge", "I'm terrible at this"—and start relying on observations: "they waived the fee once when I asked within seven days", "the chat agent was limited but the phone agent had options", "my tone changed the conversation".

The habit also requires a form of commitment, but not the kind people usually imagine. The common model of commitment is dramatic: make a vow, announce a goal, transform overnight. That model is brittle. A micro-negotiation habit uses quieter commitments: choose a small number of recurring situations and decide that, in those situations, you will test a request. Not every time. Often enough. The commitment is to the experiment, not to the outcome. The visible decision is simple: when the situation occurs, you will not default to silence. You will ask one clean question.

The emphasis on a few recurring situations matters because it prevents diffusion. People who try to negotiate everything quickly exhaust themselves and become performative. A tight selection creates a manageable practice set. In the language of skill acquisition, you are choosing drills. A drill is valuable because it repeats the same basic motion under slightly different conditions. If you choose too many drills, you never repeat any of them enough to learn. The implication is that constraint accelerates competence.

There is also an ethical comfort in starting small. Asking for a calmer room in a hotel, requesting clarification on what is included in a quote, querying an unexpected fee—these are reasonable requests. They do not require deception. They do not require aggression. They do not require you to become a different sort of person. That matters for thoughtful professionals and students because identity conflicts are a major barrier. People resist negotiation not because they dislike savings, but because they dislike what negotiation symbolises in their imagination: manipulation, selfishness, dominance. A habit built on modest, fair asks rewrites that symbol. Negotiation becomes what it actually is in most daily contexts: collaborative adjustment.

The language of "practice goals" can sound suspiciously like self-help, so it is worth grounding it in concrete behaviour. A practice goal might be as plain as this: in the next month, in two routine service interactions, you will ask one clarifying question about options. Or: the next time a price rises, you will ask what alternatives exist. These are behavioural commitments, not identity statements. They do not require perfect wording. They require only that you do not skip the attempt.

The fear that stops many people is not the fear of losing money; it is the fear of social friction. They imagine an awkward pause, a judgemental tone, a slow "no". Habit does not eliminate that possibility. It reduces its power. When you have asked twenty times, a single awkward pause loses its sting. It becomes one datapoint in a set. The concept is *desensitisation by repetition*. The implication is that courage is not the point; exposure is.

Yet even exposure must be handled wisely. Some people, once they begin, become impatient with themselves. They expect fluency in a week. They judge their stumbles. They interpret their discomfort as failure. That is the wrong metric. The right metric is whether the habit is sustainable. Sustainability is a design problem. You design a habit by making it small enough to fit real life. The visible sign of good design is that you can do it on a bad week. If your micro-negotiation habit requires perfect energy, it will collapse at the first stress. If it requires only that you notice and ask one question occasionally, it will survive.

The lab notebook returns here. In a lab, you do not abandon a project because an experiment is messy. You adjust the method. You change the conditions. You refine the protocol. The same is true of micro-negotiations. If phone calls make you tense, you test written messages. If mornings make you rushed, you test afternoons. If you over-explain, you test shorter phrasing. The habit is not merely "ask more"; it is "learn how you ask best".

The forward tension that closes this section is simple and sharp. An adult life offers endless opportunities to accept terms without noticing. It also offers endless opportunities to test those terms politely. The question is not whether you will ever negotiate; you already do, every time you accept or resist a condition. The question is whether you will treat your own agency as a sporadic burst of bravery or as a habit built from small, repeatable experiments—recorded in a quiet notebook, refined over time, and carried with you into the higher-stakes moments when you will be glad you practised.

Debriefing Every Conversation

In February 1944, in Cambridge, Massachusetts, B. F. Skinner published *The Behavior of Organisms*, arguing—sometimes to the discomfort of his readers—that behaviour changes most reliably when consequences are observed, recorded, and adjusted. The book is often remembered for its laboratory apparatus, the "box", but the more useful image is quieter: a scientist watching what happens, writing it down, and refusing to be sentimental about the data. There is a faint scratch of pencil on paper in that image, the stubborn sound of attention. Skinner's framework has limits, especially when applied to complex human motives, but one lesson holds: without feedback, repetition is not practice; it is habit without improvement.

Five minutes is enough.

Debriefing turns a single micro-negotiation from a moment into a method. It is the difference between "that was awkward" and "that was informative". It is the difference between repeating the same clumsy phrasing for years and refining your approach until it becomes almost effortless. Most people collect experiences the way they collect loose change: scattered, uncounted, forgotten in the bottom of a bag. The debrief is the act of putting experiences on the table and sorting them. Not for self-flagellation. For learning.

Show what happens without a debrief. A person finishes a call to query a late fee. They feel slightly tense, like someone has turned the volume up inside their chest. The representative says, politely, "I'm afraid that's our policy." The person thanks them, ends the call, and immediately begins an inner trial: I sounded foolish. I should have said something smarter. I'm not good at this. Name the pattern: *post-event rumination.* Explain it: after social encounters, the mind often replays fragments, seeking safety by imagining better lines, but it does so emotionally rather than analytically, reinforcing shame instead of producing insight. Implication: the person becomes less likely to ask next time, not because the world has changed, but because their interpretation has poisoned the practice.

Now show the same call with a debrief. The person ends the call and, while the details are still fresh, captures four facts: what they wanted, what they said, how the representative responded, what they will test next time. The act is simple. It is also transformative. Name the method: *structured reflection.* Explain it: a small structure interrupts rumination by forcing the mind to move from self-judgement to observation; it shifts the question from "What does this say about me?" to "What does this say about the situation?" Implication: learning becomes cumulative. The next attempt begins from a higher rung.

The debrief questions are not profound. That is precisely why they work. Profound questions tempt grand narratives—identity, fairness, destiny—and grand narratives make people defensive. A debrief is deliberately plain. What did you want? That is a question about aim, and aim can be refined. What did you say? That is a question about behaviour, and behaviour can be adjusted. How did they respond? That is a question about constraints, and constraints can be navigated. What might you try next time? That is a question about experimentation, and experimentation reduces fear. Each question has a visible output: a sentence, a phrase, a decision. None requires self-mythology.

The first question—what you wanted—matters more than it seems. Many micro-negotiations fail because the person asking has not decided what they want, so they drift into vague dissatisfaction. "I'm calling because the bill seems high" is not an ask. It is a mood. When you debrief, you notice whether your aim was clear enough to be actionable. Did you want the fee waived, a discount applied, a quieter room, a later deadline, a written confirmation? Precision is not pedantry. Precision is kindness to the other person, because it tells them what problem you are actually trying to solve. The concept is *aim clarity*. The implication is that when you improve aim, you often improve outcome without changing anything else.

The second question—what you said—forces accountability without cruelty. Most people remember how they felt, not what they said. Feelings are loud. Words are slippery. The debrief pulls words into view. Did you open with accusation or curiosity? Did you over-explain? Did you ask a single clear question, or did you scatter several requests and hope one would land? These are behavioural facts. They can be measured. They can be changed. The concept is *behavioural specificity*. The implication is that you stop treating communication as personality and start treating it as craft.

The third question—how they responded—protects you from a common distortion: assuming the response was a judgement of you. Often, it is not. Often, it is a constraint: the representative has limited authority, the system has limited options, the policy has a hard edge. Sometimes, the response is a cue: a pause that suggests there might be room, a phrase like "what I can do is…" that signals discretion, a mention of a different team that signals a better path. When you debrief, you listen for those cues. You notice the difference between "no" as refusal and "no" as the first line of a script. The concept is *constraint reading*. The implication is that you become calmer, because you stop taking policy as personal.

The fourth question—what you might try next time—keeps the debrief from becoming a post-mortem. It turns it into a plan for a new trial. "Next time I will ask if there is a one-off waiver available." "Next time I will call midweek." "Next time I will ask what options exist if I stay versus if I cancel." These are not declarations of self-improvement. They are hypotheses. Hypotheses reduce shame because they imply uncertainty is normal. A hypothesis also suggests a timeline: there will be a next time. The concept is *iterative testing*. The implication is that a single conversation stops feeling final.

A bill-call example shows the method in action without turning it into theatre. Imagine a mobile provider has applied an out-of-bundle charge that surprises you. You call. The representative explains that the charge reflects usage outside your plan. You feel a flare of annoyance and start listing every reason it is unreasonable. The representative becomes defensive. The call ends with no adjustment. Without debriefing, you might label the experience as proof that calling is pointless. With debriefing, you notice something sharper. What you wanted was either a waiver of the charge or a plan adjustment that prevents repeat charges. What you said began as complaint rather than request. The representative responded by describing policy, not options—an indicator that you never gave them a problem to solve. Next time, you might test a different opening: state the charge, state your aim, then ask for options. The difference is not moral. It is procedural.

The travel desk example is equally instructive because it reveals how debriefing trains judgement as well as language. You arrive at a hotel and your room faces a noisy street. You return to the desk and ask for something quieter. The receptionist checks and says nothing is available. You accept and return upstairs, then spend a night listening to traffic. Debriefing the next morning reveals two useful facts. Your aim was reasonable: a quieter room is a common request. Your phrasing may have been too vague—"anything quieter?"—which gives the receptionist little to search for. The response contained a key piece of information: "nothing available now." That implies "later" may be different. Next time, you might test a follow-up question: is there a move later in the evening or in the morning? The debrief does not promise a different outcome. It makes you more precise, and precision is often rewarded.

A credible limitation must be acknowledged: debriefing can slide into obsessive self-surveillance. Some people, especially those prone to anxiety or perfectionism, can turn debriefs into evidence dossiers against themselves. They rewrite every sentence, searching for the "perfect" line. That is not learning; it is self-punishment dressed as method. The reconciliation is to keep the debrief short, factual, and finite. The purpose is not to build an encyclopaedia of your mistakes. The purpose is to extract one improvement per encounter. One. That restraint matters. It keeps the practice sustainable.

Debriefing also sharpens judgement about when not to push. Not every "no" invites another attempt. Sometimes the world is genuinely constrained: the flight is full, the policy is explicit, the person has no discretion. A good debrief notices that too. It records, without drama, that the refusal was clean and that further pushing would have been inefficient or unkind. Efficiency here is visible: fewer calls, fewer emails, fewer wasted minutes. Risk is visible too: pushing beyond reason can damage relationships and reputations. The debrief teaches you the difference between persistence and nagging because it forces you to observe outcomes rather than justify impulses.

There is a subtle dignity in debriefing. It treats your time as valuable enough to learn from. It treats the other person's role as structured enough to understand. It treats the interaction as part of a larger pattern rather than a single moral episode. This is particularly important for thoughtful professionals and students, who often carry high standards into social situations and then suffer when reality is messy. Debriefing allows mess without despair. It acknowledges imperfection without indulging it.

The motif threading this section is the field note. A field note is not a diary entry. It is a brief record made while the observation is still alive: what happened, what was said, what changed. Anthropologists use field notes to avoid letting memory rewrite encounters into neat stories. Micro-negotiators benefit from the same discipline. Memory is not a neutral archive. It is a storyteller. It edits. It flatters. It exaggerates. Field notes anchor learning to what actually occurred.

The most practical effect of debriefing is linguistic. Over time, you develop phrases that fit you: openings that feel natural, follow-ups that invite options, closings that keep doors open. You also develop timing instincts. You begin to notice which channels work for which problems. You become faster because you stop reinventing your approach each time. That speed is not a trivial benefit. It is the difference between negotiating as a draining event and negotiating as a brief, ordinary task.

The forward test that remains is uncomfortable in a useful way. After the next micro-negotiation—successful, partial, or refused—will you let the experience dissolve into feeling, or will you capture it as a field note: what you wanted, what you said, how they responded, what you will test next time? The difference is small. It is also decisive.

Tracking Wins and Adjustments

On 12 July 2016, in Geneva, Switzerland, the World Health Organization published a document with a title that sounds almost comically dry: *Guidelines on Ethical Issues in Public Health Surveillance.* Buried beneath the bureaucratic surface is a simple insistence: if you collect data, you owe it attention; if you look at patterns, you inherit responsibilities. The document is about health, not household bills, yet it begins where any serious practice begins—with the refusal to let observations evaporate. There is a particular feeling to that refusal: the cool edge of a clipboard, the small discipline of writing things down even when the numbers are not dramatic.

Keep a record.

Micro-negotiations are not only conversations; they are *outcomes*—a changed fee, a different appointment slot, a clearer scope, a quieter room. The outcomes are often small, and small outcomes are notoriously hard for the human mind to honour. Memory prefers the theatrical: a single big win or a single humiliating rejection. Everything else fades. That fading is costly. It makes progress feel imaginary, and when progress feels imaginary, people stop practising. Tracking is the antidote, not because it turns life into an audit, but because it makes improvement visible enough to sustain.

Show the default state. A person spends an hour on a call and secures a £8 monthly reduction on a broadband contract. They feel a flicker of satisfaction. Then dinner happens, emails happen, an urgent task happens, and the win dissolves into the week. Two months later, they cannot remember whether the saving was £5 or £10, whether it lasts six months or twelve, whether there was a note about calling back. Name the problem: *vanishing gains*. Explain it: small improvements lack emotional salience, so they are not encoded strongly; without a record, the benefit becomes vague and therefore psychologically weightless. Implication: the person's future motivation is undermined by their own forgetfulness.

Tracking wins is not vanity. It is feedback. It is also the only reliable way to distinguish between a good month and a good method. A good month can be luck: an unusually helpful agent, a temporary promotion, an overbooked hotel desperate to placate. A good method repeats across contexts. Tracking allows you to see repetition. It answers questions that matter. Which types of ask produce movement? Which channels produce stone walls? Which timing choices reduce friction? Which language triggers options? These are not philosophical curiosities; they are operational realities, and operational realities are what save time and money.

The first objection many thoughtful people have is ethical and aesthetic. They worry that tracking turns them into a penny-counting nuisance. They fear it will make them calculating. That fear often comes from confusing measurement with greed. Measurement is not greed; it is clarity. A researcher measures not because they worship the number, but because the number prevents self-deception. A professional tracks project outcomes for the same reason. Micro-negotiation tracking is a modest extension of that competence into the spaces where adults routinely accept terms without scrutiny. The concept is *evidence of agency*. The implication is that tracking restores a sense of control without requiring aggression.

A second objection is practical. People imagine a complex spreadsheet. They imagine a new habit that competes with their already crowded life. That is a legitimate worry, and it points to an important principle: the record must be *low-friction*. If it requires too much effort, it will collapse, and then it will become one more thing that makes you feel guilty. The record is a tool, not a shrine. It is a quick note that captures three kinds of outcomes: money saved, time saved, and terms improved. Each outcome is visible. Money is a figure. Time is minutes. Terms are statements: "fee waived once", "late checkout granted", "scope confirmed in writing". When you can see the outcome, you can respect it.

Yet tracking is not only about wins. A practice that records only victories becomes distorted. It encourages the fantasy that success is the norm and "no" is an anomaly. Then, when "no" arrives—as it will—it feels like catastrophe. A mature record includes near-misses and respectful refusals because those contain high-quality information. A near-miss might be a representative who cannot change the price but offers a different plan. A respectful refusal might reveal a hard constraint or a policy boundary. Those are not failures; they are map updates. The concept is *data from no*. The implication is that you remain stable, because the record validates learning even when the outcome is unchanged.

Two named, checkable examples show how tracking changes behaviour in domains far from negotiation. In 1981, Benjamin Graham's ideas about disciplined investing were already well established, and while markets are not our concern here, one lesson translates cleanly: without a record, people confuse feelings with results. Investors who track decisions can separate good process from lucky outcomes; those who do not tend to invent narratives after the fact. A second example is more behavioural. In 1977, psychologist Albert Bandura described self-efficacy—people's belief in their capacity to execute actions that affect outcomes—as a key driver of behaviour. Tracking wins is a concrete way to build that belief without self-hype, because it provides evidence that actions sometimes change outcomes. The implication is not that every ask works; it is that your behaviour is not irrelevant.

A credible limitation must be admitted here: tracking can become a private scoreboard that corrodes relationships. If someone begins to treat every interaction as a game to "win", the tone shifts. Staff members sense it. Friends and colleagues sense it. The practice becomes extractive. The reconciliation is to track outcomes while also tracking *costs*—not financial costs, but relational and emotional ones. Did the interaction remain respectful? Did the request feel fair? Did you accept a clean "no" without sulking? These are visible behaviours. If tracking is paired with a commitment to kindness, it supports character rather than eroding it.

The motif for this section is the ledger. Not the grand ledger of a corporation, but a personal ledger—a small record that keeps you honest about what you gained and what you learned. A ledger is not only about totals. It is about categories. Once you begin to record outcomes, you start to notice what kind of value you are actually chasing. Some people think they want money saved, but their ledger shows that time saved is the real prize: fewer hours on hold, fewer follow-up emails, fewer wasted errands. Others discover that clarity is their dominant value: written scope, explicit cancellation terms, predictable billing. The record teaches you what you truly care about by showing what you consistently pursue.

Tracking also corrects a subtle psychological distortion: people overestimate the discomfort of asking and underestimate the cost of not asking. The discomfort is vivid; it happens in a moment. The cost of not asking is diffuse; it leaks over months. A ledger makes the leak visible. When you see, in your own handwriting, that a single ten-minute call reduced a monthly cost for a year, the relationship between discomfort and reward becomes less theoretical. This is not motivation by slogans; it is motivation by evidence. The concept is *cost visibility*. The implication is that you are less likely to drift into passive acceptance.

A bill example makes this tangible without becoming prescriptive. Imagine a person calls a service provider after a price rise notice. The provider will not restore the previous rate, but offers an alternative plan that reduces the increase. The person accepts. If they track only the fact that they did not "win" the old rate, they will feel disappointed. If they track the outcome precisely—how much the increase was reduced, what the term is, whether there is a future review date—they can treat it as a partial success and as information about that company's boundaries. Next time, they approach with better calibration: they know what is negotiable and what is not. The ledger turns disappointment into a useful constraint map.

A travel example shows the value of recording terms rather than money. A guest requests a late checkout and is granted an extra hour. That hour is not a discount. It is time. It can mean a shower before a meeting, a calmer departure, one less hour guarding luggage. If it is not recorded, it is not appreciated, and the practice does not grow. If it is recorded, it becomes part of a pattern: small requests for time and convenience often succeed when framed clearly and asked at the right moment. The ledger teaches the person which domains yield which types of value.

Tracking across months reveals another important truth: micro-negotiation outcomes are seasonal. At work, budget cycles matter. In travel, peak season matters. In services, contract renewal windows matter. If you record dates, you begin to see rhythms. You may notice that your best outcomes occur in the last month of a contract, or that midweek calls yield faster resolutions, or that the first response is often rigid but a second contact in a different channel surfaces options. These are not guarantees. They are patterns. Patterns do not eliminate uncertainty, but they reduce randomness. The concept is *rhythmic advantage*. The implication is that you stop attributing outcomes to luck alone.

There is also a moral dimension to tracking that is easy to miss. When you record respectful refusals alongside wins, you become better at accepting limits. You see, on paper, that not every boundary is negotiable and that this is normal. That helps prevent cynicism. Cynicism often emerges when people believe the system is arbitrary and hostile. A ledger can reveal a more nuanced truth: some systems are rigid, some are flexible, and many are inconsistently applied. This is not comforting, but it is accurate. Accuracy is calming. It replaces grievance with discernment.

The record also protects you against a peculiar form of self-sabotage: moving the goalposts. If you do not track, you may win a discount and then dismiss it as "not much". You may secure a clearer scope at work and then forget how many future headaches it prevented. Tracking freezes the moment before the mind minimises it. This is not self-congratulation. It is honesty about causation. You acted; something changed. That relationship deserves recognition, not because you need praise, but because you need feedback.

And yet, the ledger is not a promise. It does not guarantee a particular annual saving. It does not predict a perfect success rate. What it does is establish a loop: ask, observe, record, adjust. That loop is the difference between drifting through policies and engaging with them. Over time, the ledger becomes a personal research archive. It tells you which forms of asking fit you, which organisations respond to which cues, and where your energy is best spent.

The forward test that remains is unglamorous and therefore decisive. After the next micro-negotiation—whether it changes a price, a term, or nothing at all—will you let the outcome blur into a feeling, or will you place it in your ledger with a date and a note: what changed, what did not, and what you will adjust next time? The practice is small. The pattern it reveals is not.

Staying Kind and Firm Long-Term

On 10 December 1948, at the Palais de Chaillot in Paris, the United Nations General Assembly adopted the Universal Declaration of Human Rights. The document is famous for its moral reach, yet its texture is strikingly practical: articles, clauses, a language of "everyone" and "no one", a determination to write values into terms. Outside, the Seine moved through winter light, and inside, the delegates argued about words—what counts, what binds, what can be asked of institutions without collapsing into cruelty. The point was not to create saints. The point was to design a way of speaking that protects dignity under pressure.

Be firm. Stay kind.

Micro-negotiation is a craft of repeated asking. Repetition shapes the asker as much as it shapes the outcome. This is the final and most intimate problem of the entire practice: not whether you can secure a discount or a better room, but whether the act of seeking better terms slowly changes the kind of person you are. Many people avoid asking because they fear conflict. Others ask a few times, get a few wins, and then discover a new fear: that they are becoming sharp-edged, mistrustful, always scanning for advantage. The trouble is not that negotiation is inherently corrosive; the trouble is that repeated exposure to systems that say "no" can make even decent people harden into cynics. That hardening feels like realism. It is often a loss of imagination.

Show the slow slide. A person phones their bank about a fee. The representative refuses, politely. The person tries again next month with a different provider; this time, they secure a small concession. They feel clever. Soon, they begin to assume every policy is a bluff and every staff member is an obstacle. Their tone becomes clipped. They stop listening for constraints and start hunting for loopholes. Name the drift: *instrumentalisation.* Explain it: when the aim becomes dominant—save money, secure perks—the other party is reduced to a mechanism, and the interaction becomes a contest of extraction. Implication: even when the person succeeds, the costs accumulate: more tension, more impatience, more resentment, and eventually worse outcomes because people withdraw cooperation when they feel used.

Kindness and firmness are often treated as opposites. They are not. They are different dimensions of the same encounter. Firmness is about clarity: a precise ask, a boundary, a refusal to be brushed off by vague language. Kindness is about recognition: the other person's humanity, the limits of their role, the fact that they are not the policy. When firmness exists without kindness, it becomes intimidation. When kindness exists without firmness, it becomes self-erasure. The practice is to hold both at once. That is difficult. It is also learnable, because it lives in visible behaviours: how you open, how you pause, how you respond to "no", how you close.

A brief story makes the distinction concrete. A tenant in a rented flat notices a leak under the sink. The letting agent sends a contractor, who arrives late and announces that the job will cost more than expected because "it's more complicated". The tenant feels the familiar temptation: either swallow the extra cost silently or launch into accusation. Instead, they ask two questions: what exactly changed in the scope, and what is the revised figure before work continues. The contractor explains that a corroded valve needs replacement. The tenant replies, calmly, that they understand the issue but need the update recorded before agreeing. The tone remains polite. The boundary remains real. Name the move: *respectful insistence*. Explain it: by separating the person from the terms, the tenant can be firm about process without making it personal; by requesting specificity, they reduce the space where surprises breed. Implication: the negotiation becomes a joint effort to clarify reality, not a fight about character.

Kindness has a mistaken reputation. People imagine it as softness, as giving in, as apologising for existing. In micro-negotiations, kindness is often strategic in the best sense: it makes cooperation psychologically easier. A staff member who feels respected is more likely to search for options, to explain constraints, to take initiative. This is not sentimental; it is behavioural. A classic finding in social psychology is that people tend to reciprocate perceived goodwill. Robert Cialdini's *Influence* (first published 1984) popularised reciprocity as a powerful social principle, though the idea long predates him. The implication is not that politeness guarantees concessions—systems have limits—but that it increases the probability of helpful engagement when discretion exists.

Firmness also has a mistaken reputation. People imagine it as aggression, as raising one's voice, as "being tough". In practice, firmness is often quiet. It is measured questions. It is refusal to accept vagueness as an answer. It is the ability to repeat an ask in slightly different language without sounding wounded. It is also the discipline to accept a clean refusal without turning it into theatre. Firmness is a way of protecting your own attention. Attention is finite. A micro-negotiation that drags into argument is not only unpleasant; it is inefficient. Efficiency here is visible: fewer minutes on the phone, fewer follow-up messages, fewer emotional aftershocks.

The balance becomes harder over time because repeated exposure to bureaucracy invites a particular form of contempt. Policies can feel like walls built out of phrases: “computer says no”, “that’s the system”, “there’s nothing I can do”. The contempt is understandable. It is also dangerous. It turns every interaction into a moral drama and makes staff members stand in for institutions. That is how people become cynical: they start treating the nearest human as the embodiment of the machine. The counter-practice is to recognise constraint without surrendering agency. You can be firm about seeking options while also acknowledging the person’s role. You can say, in effect, I know you didn’t design this; I’m asking what you can do within it. This is not flattery. It is accurate.

A named, checkable example of institutional constraint helps here because it reminds us that limits are not always personal. In March 2020, as the COVID-19 pandemic disrupted travel globally, airlines and governments issued rapidly changing policies on cancellations and refunds. In the United Kingdom, the Civil Aviation Authority published guidance for passengers navigating cancellations and refunds, and many travellers discovered that front-line staff could not instantly resolve systemic uncertainty. The practical lesson is not a specific travel rule—those change—but the structure: when systems are under strain, individual discretion shrinks. Kindness becomes even more important because staff are overwhelmed. Firmness becomes even more important because chaos breeds miscommunication. The reconciliation is to adjust expectations without abandoning the practice: sometimes the best outcome is clarity, not compensation.

A second example can be smaller and domestic, because long-term character is shaped more by ordinary encounters than by crises. Imagine a university student disputing a small library fine. The fine is not ruinous. The point is symbolic: a sense of unfairness. If the student approaches as a prosecutor, they may win nothing and leave angry. If they approach as a supplicant, they may leave resentful even if the fine is waived. If they approach with kind firmness—state the facts, acknowledge the rules, request a review—they preserve dignity on both sides. The outcome may still be “no”, but the student learns a crucial thing: self-advocacy does not require hostility. Over months and years, that lesson matters more than the fine.

A credible limitation must be faced honestly: some organisations respond only to escalation, and some staff members respond poorly to any request. Kindness can be mistaken for weakness. Firmness can be read as insolence. The reconciliation is not to abandon either; it is to recognise that the goal is not to control the other person's interpretation. The goal is to control your own conduct. In other words, your standard is internal, not dependent on whether you receive a reward. This is where values become practical. A value is not a slogan you believe; it is a rule you follow when the outcome is uncertain.

The motif threading this section is the compass. A compass does not remove storms. It prevents drift. Over time, micro-negotiation practice can pull you towards two unhelpful extremes: appeasement and predation. The compass is the set of choices that keep you out of both. It is not a dramatic oath. It is small decisions: to ask clearly, to listen carefully, to accept limits, to persist without menace, to leave an interaction cleaner than you found it. Each choice seems minor. Together, they form a style of living.

How does one sustain that style over years? Partly by treating kindness as a behaviour rather than a mood. You may not feel warm. You can still speak respectfully. You can still thank someone for checking, even if you dislike the answer. You can still avoid sarcasm. These are visible actions. Partly by treating firmness as a structure rather than a performance. You do not need bravado. You need a clear ask, a clear boundary, and a willingness to restate both without escalation. You can pause. You can breathe. You can choose fewer words. That restraint is a form of power.

There is a deeper philosophical point hiding in the practicalities. Micro-negotiations are small tests of how we believe society should work. They ask: are policies absolute, or do humans still interpret them? Are customers and employees enemies, or can they cooperate within constraints? Is dignity preserved by silence, or by speech? Each conversation is a miniature civic act. That does not mean it must be solemn. It means it matters. If you consistently ask in ways that preserve the other person's dignity while protecting your own, you are quietly practising a version of public life where people can disagree without dehumanising one another.

Tracking, from the previous section, supports this too. A ledger that includes notes about tone and conduct—whether you remained respectful, whether you accepted a clean refusal—becomes a moral instrument as well as a practical one. It keeps you from rewriting yourself as either victim or conqueror. It shows you, with the plainness of a field note, who you were in the moment. That is uncomfortable. It is also clarifying. If you see a pattern of impatience, you can correct it. If you see a pattern of timidity, you can correct that too. The compass and the ledger work together: values steer; records verify.

A final brief story, because long-term practices are sustained by images as much as by arguments. A person calls their energy provider after noticing an unexplained charge. The representative is new, their voice slightly uncertain. The caller could exploit that uncertainty, pressing hard for a concession. Instead, the caller asks for an explanation first, then requests a review if the charge appears incorrect. The representative searches, consults a supervisor, and corrects an error. The caller thanks them and ends the call without lingering for extra demands. Kindness did not weaken firmness. Firmness did not erase kindness. The caller got what was fair and left the interaction intact. That is the kind of outcome that does not breed cynicism.

The unresolved tension to carry forward is a question of identity dressed as a practical choice. After the next micro-negotiation—especially the frustrating ones—will you treat the other person as a barrier to defeat, or as a constrained human with whom you can still speak clearly and respectfully? The answer will not be decided by a single conversation. It will be decided by the habits you repeat. The compass is already in your hand.

About the Author

Safiya Montrel helps people find calm, confident words for situations they once avoided. Over many years of working with individuals, small businesses and community groups, she has seen that most negotiation does not happen in boardrooms; it happens in kitchen-table calls to providers, quick chats with tradespeople, and quiet conversations at work about scope and recognition.

Her interest in everyday negotiation began early, listening to older relatives bargain over fruit and fabric in open-air markets. Those exchanges were rarely adversarial. They were part of a social ritual: a way of testing what was possible while preserving relationships. Safiya carries that spirit into her writing, treating negotiation as a normal human skill rather than a specialist talent.

She has spent much of her career translating complex ideas about behaviour, incentives and communication into plain language. In workshops and private coaching, she has watched people go from dreading difficult conversations to initiating them with poise. Micro-Negotiations is her way of putting those tools into as many hands as possible. She believes that when more people can ask clearly for what they need, everyday life becomes fairer, kinder and less wasteful for everyone involved.

www.ingramcontent.com/pod-product-compliance
Lightning Source LLC
Chambersburg PA
CBHW031338230926
51848CB00002B/292
* 9 7 8 9 3 7 6 5 5 3 9 3 8 *